Karl Marx

KU-477-264

Karl Marx claimed that the chains of the exploited were obscured by the flowers of ideology and religion. He set out both to remove the flowers and to break the chains. But was his solution really radical enough?

This book traces the development of Marx' ideas against his nineteenth-century background: his early life and writings, the 1848 revolutions, Marx' major work in economics, his views of history, class, women and property; trade unionism and revolution are major topics.

The book is not only a biography: it is also an analysis of Marx' ideas from a Christian viewpoint. As such it shares a concern, not just for Marx in history, but for the way his ideas are working today.

Dr David Lyon is Senior Lecturer in Sociology at Ilkley College, West Yorkshire. He was Visiting Assistant Professor in the Department of Sociology and Anthropology at Wilfrid Laurier University, Ontario, in 1976–77. He is married with two children.

For Sue, Tim and Abigail

An Aslan Lion Book

Karl Marx

A Christian appreciation of his life and thought

David Lyon

Lion Publishing

Inter-Varsity Press

Copyright © David Lyon 1979

LION PUBLISHING
Icknield Way, Tring, Herts

First edition 1979

ISBN 0 85648 161 0

This book is sold subject to the condition that it shall not by way
of trade or otherwise be lent, re-sold, hired or otherwise
circulated without the publisher's prior consent in any form of
binding other than that in which it is published and without
a similar condition including this condition being imposed on the
subsequent purchaser.

Text set in 10/11 pt Photon Imprint, printed and bound
in Great Britain at The Pitman Press, Bath

CONTENTS

ILLUSTRATIONS

Acknowledgements
Barnaby's Picture Library, pages 126, 158
Mary Evans Picture Library, pages 24, 42, 74, 98

PREFACE

There are two main themes to this book. First, it is a biography of Marx, tracing the development of his ideas through his lifetime and against the nineteenth-century European backdrop. Each chapter corresponds roughly to a stage in his life and a phase of his thought.

The Introduction sets out the framework of interpretation. (The reader may prefer to skip it and move straight into the biographical chapters. It can be referred to later.) Chapter two is about his early life and the influences of rationalism, Romanticism and Hegel. Three concerns Marx' early writings, especially relating to personhood and the meaning of labour. Four and Five deal with the 1848 revolutions and Marx' major work in economics. But other themes are also discussed, including views of history, class, women and property. Trade unionism and revolution are the major topics of chapter six, relating to Marx' involvement with the International Workingmen's Association.

Chapter seven goes beyond Marx to show how some of his ideas (and their ambiguities) have worked themselves out in the twentieth century. Different strands of Marxism are explored and finally threads are drawn together for a concluding assessment. The aim throughout is to be fair to Marx and to do him justice for his particular achievement.

It does not pretend to be any kind of definitive biography. There are other, fuller biographies on the market. By far the best of these is David McLellan's *Karl Marx: His Life and Thought*. I have relied heavily upon this in particular. I have not discovered anything 'new'.

What makes this book different is its second theme, which is a Christian commentary on the development of Marx' thought. At each stage there is an ongoing evaluation of the roots and practical implications of his outlook. I hope that misunderstandings on both 'sides' will be reduced, and that Christians and Marxists might more clearly discern what each is saying. The real connections and the real divergences will be explored, though the treatment is not so much comprehensive as suggestive. All along, however, the guiding perspective is one which attempts to be true to the biblical account of God, the world and persons. But in the process I also take Marx extremely seriously, as anyone of his stature deserves.

As with most books of this kind, I suspect, this one reflects a personal quest: the desire to understand the attraction of Marx and

Marxism; to set them in their proper social and historical context; and the call to appreciate and respond to what is going on from a Christian world-view. But this is not easy. For I am forced into a painful awareness of how often Marx and Marxists have been right about the complicity of the institutional church in an uncritical capitalist ethos and its condoning by default and implication local and international injustice. At the outset, I ought not only to mention my quest and my fundamental faith-commitment to Jesus Christ but also the fact that I am a white, male, salaried Briton. I hope that the latter does not colour the pages as much as the former.

A reminder that this is an ongoing quest came from a friend in Novi Sad, Yugoslavia, whose comments came too late to make any alteration feasible. He made me realize that much more could be said about the church as a radical alternative social reality, as many (particularly in the Anabaptist tradition) are rediscovering today. That this topic is unelaborated here in no way indicates any lack of confidence in the potential for social change of a church-community of committed Christians.

I have tried to make clear, when quoting Marx himself, which of his writings is in question. I have not footnoted most of the Marx quotes, because they may all be found in one source: David McLellan's *Karl Marx: Selected Writings*. Those uninterested in the exact location of the quote need no footnotes. Those wishing to follow something up should have no difficulty in finding the reference in McLellan.

Footnotes, by which significant quotations and authors may be traced, also serve as a guide to sources, and should be treated as such. This is not intended to be a scholarly book, so there is no formal bibliography, but many of the books which I found particularly helpful are mentioned in the footnotes. It hardly needs to be said that the literature on Marx is immense; he is, after all, the most influential philosopher of the last hundred years. My penchants for sociology and the history of ideas are probably reflected in my choice of books. Those who wish to take further the kind of Christian perspective on Marxism which I have attempted to outline here may be helped if I acknowledge my debt to the insights of Robert Banks, Jose Míguez Bonino and Johan van der Hoeven, along with several others mentioned below, but especially Andrew Kirk and Richard Mouw.

I would not have come far with this ambitious project without numerous friends who have offered their critical encouragement. While they cannot be held responsible for what I say, nevertheless they shared the task, so their influence permeates the following pages. Special thanks to those who have patiently read and commented on all or part of the manuscript. To take on Marx is to plunge into philosophy, politics, economics, sociology, history and anthropology. I also needed help from theology. My helpers represent all these different fields. Thank you Oliver Barclay (Leicester), Howard Davis (Canterbury), Shirley Dex (Birmingham), Steve Evans (Wheaton), Sander Griffioen (Toronto), Os Guinness (Oxford), Andrew Kirk (Buenos Aires), Sue Lyon (Kitchener and Bradford), Rich Mouw (Grand Rapids), David Potter (Reading), Alan Storkey (Worksop); my two helpful 'lay' people, Dave Hodgson and Dave Tordoff (Bradford and Bingley), and my perceptive editors at Lion, Tim Dowley and Derek Williams.

Most indispensable among my earthly friends is my wife, Sue, who has borne but not always enjoyed the many months of my incarceration in the study. I hope that my actions over the next years will express my gratitude to her and to Tim and Abigail; words are insufficient.

David Lyon

A CHRONOLOGY OF MARX

1818   Birth in Trier
1835   Student at University of Bonn
1836   Student at University of Berlin
1841   Doctoral thesis accepted at Jena
1842   Articles for *Rheinische Zeitung*
1843   Marries Jenny von Westphalen; moves to Paris;
        Critique of Hegel's *Philosophy of Right*; *The
        Jewish Question*
1844   Editor of *Deutsche-Französische Jahrbücher*;
        Economic and Philosophical Manuscripts; met
        Engels; Jenny born
1845   Move to Belgium; *Theses on Feuerbach*;
        summer visit to England
1846   *The German Ideology*; birth of Edgar
1847   Joins Communist League
1848   *Communist Manifesto*; editor of *Neue
        Rheinische Zeitung* in Cologne
1849   *Wage Labour and Capital*; moves to Paris, then
        London; birth of Guido
1850   *The Class Struggles in France*; death of Guido
1851   Birth of Frederick Demuth; year of the Great
        Exhibition
1852   *The Eighteenth Brumaire of Louis Bonaparte*
1855   Birth of Eleanor; death of Edgar
1857/8 *Grundrisse*
1859   *Critique of Political Economy*
1862/3 *Theories of Surplus-Value*
1863   Death of mother
1864   *Inaugural Address* for the First International
1865   Drafted *Capital* volume III
1867   *Capital* volume I
1869   Engels retires from Manchester to London
1871   The Paris Commune; *The Civil War in France*
1875   *Critique of the Gotha Programme*
1881   Death of Jenny Marx
1883   Death of Jenny Longuet; death of Marx

Flowers on the chains

*Criticism has plucked imaginary flowers from the chains,
not so that man may bear chains without any imagination
or comfort, but so that he may throw away the chains
and pluck living flowers.*
Marx, Critique of Hegel's 'Philosophy of Right'

Marx wrote these words while staying at his mother-in-law's house, having recently returned home from his honeymoon in Switzerland and Baden. Enthusiastically in love with Jenny and without the financial worries which would soon dog him, he prepared to take on the world. Abounding in vigour, he made ready to pluck the imaginary flowers from the chains of human bondage.

Marx possessed a powerful sense of his own destiny. In his doctoral dissertation he described the crisis of Greek philosophy after Aristotle, comparing it to his own time. Who would follow the great master Hegel in European philosophy? The upheaval demanded a decisive change in direction. Karl Marx announced that he would 'seek to discover the new world by criticism of the old'.

There is a sense in which Western culture is in a similar condition in the late twentieth century. Most 'grand systems' of philosophy are apparently out of favour. Yet many voices seem to cry out for an escape from the 'adhocracy' where 'if it works for the time being, do it'. Western culture especially has no concept of principled direction. No clear signposts are erected. Marx is posthumously stepping back into this void and offering again to discover the new world by criticism of the old.

One aspect of the old world for which he reserved particularly biting criticism was the formal religion of Germany. Religion, for Marx, constituted 'imaginary flowers'. This important claim must be carefully checked out, for it affects everyday life at the deepest possible level.

The crucial question

'Christianity', Oswald Spengler once declared, 'is the grandmother of Bolshevism.' Others, too, have claimed that Christianity and

Marxism belong to the same family and that the latter is the descendant of the former. Yet, paradoxically, Marx himself included the abolition of religion in his programme and Christians have not been slow in dismissing Marxism as an insidious enemy of the church. Are we observing a family feud, or real animosity between deeply-opposed extremes? This is a crucial question which runs like a guiding thread through this book.

In 1937 Nicolai Berdyaev suggested that the reason for communist antagonism towards Christianity lay in its being a rival religion: he felt there was fundamental opposition between the two world-views. But William Temple, then an archbishop in the Church of England, took the other view. He maintained that the purposes of Marx' social concepts come so close to those of Christianity that Marxism counts as a Christian heresy. Both alternatives are plausible, although 'religion' and 'heresy' must be carefully defined. But before we become immersed in the opinions of Marx' interpreters, we must ask the question: what did Marx think?

There is no doubt, to begin with, that he was an atheist. Rejecting the God of the Bible was an early step – and with it went religion in general. The angry young Marx had as a slogan: 'The criticism of religion is the presupposition of all criticism.' And as more than one scholar has demonstrated, he was opposed to belief in God because he thought it a mistake, quite apart from the alleged damage done by religious institutions and ideas. Zylstra, a Christian student of Marx, has convincingly shown that he was a post-Christian humanist, profoundly at odds with the Christians' God.

Religion, as condemned by Marx, was the 'imaginary flowers' which decorate and camouflage the chains of human servitude. As long as the flowers of 'contentment with one's lot' and a 'happy hereafter' remain, the chains are invisible. Religion makes the suffering bearable. And philosophy, while it stands aloof from the real world, simply condones things-as-they-are.

But Marx had a new task for philosophy – to play its part in world-changing. So when philosophical criticism plucks those sham flowers, the powerless human condition in all its true wretchedness is revealed. Social misery is caught in the floodlight of reason and observation. People are slaves to capitalist society, with nothing to lose but their chains. Religion, like a camera obscura picture, makes the world appear upside-down, with the authority of the powers-that-be allegedly coming direct from God.

So it never dawns on these captives, whose religion situates them at the bottom of this chain of being, that they might control their own destiny. (For Marx, the chain of being would undoubtedly be a chain of bondage.) Religion is thus kept alive through this alienation, for it gives meaning to it. Real human life, says Marx, is lost in God and in work – people are cut off from themselves at both levels. 'Forget God,' he would have counselled, 'for you do not need him (except as a false comfort in suffering). I speak of things we can see and test: pluck the illusory flowers from your chains as a first step towards liberation. Real flowers still wait to be gathered!'

Marx obviously believed that he was involved in no mere family feud but that religion was inimical to his aims. As a would-be social scientist he would have hated the thought that he might be heralded as the prophet of a new religion, as his impatience with Comte shows. Auguste Comte, the French founder of sociology and the Religion of Humanity, had made himself a laughing-stock by marrying social science and religion. Not for Marx was Comte's papal aspirations, his theological and sectarian spirit, or his prophetic frenzy. Ironically (in view of his own rather similar exploits) Marx showed hostility towards Comte's attempts to impose a particular philosophical doctrine on the labour movement, which he saw as evidence of Comte's misguided religious zeal.

There is no doubt that Marx was an atheist, whose humanism followed his atheism. He held that religion was obsolete and would necessarily be destroyed. In its destruction lay the hope of a new social order and authentic human life.

Marx' gospel

Later generations, however, have refused to believe that Marx was somehow 'a-religious'. He looked and sounded too much like a prophet of the apocalypse for his own disclaimers to be taken at face-value. For he was more than an obscure German immigrant scribbling away in the British Museum. Frequently, in this century, he has been regarded as some one who appropriated the messianic role of the Jewish-Christian faith and in whose outlook there are many religious themes. Just as many novels and films exude redemptive motifs (think of *Star Wars*), so Marx' drama of class-struggle and revolution is reminiscent of the salvation rescue-plan of the Jewish-Christian scriptures.

Marx' most significant mentor, Hegel, was a rather unorthodox Protestant philosopher. Like Feuerbach, Hegel tried to reframe Christianity in secular terms. What they produced amounted to a new religion, based on humanism, for post-Christian Germany. Many argue that Marx inherited aspects of this tradition. According to such interpretations, the proletariat (the urban-industrial working class) is supposed to play the role of Isaiah's suffering servant. With his own

Jewish background and stark, commanding appearance, Marx himself could have been taken for an Old Testament prophet, thundering his denunciations of the 'cows of Bashan'. (Thus Amos impolitely attacked the wealthy and oppressing *female* class of his day!)

Robert Tucker, whose elaboration of this theme is probably the best known, puts Marx squarely into the Judeo-Christian tradition: 'The religious essence of Marxism is superficially obscured by Marx's rejection of traditional religions.' 'Marxism', he continues, 'follows in certain ways the pattern of the great religious conceptions of Western culture. In particular it has a number of basic characteristics in common with the Christian system in its Augustinian and later medieval expression.'[1]

But it is not only that some theological baggage from a religious past seems to have accompanied Marx into the present but that his teachings still resemble religious ones. C. Wright Mills, an angry American sociologist of the 1960s, said that it is 'little wonder that clergymen regularly complain that the communists have "stolen our stuff". Indeed, Marxism as ideology is less a message than a "gospel" which in the literal sense means "glad tidings"'.[2] Marxism has an appeal similar to that of the Christian gospel. A root problem is isolated, its manifestations described, release is promised, a saviour is available and new life will follow.

The 'Creator' is now man; creation, work; the fall, division of labour; sin, capitalism; the saviour, intelligentsia plus working class; salvation, revolution; the church, the people or the party.

But even that is not the end of the story. Those who believe the gospel are accepted into the church. Some have seen an ecclesiastical structure in Marxism, in which the new canon of sacred writings points beyond itself, revealing truths about the universe and history, and the great drama in which all are participants. Kovesi writes that: 'If we want to understand the religious dimensions and aspects of Marx's achievement we have to take into account the peculiar nature of these attitudes towards Marx as much as ... Marx's writings themselves.'[3] He goes on to liken the changes in Marxism which are due to new interpretations of his writing, to changes in churches due to biblical criticism. He asserts that 'Marx's system is capable of being interpreted by others coming after him as referring to them, as allocating a *role* to them in a drama'. Thus there is a sense both of 'progressive revelation' and of the need for new apostles of that revelation in fresh historical contexts.

But the Judeo-Christian tradition is not the only one with which Marx is alleged to have some affinities. Interestingly, it is a Christian writer, Gary North, who has argued against the association of Marx with the biblical gospel and church-life. Rather, he sees Marxism as a revival of the 'chaos cults' of the ancient world, where creative destruction is the key symbol.[4] The pristine power of creative destruction is all distilled in Marx' idea of revolution: out of the wreckage of an old order, new life will mysteriously spring into being. For Marx, according to North, 'all roads lead to revolution', a belief which seems to be a throwback to primitive, destructive ritual.

This is a useful corrective for those who would jump to the common conclusion that Marx was a direct product of his Jewish and German Protestant background. But judgement will have to be reserved on the question of Marx' religious obsession with revolution. Crucial as the concept of revolution is, it is arguable whether it constitutes the linchpin of Marxism.

Science or religion?

How then did Marx, who claimed that his ideas were scientific in a way that religion is not, give birth to what others have construed as an alternative religion or a Christian heresy? The answer is simply that some of Marx' assumptions are untestable. The idea, to which Marx became increasingly attracted towards the end of his life, that it is possible to talk of 'certainties' in science, is far less plausible today. In fact, all scientific study is done within the framework of a particular world-view. Assumptions which may not necessarily be part of a theory are nevertheless built into it.

In Marx' early work, for example, several essentially romantic ideals made up his world-view and guided his scientific reflection. The lonely defiance of huge forces is one instance of this. It is seen in his love for the myth of Prometheus. Such a world-view may only be 'tested' in the crucible of experience and against some concept of truth. Ideals may make sense of human experience, for a while at least, in the same way as any religion might: they give meaning to life. Indeed, it is helpful to think of a world-view as something which derives from one's basic religious commitment. This, in turn, is something which all have. Religion is fundamental to our humanity. The human heart is either directed towards God, or, no less religiously, but less truly, to some substitute.

One of Marx' beliefs was in a hypothetical condition of communal, unalienated labour, when people worked together freely and without exploitation. This state of affairs, he prophesied, would return after the passing of capitalism. This romantic ideal, which both looked back to a past golden age and forward to its reinstatement, was enthused over with what may only be described as religious fervour. Consider these words which Marx uttered on coming across a German immigrant workers' association in Paris: 'the brotherhood of man is no empty phrase but a reality, and the nobility of man shines forth upon us from their toil-worn bodies.'

The direction of Marx' ultimate (or religious) commitment became evident in his world-view. This has been aptly described by Bernard Zylstra as 'post-Christian humanism'. All of Marx' theories embody beliefs – on the identity of persons, nature and history, for example – which relate to his religiously-rooted world-view.

Marx' failure to understand the religious dimension of what he was doing has caused problems. Here is a warning of the dangers of a consistent Marxism. Reinhold Niebuhr[5] suggests that this confusion between genuine, self-conscious scientific activity and the utopian ideals allows the Soviet leaders to use Marxism to legitimize what is done to the faceless masses of Russia. Soviet Marxism, for Niebuhr, is in a state of 'dogmatic atrophy'. The pretence is maintained that scientific laws govern both what has happened and what will happen in the transition to fully socialist society. Niebuhr would blame not Lenin and Stalin for 'corrupting' Marxism but Marx himself for making no distinction between what he observed in nineteenth-century Europe and what he claimed would emerge from the ruins of that society.

What Marx meant by 'science' and how this related to his prognosis for future society is a question to which we must repeatedly return. Niebuhr, among others, is in no doubt about it. Marx could not decide whether to be the Darwin of the social world or the liberator of the workers, so he attempted to be both. Thus he blurred the distinction between his philosophical *criticism* of social relationships and his scientific *description* of such relationships. Because his ideal of scientific description was taken from *natural* science, he also shared Engels' belief that one could distinguish between 'scientific' and 'utopian' socialism.

Marx offered hope to suffering people but hope cannot be produced in a test-tube. Hope might be the context in which science is done but Marx approached the two as if they were one. Such an inconsistency is the starting-point for the Marxist-Leninist dogmatic and manipulative interpretation. It can have tragic practical implications.

Can Marxism replace Christianity?

Alasdair MacIntyre once put the emergence of Marxism in the context of the de-Christianization of the West. He said that although heroes of the eighteenth-century Enlightenment hoped that rational thought would one day provide answers to the great questions of immortality, freedom and morality, people have simply learned not to ask the questions. The self-styled nineteenth-century humanists, with their attempts to provide a 'scientific' alternative to everything religious, present a pathetic picture. But, continues MacIntyre, 'Only one secular doctrine retains the scope of traditional religion in offering an interpretation of human existence by means of which men may situate themselves in the world and direct their actions to ends that transcend those offered by their immediate situation: Marxism.'[6]

MacIntyre is saying that Marxism is a worthy successor to Christianity because it gives plausible answers to some of the momentous questions about human origin and destiny. Marxism, like Christianity, may be seen as an all-encompassing system of belief and practice which gives meaning to human existence. Through Marx we may understand who we are and why the world is in its present state, as well as what to do about it. Put like this, we have a more sociological dimension of the definition of religion, focusing on the way it gives meaning to social life.

But MacIntyre has more to add. He held (but has since moved on from this position) that Marxism may compensate for the deficiencies in practised Christianity when the latter has lost its sense of direction. This is an acerbic and penetrating criticism which Christians cannot afford to ignore: 'That function of religion which consisted in providing a radical criticism of the secular present is lost by those contemporary demythologizers whose goal is to assimilate Christianity into the secular present.'

MacIntyre, taking the role of an outside observer, sees 'Christians' doing all they can to wriggle out of saying that Jesus came to be '*the* way', that he rose from the dead and that the church is supposed to be a living, corporate 'No!' to self-seeking, power-lusting and injustice. Rather, Christians seem intent on making themselves indistinguishable from the God-rejecting world, their theology-come-of-age finally publishing God's obituary notice. Marxism, for MacIntyre, humanizes certain Christian beliefs, presenting them as a secular version of the Christian judgement upon (rather than compromising adaptation to) contemporary 'secular' society.

But can Marxism really have the *scope* of Christianity as an 'alternative religion' – does it really answer all the human needs and provide the life-direction of biblical religion? This is an important trail to be followed. For it can be highly misleading to speak of 'alternative religion', and especially 'Christian heresies'. A sociological understanding helps us to avoid minimizing the potential scope of alternative religions (as 'meaning systems'). For it is a misuse of the term 'religion' to identify it merely with the institutional (the 'church') or the intellectual (the 'creed'). To talk of 'heresy', for example, invokes the caricature of religion-as-creed, where assent to essentially intellectual assertions is the sole criterion of 'what religion is'. To think of either Christianity or Marxism as a 'set of ideas' is to miss their genius, to deflect their impact onto a soft cerebral cushion.

Raymond Aron, in his trenchant critique of Marxism, indicates its credal character by referring to it as 'the opium of the intellectuals'. As for the Christian view of religion-as-creed, it is implicitly scorned by the apostle John when he says 'let us not love with word or with tongue, but in deed and in truth'. Neither consistent Christianity nor consistent Marxism can divorce theory from practice. Having said that, however, practice throws up institutional forms – and there is always a danger that *they* might be mistaken for the 'real thing'. The Methodist Conference no more sums up 'Christianity' than the Italian Communist Party sums up Marxism.

In an intriguingly circular way, it is Marx' own view of religion which points to the broad *scope* of religion in the sociological sense. For Marx suggested not only that religion is a means of self-awareness by which people make sense of the world but also that its character varies in different social and material circumstances. Christians must not only ask why Marxism seems to make sense of the world for so many people but also why Christianity so often resembles the religion attacked so acidly by Marx.

The unfinished debate

We live in an age when numerous Christians all over the world find themselves affected by Marx. In the USSR and her satellites, China and other countries, some variety of Marxist–Leninism is the official creed. It is used in a conservative way to justify the regimes of totalitarian state control which includes limitations upon and often active and bitter opposition to churches and believers. In Latin America, on the other hand, where Marxism is still a revolutionary force, theology has come to look very like it and many (especially Catholic) theologians frankly acknowledge that they stand on Marx' shoulders.

Others, especially in Europe, have been drawn into the rather inconclusive Christian–Marxist dialogue which has had two unfortunate characteristics. In the search for some 'bridge' between the two outlooks – such as 'transcendence' or the concept of personhood – crucial aspects of their own commitment have been conveniently overlooked or soft-pedalled by both sides. Marxists may forget their antipathy to religion, or Christians their belief that the fundamental alienation is that of persons from God. Misunderstandings which may have been cleared up have all too often been exchanged for new ones. The other characteristic, untrue to the nature of each persuasion, is that discussion has taken place at a rarified intellectual level.

Yet another group who take seriously the Christ of the Bible are encountering Marx more frequently. As social concern grows among evangelical Christians in Britain, North America, Latin America and Africa, so the Marxian categories often surface as the most likely alternative to affluent, wasteful and dominating capitalist 'civilization'. More and more find that grappling with Marx is an unavoidable necessity. To ignore him is to opt out of the real struggle.

So how should Christians approach Marx? On what terms should the debate be carried out? Obviously, the Christianity of one country will not resemble that of another in every particular: differences of climate and custom see to that. Furthermore, it must be said that the response to Marx may have to differ according to social circumstances. But this is by no means to capitulate to some merely relative view of Christian commitment.

In essence, Christian faith is unified. There is a distinctive Christian gospel of good news which transcends cultural differences of expression. It centres on Jesus Christ, the saviour and Lord who frees from sin and to whom all are accountable. How should those who share a fundamental commitment to Christ, who try to live everyday life in authentic and communal imitation of him, approach Marx? Are there some abiding principles and distinctive traits of biblical Christianity which confront or contain Marxism? May Christians countenance the 'family feud' idea, or is mindful heart-commitment to Christ incompatible with the acceptance of Marxian attitudes?

At this point, we may only hint at answers. It is necessary to put Marxism in perspective by considering Marx' own life and the development of his thought against the backdrop of European revolutionary movements and Victorian England. While fairness and the willingness not to prejudge issues are essential, all things must also be carefully evaluated and a final discernment between good and bad must take place. Marx wished to produce a world-changing theory of society and it is on this claim that he must be judged. His life *was* his work, as this description of him in his twenties shows:

> He reads a lot. He works in an extraordinarily intense way. He has a critical talent that degenerates sometimes into something which is simply a dialectical game, but he never finishes anything – he interrupts every bit of research to plunge into a fresh ocean of books.[7]

His work was essentially intellectual, even though he believed that it was practical and that his ideas would only be verified in practice. In our evaluation of Marx and Marxism, therefore, we have his invitation to judge the theory on the results. A child of the nineteenth century, his writing continues to inspire those today who have seen all too clearly the inhumanity of 'the system'. His basic gospel lives on.

But while we start by trying to assess Marx' life and thought, Christian commitment does not allow him to raise all the questions. A thorough Christian appreciation of Marx must involve critical reflection on his work from a full-orbed biblical perspective. Christians, all too often characterized by their defensiveness, can become captivated by the *questions* thrown up by 'challenges' to the faith. No one denies that Jesus gave answers to real questions thrust at him but the amazement of his hearers stemmed from the fact that his answers revealed a totally new perspective: an alternative metaphysic.

Simply to 'answer Marx' in a woodenly 'prooftexting' manner would be to let him set the agenda. Our aim is an evaluation of Marx from the perspective of a biblical world-view. Such a world-view is informed by careful biblical study and derives from the principles of life offered by those scriptures. This has two implications. One is that we may have to raise questions untouched or sidestepped by Marx. What he did not say may be as significant as what he did say. The other implication is that, taking the Bible to be a unified and coherent whole which itself contains guidance as to how it should be interpreted, we shall not be raiding it at random for prooftexts. There is no 'Handbook of Christian Replies' through which we may thumb for instant answers.

But there are historical as well as Christian reasons for not simply allowing Marx to raise all the questions. Things have changed since his day. Revolutions have been made in his name, though not in the kinds of context he expected. The problem of revolution in non-industrial society is one we must face. Likewise, the issue of what *has* happened in industrial areas of the world also deserves attention. The state has grown to unforeseen proportions: is this a threat to all industrial societies?

The oppression of ethnic minorities, the exploitation of the Third World, student movements, discrimination against women – all these have been proposed as new catalysts to revolution in the late twentieth century. Does Marxism have to be modified to allow for these as authentic co-workers with the proletariat? Is feminism, often closely associated with socialism, inseparable from Marxism? These are important issues, generated in different parts of the contemporary world, which demand consistent and coherent thought and action.

Marxism has tried to face them but is the Marxist analysis adequate? Is there a credible Christian alternative?

Again, if one is after some pat answer, it will not be found here. There are no easy answers. The Christian does not stand in some isolated social vacuum, Bible in hand, fending off the bombarding ideas incompatible with a Christian world-view – far from it. All are immersed in a specific social, historical, economic and religious milieu. All are answerable to God in an ongoing way, from within the dilemmas, agonies and complexities of everyday life. The Christian community must be radically self-critical as it engages with human struggles and with the insistent challenges thrown up by Marxism. There can be no clinical dissection of Marxism for minute examination. Human social existence is profoundly unhygienic and we are in it together. While Marxism may not be permitted a monopoly on asking questions, Christians must themselves be open to the Marxist critique of their position. God is judge, not Marx; but the latter may sometimes be a truthful witness for the prosecution.

Christians *have* often been bourgeois in attitude and paternalistic in approach, especially in industrial relations and social policy. The bourgeois person is one who slides easily into an economic evaluation of life, gauging people and things in terms of costs and benefits. Personal interest and gain becomes uppermost in the bourgeois mind. Property, the secluded suburban house and the fuel-thirsty automobile, take on an immense significance. The economic evaluation seeps into all of life.

Paternalism is linked to this. Christian employers have been known to treat their employees not as partners co-operating in the enterprise but as 'hands' or 'the work-force'. In social welfare Christians have supported policies which tend to manipulate the disadvantaged by strictly defining who does and who does not 'deserve' help and covertly stipulating *how* financial aid should be used. Persons are thus treated as less than fully responsible. This is a kind of moral control quite incompatible with a Christian social ethic.

All this may partly be traced back to certain attitudes held by some Christians, especially that which divides 'nature and grace' – the 'material' and the 'spiritual'. Rather than seeing the whole world as God's, they have isolated some so-called 'spiritual' areas as somehow being more subject to God's direction and control than others. Thus, for example, industrial relations may be placed in an entirely different compartment from, say, inter-church relations. The sins of the fathers may well be visited on the children so that contemporary Christians have to do much uncomfortable reflection in the process of coming to terms with Marx. Marxists may initiate the action against

Christians – and Christians may be weighed and found wanting.

One hint may be given about the general framework in which our evaluation of Marx is couched. Throughout the biblical account of human existence, people are regarded as having a basic religious orientation, either towards or away from God-the-Maker. Two processes go on in those who, like Marx, orient themselves away from God and towards his creation. On the one hand, they may be indistinguishable from those whose lives are directed towards God and may have many ideas and life-patterns which are compatible with belief in God. As scientists, for example, they may come up with truths about the world and theories of social life which comport well with Christian faith.

On the other hand, however, not having a radical commitment to God, they will tend to focus on some substitute, to which they look for meaning and purpose in life. This becomes their 'religion'. It will be evident that this complicates things for the person who wants to evaluate something from a Christian perspective. With regard to Marx, it means that his work must be taken extremely seriously, for it contains many true insights. The Christian task is to 'examine all things carefully' and to 'hold fast to the good'. But it also means that there will be a constant possibility that the true insights are elevated to a position of explaining everything. If something in the creation, rather than the Creator himself, is given ultimate status, then anything may become the focus of faith.[8]

But these are only hints about the framework – not a rigid sieve. They only give us clues as to what we might expect; the reality is riddled with all the ambiguities and complexities already mentioned. To sketch a framework is a far cry from making final judgements.

Feuding family or rival species?

So we return to the original question: Are Christians and Marxists feuding members of the same family, or are they different species locked in a fundamental conflict? The answer depends to an extent on the vantage-point of the observer.[9]

If the question is approached from the position which recognizes that all people, whether Christian or not, can discover truths about the human situation, then the antagonism would seem to be that of a feud. But if it is approached with an awareness that human insights are frequently raised to the level of ultimate truth, then it is more than possible that those insights may come into direct conflict with God himself. It is also possible to hold both views simultaneously. My own convictions will become clear as we proceed, but it is of course a matter for each reader to decide.

I shall try to follow Marx' own method of 'critique' though allowing rather different assumptions to guide my assessment of his work. But it should be clear already that I stand in a different place from Marx in order to make the critique. More than one use can be made of the metaphor of the flowers and the chains. By the end of the book, we may possibly be left wondering which are the imaginary flowers and which are the real – not to mention the chains.

Notes and references

1 R. Tucker, *Philosophy and Myth in Karl Marx*, Cambridge University Press, 1972, p. 22.

2 C. W. Mills, *The Marxists*, Dell, 1962, Penguin, 1963, p. 35

3 J. Kovesi, 'Marxist ecclesiology and biblical criticism', *Journal of the History of Ideas*, 1976, vol. 37, 1.

4 G. North, *Marx's Religion of Revolution*, Nutley, New Jersey, Presbyterian and Reformed Publishing Co., 1968, p. 119.

5 R. Niebuhr, 'Introduction' to *Marx and Engels on Religion*, Schocken, 1964, p. 10.

6 A. MacIntyre, *Marxism and Christianity*, Penguin and Schocken, 1971, p.10.

7 David McLellan, *Marx*, Fontana Modern Masters, 1975, Penguin Modern Masters, 1976, p. 13.

8 This is elaborated in my article 'Approaching Marx' in *Third Way*, vol. I, 19, October 1977.

9 The Christian-Marxist dialogue and various theologies of liberation have recently raised these issues in an acute way. Marx' own position is clear from Bernard Zylstra, 'Karl Marx: Radical Humanist', *Vanguard*, December 1973, and P. M. Schuller, 'Karl Marx' Atheism', in *Science and Society*, vol. 39, 3, 1975. Theologians of liberation, whose work often highlights important matters, but who also tend to use Marx rather uncritically and thus sometimes defuse and divert attention from the biblical gospel's potential power, include Gustavo Gutierrez *A Theology of Liberation*, SCM Press and Orbis Books 1973, and Jose Miranda, *Marx and the Bible*, Orbis Books 1974 and SCM Press 1977. Warning voices from Roman Catholic and Anglo-Catholic quarters are Peter Hebblethwaite, *The Christian-Marxist Dialogue*, Darton, Longman and Todd, 1978, and Dale Vree, *On Synthesizing Christianity and Marxism*, Wiley Inter-Science 1976. Due soon is Andrew Kirk's important contribution, *Liberation Theology: An Evangelical Contribution from the Third World*, Marshall, Morgan and Scott.

Karl Marx

CHAPTER 1

The young Prometheus

*Prometheus' declaration, 'In a word, I hate all gods' is its
own confession, its motto against all gods, in heaven or on
earth, who do not recognize man's self-consciousness as
the highest divinity.*
Marx, PhD thesis.

Karl Marx was born into a German Jewish family who had adopted
Lutheranism for the sake of social convenience. He spent his university days studying under radical critics of Christianity. So it comes as
little surprise that Marx is often remembered as an aggressive oppo-
nent of Christianity. But it would be too easy to think of his early
development simply in these terms. He was far more than a deviant
rabbi or a militant atheist. Nevertheless, his feelings about the Christian faith and his response to current world-views are essential clues
to a proper understanding of his life.

Marx' birthplace was Trier, an old town in the green vine-growing
region of Germany's Rhineland. He was born, on 5 May 1818, in
troubled times both for Prussia and his family. In 1803 the area had
been over-run by Napoleon and incorporated into the Federation of
the Rhine. A new liberty was enjoyed by those who had been
thwarted for years by the iron hand of the hereditary monarchy. It
was as if the inhabitants of the German states were waking up to a
new day of promise under the 'Napoleonic Code', a framework of
laws which dissolved traditional hierarchies of social rank and
privilege.

But hardly had the eye-rubbing begun when, in 1814, the
Rhineland was incorporated into Prussia. To the disgust of many
Trier folk, a vigorous campaign was set in motion by the reactionary
German authorities to return to the old *status quo*. The new rights
and freedoms were withdrawn. In Prussia (where Trier was now
situated), Frederick William III was among the keenest to banish all
French ideas from the land.

He was determined to reproduce a virtually medieval state, replete
with restrictions and barriers not only against ideas but against the
development of trade and industry. The king clamped down, using

reinforced police powers, on private as well as public life, in the attempt to seal off his kingdom from any contaminating influences which might still be lurking in the homes of the bourgeoisie. Having once tasted a degree of liberty, however, few were prepared to relinquish it easily and many continued to read and write about the new ideas, even though penalties for such activities were stiff.

Specifically anti-Jewish laws were introduced in 1816, which deeply affected Marx' family. Both his father and mother came from a long line of Jewish rabbis, although only his mother continued practising Judaism during Karl's childhood. Life was always difficult for German Jews. They had tended to insulate themselves from hostile regimes by an almost fanatical adherence to their own culture and life-style. Many Jews had welcomed Napoleon's legal code, however, because it cleared their path to various occupations which had previously been closed to them.

So the Jews above all were disheartened and frustrated when the doors of opportunity were slammed in their faces. Suddenly finding themselves in a no-man's-land between the ghetto they had left and the careers they could no longer follow, rapid decisions had to be made. Some chose to return to their families in the ghetto and once more identify with the most underprivileged sector of the population. Others did the opposite, forsaking the ghetto for a wider life.

Heschel Marx, Karl's father, was one of the latter. He was a promising lawyer but his racial background now prevented him from holding public office unless he could obtain a royal dispensation. The practical alternative was to forsake his origins by changing his religion. It was on this course that he decided. Even his name had been an obstacle, Marx being a corruption and abbreviation of Mordechai. Thinking his first name to be even more Jewish, however, he changed that to Heinrich.

With the name change came baptism in the Lutheran church (even though Catholicism was the majority religion), and the transition was complete. In fact, the change to Protestantism made precious little difference to the actual beliefs and opinions which he held. His secular French education had left him without much sympathy for the synagogue and the Lutheran baptism did not involve him in any particular church routine. He was baptized in 1817 and kept his job. By 1818 he had become counsellor-at-law in the High Court of Appeal in Trier: the 'conversion' had paid off.

According to Eleanor, Karl Marx' daughter, her grandfather never gave the impression that he was seriously committed to any formally religious viewpoint. Rather, he was 'steeped in the free French ideas of the eighteenth century on politics, religion, life, and art'. He shared the Enlightenment belief in the power of unaided reason to explain the mysteries of the universe and to transform society. God, for him, was one to whom he prayed 'against his will' when all else had failed. At first, Karl was to follow his father very closely in his attitude to French rationalist thought. Alongside Romanticism, it was one of the main influences on his early outlook (even though, for many, rationalism and Romanticism were unlikely bedfellows).

Hopeful dreams and social upheaval

The leaven of French thought and social policy had deeply permeated the Rhineland ever since those relatively glad days of annexation during the Napoleonic regime. The key ideas of this so-called Enlightenment were that human beings are fundamentally good (in a moral sense) but have the potential for improvement by becoming more rational. A deep-flowing current in eighteenth-century Enlightenment thought was the belief in human progress and even perfectibility. It was the age of Newton, in which the world was conceived as a vast machine. This explained everything. The poet enthused:

Nature and Nature's Law's lay hid in Night,
God said, Let Newton be! and all was Light!

The French Enlightenment philosophers felt no need for the 'hypothesis' of God – the system worked without him. He was more or less gently pushed out of the picture.

But at least one inherent contradiction muddied the waters of this humanistic optimism. Two basic beliefs were in competition. Marx himself may be understood as someone grappling with these issues. We may call them 'nature and freedom'. On the one hand, there was a proud belief that human beings are on their own in the world, liberated from any outside authority (especially God) and in complete control of their destiny. But on the other hand, the ideal of science threatened this. For if everything in the world is predetermined by certain unavoidable laws, how do people themselves avoid this trap of determinism? Can one speak of a free person in a mechanistic universe?[1]

Enlightenment heroes, undaunted by this difficulty, fostered great optimism in early nineteenth-century Europe. For they not only proclaimed that everything in the world operated mechanically but that all evils could be cured by appropriate technological steps. One may smile at such grandiose beliefs, even call them delusions, but those who held them were intensely committed to them, just as their descendants are today. At any rate, their doctrines made very good sense to those who were participating in the massive social upheaval of that epoch, the *industrial* revolutionists.

But progress could not occur, these philosophers agreed, while social convention supported by a traditional church obstructed its path. The medieval-style Catholic church and the feudal aristocracy were regarded as the chief hindrances to free and triumphant human development. They were barriers to be removed. Once the night of ignorance and superstition had faded with the demise of priests and rulers – the last king strangled in the guts of the last priest – a new day of liberty, equality and fraternity would dawn. With it would come new opportunities for social progress and self-realization.

Two revolutions formed the womb within which Marx' thought would grow and develop. The first is really misnamed, for the 'industrial revolution' hardly happened overnight. But however long it took, the process of industrialization was revolutionary in the sense that the whole course of human history was fundamentally altered by it. The profoundly unsettling experience for Hegel, whose philosophy was to play a leading part in Marx' social imagination, was that of being in the artificial environment of an industrializing society. The 'man-made world' turned out to be more than a philosopher's dream. It was an iron-and-steel reality. Technology 'carried' the idea.

The other revolution, though its shock-waves also rolled round the world, was a more coherent thing. The impact of the French Revolution on Marx' thinking cannot be overestimated. For him, and those with whom he was to study later, it was *the* revolution. (Industrialization was not yet described as a 'revolution'.) Hegel, again, wrote of the French Revolution as a 'glorious dawn'. He enthused about the role of reason in the revolution, claiming that human existence is centred in the head. Reason (the head) inspires people to build up their own worlds of reality – such as the new France.

The revolution was an attempt to make all things new: to frame laws based on reason, not revelation or church-doctrine, to make rulers answerable to law, not just themselves, and to involve 'the people' in decision-making processes in an unprecedented way. There is no doubt that many of the revolutionaries' ideals were laudable, though question marks remain over some of the means used to attain them and the real interests in which they acted. Christians, for instance, whole-heartedly endorse efforts to make all leaders accountable to higher authority than themselves but not simply to curb possible misuse of power against them. In making reason rather than (biblical) revelation their sole guide, the revolutionaries opened the doors, ironically, to a highly subjective and arbitrary understanding of law and the state.

French ideas had been popular for some time in Trier and the high school which Marx attended had not escaped their influence. Conflict existed, of course, between the new and the old ways of thinking. The city was predominantly Catholic (which may be another reason why Heinrich Marx plumped for Protestantism rather than the socially-dominant but reactionary Catholicism), and the Catholics rightly sensed that the humanism of revolutionary France was inimical to all their cherished beliefs. They trusted above all in the authority of the church, even over the state and education. The new humanists, however, had no guide but reason and wished to exclude God from their every thought and especially from politics and science.

Marx, along with all other social theorists, found that it was essential to comment on the French Revolution as the starting-point of a new era in history. The events of the closing years of the eighteenth century intrigued and excited the greatest minds of the following century, both to praise and to scorn. Little wonder that the Revolution has been spoken of as the 'greatest event of the *nineteenth* century'.

Pranks and piety

Marx' performance at school was much like that of any other boy. He was not an outstanding pupil. Socially, he was popular as a practical joker, although he had a knack of writing satirical poems about those whom he disliked. He retained all his life this ability to produce criticism, though not always with the poetic element. Academically, he was above average: he described some of his class-mates as 'country bumpkins'. But strangely enough it was at Greek and Latin that he excelled; history, which was in a sense to become his life's work, was his weakest subject. Two essays, written for the school-leaving examination, are worth comment.

The first, on religion, was 'a demonstration, according to John's Gospel, chapter 15, verses 1–14, of the reason, nature, necessity and effects of the union of believers with Christ'. However, it was clear from this essay that he had no biblical understanding of Christian faith. He wrote that men always tried to raise themselves to a higher moral plane and 'thus the history of mankind teaches us the necessity of union with Christ'.[2] By this he meant that the full potential moral development of man came with the advent of Christianity and throughout his life he was to imply that such human self-development could eventually lead to a perfect society.

He evidently regarded Christianity as a means of moral education and no more, an opinion which probably coincided with his teacher's. His notion of God, like his father's before him, was vague and distant. Quite unlike the God portrayed in the Bible, he was a being altogether outside human experience, an absent architect who never acted or spoke into human history.

'Reflections of a young man on the choice of a career' was the title of the other essay and once again, the underlying Enlightenment humanism continually surfaced. It was free choice, he asserted, which distinguished him as human from the animals and so his choice of a career would not be completely arbitrary and random. While he saw that his social background determined to some extent the type of career chosen, the guiding value in occupational choice should properly be sacrifice for the good of mankind. The aim of all endeavour, he maintained, was the 'full development' both of the individual and society. Carried along on a wave of enthusiasm, Marx concluded this essay on a high note: 'Our deeds live on quietly but eternally effective, and glowing tears of noble men will fall on our ashes.'

The use of rich expressions and poetic imagination was encouraged by a neighbour of the Marx family, Baron von Westphalen, also a lawyer and a Lutheran. The baron took young Karl for long country walks, apparently ignoring both their differences in age and in social position. They read Homer and Shakespeare together and Marx became increasingly fired with a Romantic spirit which was to set alight many of his later writings.

'Romanticism' was essentially a feeling of liberation of the imagination and thus found its prime expression in artistic activity. It was a major religious current in Europe at the turn of the nineteenth century.[3] But that in no way denies that Romanticism had deep consequences for personal and social behaviour. It was both an extension of the eighteenth-century rationalism and a major revolt against it. Similarly grounded in non-Christian humanism and perhaps even more blatantly so, Romanticism's explosive contrast lay in its exaltation of the irrational. The 'freedom ideal', gasping for air, was attempting to break out of the scientific strait-jacket.

Greek mythology often fuelled the fires of Romantic imagination. Marx was particularly attracted by Prometheus, with whom he found some affinity. Zeus had punished Prometheus for taking fire from heaven and giving it to earthlings. Chained securely to a rock, Prometheus had his liver eaten out by an eagle but daily the liver grew again. The notion of life growing out of destruction or death is what we earlier called a 'redemptive motif'. Its true significance is disclosed in the resurrection of Christ but many religions and mythologies prefigure or parody it. Marx hung onto this notion long after he had explicitly left the dwellings of the gods for a concern with the 'real world'. (His contemporary, Wagner, who was similarly post-

Romantic in his music, also retained this idea.)

The shackled but powerfully-writhing Prometheus is nowhere more vividly portrayed in Marx than in the scything syllables which close the *Communist Manifesto*:

> Let the ruling classes tremble at a communistic revolution. The proletarians have nothing to lose but their chains. They have a world to win. Working men of all countries, unite!

So, while walking in the forest, Marx gleaned from the baron his Romantic enthusiasm (though never its mere irrationalism). It was also through the baron that Marx first encountered Saint-Simon, whose ideas on the dynamic principle of history were to lace Marx' best-known theories. Saint-Simon saw human creative work as the key to the unfolding of history, as for each stage new inventions were made to produce contemporary necessities. Saint-Simon would no doubt have approved of the baron's progressive views, even though the latter had been born into the class which, according to Saint-Simon, was destined eventually to pass away.

Saint-Simon was optimistic about the positive potential of technological development in providing abundantly for all human needs. Marx (in the *Grundrisse*[4]) was to share this opinion. But a major obstacle hindered advance. History, according to Saint-Simon and after him Marx, could be understood as a series of class struggles between those who possessed the main economic resources of the community and those who did not. He maintained that repeated conflict would accompany increasing technological advance until enough was produced for all and selflessness and justice prevailed.

But Marx had to wait until he reached Paris before he had an opportunity seriously to grapple with the ideas of Saint-Simon. Meanwhile, his friendship with Baron von Westphalen grew, to the approval of his father, who little appreciated the direction in which Marx' Romantic idealism would take him. Marx was later to dedicate his doctoral thesis to the baron in an unusually sentimental manner: 'Far from retreating before the reactionary ghosts and the often dark sky of our time, you have always been able, inspired by a profound and burning idealism, to perceive, behind the veils that hide it, the shrine that burns in the heart of this world. You, my fatherly friend, have always been for me the living proof that idealism is no illusion, but the true reality.'[5]

So, by the age of seventeen, Marx was already aware of the general contours of Enlightenment thought, of several progressive social theorists, as well as of classical writers and Romantic poets. He had, however, become aware of another attraction in the von Westphalen household: the baron's eldest daughter Jenny. Since childhood, in fact, when the families had social contact, Marx had found a soft spot for her, though she was four years older than he. But 1835 saw Marx' departure for Bonn, where his father had recommended that he enrol as a law student in the university. His separation from Jenny stimulated his own attempts at writing poetry, which turned out to be one of his major preoccupations during that first academic year.

The bold knight and the alehouse

He stayed at Bonn for just one year. He drank, duelled and composed poems. Romanticism was the mood of the university there, which, though small with only 700 students, was the Rhineland's centre of higher education. He ambitiously registered for nine courses, soon reducing this to six. His interests were mainly literary, at least as far as study was concerned. He also spent much time in the Trier Tavern Club, where the main interest was alcoholic. He overspent his father's allowance and although the authorities were content with his academic work, he was in trouble with them for drunkenness and the possession of forbidden (duelling) weapons. In this, he was far from untypical of students in Bonn.

Not surprisingly, Heinrich Marx took a dim view of his son's activities, although he discovered only sporadically what was happening, as Marx hardly ever wrote home. When one of Karl's rare letters did arrive, containing a request that his father pay for the publication of some of the poems, Heinrich resolved to take a stern attitude. In any case, he found the verses quite incomprehensible and was definitely not prepared to contribute to their publication. He was generally disappointed with his son's performance and felt that the solution would be a change of environment. Maybe Karl was mixing in the wrong circles and a move to a larger, more academic university was required. In the subsequent transfer to Berlin University in 1836, neither father nor son could have guessed that the immense consequences of the move would increase rather than diminish the distance between them.

Berlin was a totally different scene. Marx must have felt provincial and unsophisticated when he arrived to present himself to the university, far removed from the placid backwaters of Trier and Bonn. Isaiah Berlin says: 'Berlin was an immensely large and populous city, modern, ugly, pretentious and intensely serious, at once the centre of the Prussian bureaucracy and the meeting place of the discontented radical intellectuals who formed the nucleus of the growing opposition to it.'[6] The fresh atmosphere had an invigorating impact on Marx, who feverishly set about working hard to understand and criticize his new environment.

His first preoccupation, however, was romance. He wrote a lengthy letter home to his father during his first year, which gives biographers considerable insight into his character. 'When I left you,' he said, 'a new world had just begun to exist for me.' Even in the Romantic world of nature, there was no 'work of art as beautiful as Jenny'. In the summer months at home, Marx had become semi-officially engaged to her, but the relationship was not disclosed to her parents. His Romanticism did not leave him short of zeal in the matter and he wrote three books of poetry in her honour. The poems were alive with gnomes and sirens, with ditties to the stars and odes to bold knights. They were a huge change from the rationalism of home and from his schoolboy humanitarianism. As with Thomas Carlyle, it seemed for Marx that 'the whole ME stood up', in his exaltation of free personality and detached genius. He wrote that when Jenny were finally his,

> Then I will wander godlike and victorious
> Through the ruins of the world
> And giving my words an active force
> I will feel equal to the creator.

His father, who took his advisory role very seriously, continually cautioned him to calm down. He suggested how he ought to write to Jenny and even helped him with the ticklish task of persuading her parents to consent to their marriage. Whether or not his aid was necessary, the permission for the couple to wed was granted in March 1837. Another six years were to elapse, however, before the event came about.

The decisive conversion

Despite the emotional turbulence of this period, Marx was immersing himself in his studies. As at Bonn, he began with law but soon felt a need to grapple with philosophy, as there was a major controversy in the Law School. One professor taught from the viewpoint of Hegel, emphasizing social questions and the benefits of the French Revolution. Another, in the 'historical school', argued that laws were derived from customs and traditions and that therefore law should have a strong connection with the past. Here was a deep dilemma – whether progress depended on rejecting or conserving the past. Marx plunged in, determined to find himself a satisfactory answer.

The sheer exertion of work, however, made him very ill, as he spent many nights reading and writing. The doctor's report suggests that he had tuberculosis. Due to the resulting weakness of his lungs he was exempted from military service and sent to a country village to convalesce. The break caused him to see his problems in a new light and he made a sudden and complete change.

The Romantic idealism, with its rift between the natural and the supernatural, which had captured his mind until then, was ousted in a moment: 'I came to seek the idea in the real itself. If the gods had before dwelt above the earth, they had now become its centre.' He had decided to follow the philosopher Hegel. David McLellan rightly points out that it was probably the most important intellectual step of Marx' whole life. For while Marx was an acidic critic of Hegel, frequently accusing him of un-earthed idealism or political reaction and while he claimed to have stood Hegel's dialectic 'on its feet', the structure of his system and even his basic concepts derive from his early mentor – Hegel.

Marx set out in a new philosophical direction, though certainly not for the last time. His early intellectual development may be seen as a series of thought-transformations. Their turbulence was not to settle into stable progress until much of his young work was written. As we have seen, previous imprints on his mind had been left by Enlightenment ideas of reason and Romanticism. Boundless faith had been placed in the power of reason and criticism to explain and improve the material and social world. Suffering and ignorance, it was thought, could be abolished simply by finding rational solutions. All the answers to human problems could be found, given time and, once established, straightforward technique would take over.

The canny Enlightenment *philosophes*, as the theoretical spokesmen of the new class of industrial entrepreneurs, were fully aware of attempts to impede progress. It was in the interests of some propertied and privileged groups, especially the official church and the court, to maintain general ignorance. If the Enlightenment dream were really to materialize, such elements in ruling classes would have to be removed. Enlightened government would enable natural human benevolence to flourish and the spread of education would, they believed, systematically erase all traces of misery. Happiness would follow on the heels of progress.

With goals such as these, it comes as no shock to find that these philosophers were never deeply perturbed by the contradictions lurking beneath the surface of their hopeful theories. The problem of freedom in a world apparently governed by causal laws was aggravated by the desire of men such as Montesquieu for a 'science of society'. The belief in progress was given a big boost in pre-Revolutionary France by the apparent success of English scientists in discovering laws by which the universe could be explained. The belief was reinforced by the idea of extending such science to the study of persons in society. At the same time however complications of the freedom/science paradox multiplied. But such hitches were insignificant in view of the pressing need to obliterate all entrenched forces of irrationality and reaction, whether in church or government.

Hegel challenged all this and condemned it as mere unrealistic dogmatism. He did not question the importance of reason. One of his most celebrated aphorisms is that 'the real is the rational, and the rational is the real'. But he said that ideas such as 'natural law' could not on their own provide the basis for human studies such as history.

Mere mechanical causation is a most inappropriate model for history, he argued. French thought may be able to see change but it cannot comprehend the direction in which history is going. No, history is *organic*. This is the dynamic principle which must be reckoned with. The past contains the seeds of the future, which one day will blossom into the plants and trees of action and events. This process is being driven by a force 'out there', which may be discerned 'down here'. That force he variously termed 'Idea', or 'Spirit', his substitute for God.

Simple mechanical causes were out. Hegel would have disagreed profoundly with those Victorian social thinkers who believed that 'drink causes poverty', as he held that much wider questions must be asked about the whole context in which any phenomenon such as poverty exists. (Marx was to make some very searching observations as to why such an equation was inappropriate, partly based on the method he learned from Hegel.) Individual events, according to Hegel, are only explicable in terms of a variety of factors – and those factors are nothing less than the manifestation of one Spirit, which continually moves history in a progressive direction. Hegel was primarily concerned with the development of thought itself, which he was sure would culminate in absolute human knowledge.

Unlike many of his predecessors, Hegel did not believe that the progress of philosophy in the direction of absolute knowledge would be smooth. On the contrary, he conceived of progress as a series of jumps from one stage to another. Put another way, he held that thought developed as contradictions were resolved. Some assertion might be challenged by a counter-argument and that would result in a compromise between the two positions. That emergent assertion would not be a conclusion but rather a proposition to be modified through further tension and conflict. Human beings cannot in any sense 'know truth', for there is always tension in a state of affairs between what is now and what is going to happen. The seed is, as it were, struggling with the tension of present existence and the knowledge that one day it will be a mighty tree. Everything is in the process of becoming something else. Hegel called this process 'dialectic'.

Hegel's philosophy was immensely popular, especially in Berlin University where he had taught. Contradictions of Enlightenment thought such as the freedom/scientific law question could be resolved by Hegelianism. Freedom, for Hegel, was a recognition of finitude, which is a manifestation of Spirit. As people became more self-aware, they became more aware of their limitations but in that knowledge there was liberation. For those who were disillusioned by the failure of the French Revolution to provide 'Liberty, Equality, and Fraternity' for all, here was a new ray of hope. The revolution could be understood as a mere stage in the unfolding of Spirit. Perhaps more was to follow.

Although it was popular and although Hegel himself allied his philosophy with Protestantism, many of its implications were by no means Christian. Hegel's notion of 'truth' for example, is impersonal. Think dispassionately enough and you will find it. Moreover, the truth can never be 'known', in the Christian sense, as one is never sure what it may next *become*. The basis for right principles of action – should I kill this person? – was severely weakened by Hegel. He began to pull the rug from under our feet. Then he left his disciples to finish the job.

Hegel's philosophy could be used by either conservatives or radicals. He himself saw the Spirit manifesting itself supremely in Prussian Protestantism and, politically, in the Prussian state. Others took an entirely different view and, basing themselves on the 'becoming' side of the dialectic, made Hegel radical. Marx was soon associating with these 'free spirits' (as they called themselves) in the heady atmosphere of the Berlin University Doctors' Club. The radical followers of Hegel came to be known generally as 'Young Hegelians'. Their discussions had begun with the criticism of religion and they had their first champion in David Strauss, whose controversial book *Life of Jesus* appeared in 1835.

Strauss tried to amputate the supernatural from Christian faith. He suggested that the Gospel records of Jesus' life were not history at all but myths originating in the Jewish *expectation* of the Messiah. As the Gospels date from an earlier stage of the self-awareness of mankind, he went on, they are important for an understanding of that time but are now quite inadequate and unreliable guides for modern life. A storm of controversy broke, not only among those who held to the orthodox Christian belief in the historical accuracy of the Gospels but among the Young Hegelians who decided that Strauss was not radical enough. Bruno Bauer, who was recognized as leader of the Doctors' Club and taught theology at Berlin University, went further and completely denied the historicity of Jesus, dismissing the Gospels simply as fictitious tales of a bygone era.

Although criticism of religion was the first task of the Young Hegelians, it was a short step from there to the criticism of politics, as the state was hopelessly mixed up with the church in Prussian society. The Doctors' Club soon became the scene of hot political debate and Marx quickly made a name for himself, as a critic of both politics and religion. Bauer's brother, Edgar, described him in a Club poem:

> But who advances here full of impetuosity?
> It is a dark form from Trier, an unleashed monster,
> With self-assured step he hammers the ground with his heels
> And raises his arms in full fury to heaven
> As though he wished to seize the celestial vault and lower it to earth.
> In rage he continually deals with his redoubtable fist,
> As if a thousand devils were gripping his hair.

Making 'Dr Marx'

A change occured in 1838, however, with the death of Heinrich Marx. With his main means of support gone, Karl had virtually to fend for himself. He began work almost immediately on a doctoral thesis, with the hope of obtaining a university teaching post. Making an explicit parallel with his own time of ferment after Hegel, he wrote about Epicurus and Democritus after the time of Aristotle. His atheistic convictions, which he sustained throughout his life, were stridently announced in the preface: 'Philosophy makes no secret of it. Prometheus' confession "in a word, I hate all gods", is its own confession, its own motto against all gods in heaven and earth who do not recognize man's self-consciousness as the highest divinity.' While this kind of sentiment was undoubtedly common among the Young Hegelians, it was not merely 'juvenilia'; Marx really meant it. This is evident, as we shall see, throughout all his later work.

Marx' self-assured style when writing against Christianity derived partly from the important influence of the Berlin philosopher Ludwig Feuerbach.[7] Marx had read his work while working on his dissertation. Although Feuerbach's *Preliminary Theses for the Reform of Philosophy* was to excite Marx' imagination even more profoundly than *The Essence of Christianity* (which came out in 1841) the basic message of the latter was adopted by Marx. For Feuerbach, God was nothing but a 'projection' of human nature onto a mythical being who exists in an entirely imaginary 'out there'. Feuerbach wanted people to see that 'God' is really mankind and that 'the knowledge of God is nothing else than the knowledge of man!'[8]

It is important to notice that Marx accepted this belief so early on. For there is a deep difference between Feuerbach's view and biblical Christianity. For the biblical God is *both* 'out there' *and* 'down here'. To misunderstand this leads straight to Feuerbach's illusion that God and humanity are the same thing. There is a distinction between Creator and creature which must be maintained if human purpose – to live for and enjoy God – is to be appreciated. The very existence and persistence of Christianity is an obstinate difficulty for those who adhere to Feuerbach and his ilk.

With pressures from lack of funds and pressures from the call of colleagues (especially Bauer) to spend his time on radical criticism, Marx was eager to complete his thesis. Though it was a good piece of work, he could not risk failing the degree, so he sent it, not to Berlin, but to Jena, which had a reputation for being something of a PhD 'factory'. He was immediately granted the degree in April 1841. He worked hard at the final qualification necessary for a university post but his hopes were dashed when Bauer, through whom he had expected to be appointed, was himself thrown out of the university for his unorthodox views.

Thus excluded from a position within the establishment, Marx was slightly at a loss as to what his next move should be. He commuted restlessly between Trier, Bonn and Cologne while he tried to find work. He wrote several articles, some of which had the distinction of being stopped by the censor, but despite their vivid style, none gained him the 'break' he needed. But he did not spend the rest of the time moping. Of a relaxing afternoon with Marx in Bonn, Bauer wrote: 'We were as carefree as ever. In Godesberg we hired a couple of donkeys and galloped on them like madmen around the hill and through the village. Bonn society gazed at us amazed as ever. We hallooed and the donkeys brayed.'

'Bonn society' was soon to know the name of Marx for more notorious reasons. Probably still in disgust at his failure to obtain a university post, he joined the 'Cologne Circle' (whose membership included at least one other previous member of the Berlin Doctors' Club), which was engaged in liberal opposition to the government. Marx readily increased his involvement in practical politics. When an enthusiastic member of the group, Moses Hess, persuaded the wealthier financiers and industrialists that a newspaper would be an ideal means of spreading their views, Marx glimpsed a possible opening for himself. Although he had offered his services to another journal, nothing in the way of regular work had come of that, so he threw his energy into the new *Rheinische Zeitung*. This proved to be a useful time for Marx, who learned to wield his pen journalistically, though it was also to culminate in his being made unwelcome in Germany.

There was little doubt in the minds of others in the Cologne Circle about Marx' volcanic potential. Hess, for example, felt that it would only be a matter of time before Marx outstripped them all. He introduced him to a friend in these words:

> Prepare to meet the greatest — perhaps the only genuine — philosopher now alive, who will soon ... attract the eyes of all Germany ... Dr Marx ... will give medieval politics and religion their *coup de grâce*. He combines the deepest philosophical seriousness with the most biting wit. Imagine Rousseau, Voltaire, Holbach, Lessing, Heine, and Hegel fused into one person — I say fused not juxtaposed — and you have Dr Marx.[9]

Hess was not exaggerating. The following year Marx was to make his famous, though ambiguous, comments on religion as an illusion, a diversion from real life, 'the opiate of the people'. Two years later he was to be internationally known to European authorities as a dangerous anti-liberal, a revolutionary communist. He did not fail to impress those who came into contact with him, whether or not they liked him, as this description from another *Rheinische Zeitung* colleague shows:

> Karl Marx from Trier was a powerful man of twenty-four whose thick black hair sprung from his cheeks, arms, nose, and ears. He was domineering, impetuous, passionate, full of boundless self-confidence, but at the same time deeply earnest and learned, a restless dialectician who with his restless Jewish penetration pushed every proposition of Young Hegelian doctrine to its final conclusion ...[10]

It was certainly Marx' desire to use his strength and skill to 'give medieval politics and religion their *coup de grâce*', and he would increase his efforts to do so as time went on. But the basis of his anti-religious feeling was already present. All he had seen of Christianity was a pathetic caricature (the Prussian state church), much of which truly deserved his biting criticism. He had observed his father exchange one 'faith' for another without it making any difference either to his convictions (which were at variance with the pure form of either religion) or to his life-style. He had shown that he could write sentimental high school essays about Jesus which were sufficient to satisfy his teacher. He had entertained a Romantic enthusiasm for the mythological gods of ancient Greece, only to spurn them as distractions from human self-consciousness, which he proclaimed the highest divinity. And he had endorsed the opinions of the Young Hegelians, that the Gospels were unreliable as history and that religion is the enemy of human progress.

Perhaps it is no accident that Marx wrote of the flowers on the chains. For both Rousseau, a leading Enlightenment philosopher, and Hegel used similar phrases. Rousseau spoke of those who 'decorate the chains (of human bondage) with garlands of flowers'. Hegel, in a slightly different connection, reused Luther's phrase 'the rose in the cross'. Luther's intention had been to show the benefits available in Christ's cross. But Hegel made the rose central, as 'reason'. The darker aspects of the present age, its suffering and its sorrow, are alleviated by the promise of reason's dawn. Marx' thought was to grow both in the context of Enlightenment liberationism and Hegelian metaphysics.[11]

His understanding of the nature and function of religion was to undergo various modifications in later life but he never retracted his fundamental atheism. Nevertheless, many commentators have suggested that there is a certain similarity between Marxism and Christianity, despite obvious differences in the basic tenets of each. Could it be that while he rejected the Christianity which he saw around him, he still came close to Christian ideas in his understanding of the social world of men and women? We must examine Marx' later development to seek an answer. But now economic questions were already engaging his attention. And he was about to grapple with the crucial issues of the nature of history and the nature of persons.

Notes and references

1 This, of course, is still a live question. See the recent statement by C. Stephen Evans, *Preserving the Person*, Inter-Varsity Press (Downers Grove), 1977.

2 David McLellan, *Karl Marx: His Life and Thought*, Macmillan, 1973, Harper and Row, 1974, p. 11.

3 J. L. Talmon, *Romanticism and Revolt*, Thames and Hudson and Harcourt, Brace, Jovanovich, 1967.

4 The *Grundrisse* is discussed in chapter 5.

5 David McLellan, 1973, p. 16.

6 Isaiah Berlin, *Karl Marx: His Life and Environment*, Oxford University Press, 1963, p. 34.

7 Johan van der Hoeven, *Karl Marx: The Roots of His Thought*, Wedge Publishing Foundation, 1976, p. 33. See Also David McLellan, *The Young Hegelians and Karl Marx*, Macmillan, 1969, p. 92f.

8 Quoted in Colin Brown, *Philosophy and the Christian Faith*, Tyndale Press (London), 1969, p. 134.

9 David McLellan, 1973, p. 47.

10 David McLellan, 1973, p. 53.

11 A helpful background to this is Peter Gay, *The Enlightenment: An Interpretation* volume I 'The Rise of Modern Paganism', Weidenfeld & Nicholson, 1967. The Enlightenment, while presenting a united attack on Christianity, was itself religious. This is also a theme of Herman Dooyeweerd, *In the Twilight of Western Thought*, The Craig Press, 1960, and, with reference to art in particular, H. R. Rookmaaker, *Modern Art and the Death of a Culture*, Inter-Varsity Press 1970.

Nineteenth-century street scene in Britain

CHAPTER 2

Alienated man

We begin with real, active men, and from their real life-process show the development of the ideological reflexes and echoes of this life-process.
Marx, 1845–46

Marx was an alienated man. Born into a family which was excluded from full social participation, unable to obtain an 'establishment' university teaching post, moved on by police from one country to another, he finally lived as a foreigner in London. Even there he was to be evicted from his lodgings for rent-arrears. As a social critic, the personal experience of not feeling at home in the world gave him a unique vantage-point. He could sympathize with the estranged.

He wove the notion of alienation into his whole social theory. Giving it a more specific meaning than just not being 'at home', alienation, for Marx, became the basic human problem.

We cannot know about the world without saying something about our relationship to it as people. As with all world-views, Marx' included a particular view of personhood, of what it means to be human. All social theories are constructed on the foundation of some open or hidden understanding of man: male and female.

Because Marx believed that to be human was to be a purposeful being developing his or her capacities through work, he could consistently demand liberation from any constraints on that development. If to be human is to labour freely, any limitations on that amount to a stunting of full personhood.

This phase of Marx' thought-development can be understood in terms of his wrestling with the riddle: who are we? why are we here? why is life problematic? The point of the exercise, however, was not simply to shape a finely-chiselled fresh definition. Marx committed himself to understanding the human condition with a view to transforming it. Just as Christian thinking on personhood does not take place in cloudy abstraction (in the Bible at least) but is rooted in real life-processes, so Marx' big questions were firmly grounded in everyday human life.

As we shall see, with the domestic backdrop of early married life, attempted communal living in Paris and an undignified banishment to Brussels, Marx' thought developed at a fast pace. His intellectual and journalistic activity was to take him from the more abstract realms of German philosophy, through French radical politics and eventually to English economics in his quest of the *practical* meaning of human existence.

Social wood

The articles he wrote for the *Rheinische Zeitung* led to that paper's wide success – and suppression. The exasperated censor finally clamped down in March 1843. This official intolerance of his writing led directly to Marx' departure for France. Ironically, Marx' final articles had concluded with a vigorous plea for a free press, the lack of which effectively gagged a large sector of the population whose views, he felt, ought to have been openly expressed. But writing the articles was important to Marx, as he began to sense for the first time that 'political' problems had deeper roots.

As Engels said later, Marx was now drawn away from pure politics to economic relationships and so to socialism. He had been attending a socialist discussion group which was stimulated by French socialist ideas, the presence of communists such as Moses Hess and by Marx' own observations of living and working conditions in the Rhineland. The last articles reflected this concern.

One article was on timber-theft. At one time everyone had been able to gather dead wood but legal restrictions were imposed when timber became scarce. Prosecutions for wood-theft suddenly became the most pressing legal problem in Prussia. The official policy, which lawgivers were to follow, suggested that only the lumber itself was to be considered in prosecutions. It was against this that Marx objected.

The timber, as he saw it, was a symbol for social-political relationships and could not be realistically considered in detachment from that context. He referred to the old customary law, which allowed the poor to gather wood for fuel (just as, in the Old Testament, the poor were allowed to 'glean' the fields at harvest time). This law, he judged, had simply been swept aside by the greed of those who now benefited from the sale of the timber. The state had a duty to protect the poor rather than simply defend the interests of the rich. The timber had become a *fetish*; an apparently innocent object which in fact camouflaged a relationship of domination of man by man.

Having made this observation, Marx began to view other matters in the same light. The deep poverty of some Mosel wine-growers could be understood in terms of the trade-agreements made by those in power. It was not for want of hard work on the part of the farmers that they were poor but rather that outside competition had crippled them. Marx wanted an arbiter between the two groups, 'which at the same time represents the citizen without being directly involved in private interests. This resolving element, composed of a political mind and a civic heart, is a free press.'

Marx was to put great store by the freedom of the press and by his own journalistic activity. He conceived of both as contributory factors to wider human freedom. But this was also the way that Marx, editor-in-chief of the *Rheinische Zeitung* from October 1842, made himself unpopular with the Prussian censor. The circulation of the paper had risen to 'dangerous' proportions and the censorship was infuriating Marx. The paper was suppressed and, almost simultaneously, Marx handed in his resignation. He declared that 'the Government have given me back my liberty', and resolved to leave the country.

The immediate difficulty, however, was to find another job, particularly as he wanted to marry Jenny without further delay. His old friends of the 'Young Hegelian' persuasion were splitting into two parties – some to pursue abstract theoretical criticism (led by Bauer), and others, led by Ruge, to more direct political action. Marx was invited by Ruge to join him as co-editor of a new journal which would link French and German social theory and politics.

He was enthusiastic about the project and optimistic that it might further the cause of 'suffering humanity' to which he now felt more urgently drawn. Agreements were drawn up, and Marx' salary was assured. At last marriage was possible! He told Ruge, 'I am head-over-heels in love and it is as serious as it can be. I have been engaged for more than seven years and my fiancée has been involved on my behalf in the toughest of struggles which have ruined her health. These have been in part against her pietist and aristocratic relations . . .'

If Jenny's relations caused trouble in her relationship with Karl, this did nothing to dampen her ardour towards him. She was passionately in love with him and was to remain a devoted wife to the end of her days. Not long before their marriage, on 19 June 1843, she told him in a letter, 'I think that you have never been as dear, as sweet, as charming . . . I did not know how dear you were to me in my deepest heart until I no longer saw you in the flesh . . .'

They honeymooned in several places during the weeks following the wedding, visiting beauty spots in Switzerland *en route*. On their return, they lived at first with Jenny's mother, who had moved to

Kreuznach some time before. Once settled there, Marx began preparing himself for work on the *Deutsche-Französische Jahrbücher*. In particular, he wished to clarify his thoughts on politics and thus plunged into Hegel once more. The resulting critical commentary on Hegel's view of the state he entitled *The Critique of Hegel's Philosophy of Right*. Though highly significant, it remained unpublished during his lifetime.

An upside-down world

Marx, with his growing awareness of socio-economic realities and inspired by the ideas of the anti-Christian philosopher Feuerbach, set out to show, as other contemporaries were also showing, that politics came to a dead-end in Hegel. Marx believed (with Feuerbach himself) that Feuerbach's *The Essence of Christianity* had struck the death-blow to Christianity and that Feuerbach, unlike Hegel, had rightly perceived the relationship between ideas and reality. Whereas with Hegel reality was the outworking of the *Idea*, for Feuerbach the opposite was true. And Feuerbach's influence was crucial.

Hegel maintained that human consciousness was manifest in legal, political and other social institutions, giving the latter rationality. Marx disagreed: it is *people* who make political constitutions and the like. Such statements simply reflect the reality of their origins. This situation is mirrored in religion. God, for Marx as for Feuerbach, is a fiction of the mind, invented because of unsatisfied needs. But when people see this, then the unreality of religion is unmasked and men can take their lives into their own hands. While people still believe in God (and similarly while they still believe in the constitution as an expression of the *Idea*), they have an upside-down view of themselves and the world and cannot properly understand their condition.

Thus, as Marx later wrote in reference to the stance of the new journal, he saw his task as the 'reform of consciousness'. Religious and political myths had to be exposed for what they were and then something new could begin. The closing remarks of an idealistic letter to Ruge made it clear that salvation lay ahead: 'To have its sins forgiven, humanity needs only to recognize them as they are.'[1]

For the very ordinary reason that Paris seemed the most appropriate place for a German–French journal to be published, Marx and Ruge started work there in 1843. Jenny Marx was already four months pregnant but at Ruge's suggestion they moved in with him and with two other families, as a Fourierist experiment in communal living. (Charles Fourier, a Parisian commercial traveller, wished to divide the world into small, self-governing groups which he dubbed 'phalansteries'. He hoped thus to avoid the tyranny of the top-heavy bureaucratic state. Phalanstery members would hold goods in common, each work according to their ability and together devote extensive periods of each day to intellectual and artistic recreation.) Within a few weeks of this particular phalanstery getting together, however, the members' different ages, class-backgrounds and ambitions ended the experiment and they left the community for their own homes in the neighbourhood.

But not only were the families a mixed bunch, the whole contributing team of the *D-F Jahrbücher* was, to say the least, eclectic. There were poets (Herwegh and Heine), anarcho-communists (Hess and Bakunin), and democrats interested in popular education (Ruge and Froebel) as well as Marx himself. Needless to say, apart from the very limited success of the journal itself, Marx would not stand such diversity of views for long. That he did put up with it for some time may partly have been because he was forming new opinions himself. Once in France, a crucial question began to nag him: why had the French Revolution ultimately failed? The socialist atmosphere of Paris and the presence of a large working class was to make a significant impression on him as he began to think out his answer.

Mainly due to lack of support, the new journal did not last long: the first double-number was also the last. However, Marx wrote two pieces for it, the first of which was 'On the Jewish Question'. As with so many of his writings, it was a response to the views of another, in this case Bauer. Still concerned with the relationship between religion, the state and human freedom, Marx wished to explore the reasons for the inferior status of German Jews.

Bauer had attacked the state for giving 'Christians' more rights than Jews, but Marx wanted to go further and question the state itself. He felt that Bauer had not considered *human* emancipation (the freedom to develop all human faculties), but only *political* rights and liberties. One only had to look at North America, wrote Marx, to see that political freedom can co-exist with 'Christian' practice; but without human liberation. The vaunted 'rights of man' were opposed to true humanity. Liberty, 'the right to do and perform what does not harm others' was, according to Marx, 'not based on the union of man with man but on the separation of man from man'. Property, the right to dispose of one's goods at will, without regard for others, was 'the right to selfishness ... it leads man to see in other men not the realization, but the limitation of his own freedom'.

Marx asserted that the 'abstract', impersonal man of charters and constitutions must once more be endowed with genuine 'citizenship'. True human identity must be conceived as 'species-being', distinguished from animal existence by the free opportunity for people to develop through their work. When a person's nature as a member of society rather than a cipher, and as a worker rather than a religious or political creature, was recognized, then there would be hope of human emancipation.

But Bauer still thought too theologically: he imagined that, while Christians would be free by ridding themselves of their religion, Jews had to take two steps to liberty. This was nonsense to Marx. He insisted that 'civil society', in which Jews and Christians were both involved, had a god of its own:

> Money is the jealous god of Israel before whom no other god may stand. Money debases all the gods of man and turns them into commodities. Money is the universal, self-constituted value of all things. It has therefore robbed the whole world, human as well as natural, of its own values. Money is the alienated essence of man's work and being; this alien essence dominates him; and he adores it.

Religion, for Marx, is something people project on to an alien, imaginary being which apparently takes on a life of its own. Here the secular god of money has become a blind, concealing real human relationships.

On self-liberation and opium

He had, of course, stumbled on a significant point and one which is repeatedly made in the Bible. The prophet Isaiah scorns the person who uses half a tree-trunk for firewood and shapes the other half into an idol, beseeching it to save him. And the apostle Paul, with a similar lively stroke, castigates those whose 'god is their belly'. People 'project' religions constantly; it is a feature of our fallen humanity. To trust a carved idol, or to worship one's appetite for gain is obviously to engage in a foolish delusion. With this Christianity and Marxism must agree.

We must part company at the point where Marx mistakes the human manufacture of gods for the whole story. It is too big a step from 'people project religions' to 'all religion is projection'. Marx hated the idea of any 'go-between' which might threaten the notion of *self-liberation*. As a post-Christian figure, he was convinced that we can redeem ourselves, without help. For him, therefore, any religion (but especially one like Christianity which announces that Jesus radically 'stepped in' to rescue and bring new life to mankind) is a distraction. Marx had no truck with any view which seemed to him to detract from real people meeting their own real needs. The 'real needs' which are met by Christ, however, are a lot deeper than the surface manifestations which Marx so bitterly fought.

The second article (related to the first) was intended as an in-troduction to the *Critique of Hegel's Philosophy of Right*, but had a significant new ingredient – the role of the proletariat (urban-industrial working class) as the emancipator of human society. Marx began with the necessary attack upon religion: 'The criticism of religion is the presupposition of all criticism.' Once the mists of out-moded religion have been cleared (and especially the religious legitimation of the German state), real problems will become visible and rational solutions made possible. Here is the point:

> The foundation of irreligious criticism is this: man makes religion, religion does not make man. But man is no abstract being squat-ting outside the world. Man is the world of man, the state, society. This state and this society produce religion's inverted attitude to the world because they are an inverted world themselves.

Thus Marx revealed again his own deepest belief. As van der Hoeven points out, the proposition that 'man makes his religion' is on the same footing as 'religion makes man'. Marx is 'confronting one religious stance with another: his own'.[2]

Marx then produced his most celebrated denunciation of religion:

> ... the struggle against religion is indirectly the struggle against that world whose spiritual aroma is religion. Religious suffering is at the same time an expression of real suffering and a protest against real suffering. Religion is the sigh of the oppressed creature, the feeling of a heartless world and the soul of soulless circumstances. It is the opium of the people ... The criticism of religion is therefore the germ of the criticism of the vale of tears whose halo is religion.

Religion both reveals and conceals suffering. On the one hand it is an escapist fantasy of alienated man, suffering oppression but looking forward to relief in heaven. On the other, it justifies social evils through the religious support of the state and through the preaching that patient endurance of suffering is a virtue. Marx was quite con-sistently revealing his atheism here. (Some commentators dis-agree – but he was referring to religion's *abolition*!) He immediately showed where his alternative commitment lay: 'The criticism of religion disillusions man so that he may think, act, and fashion his own reality as a disillusioned man come to his senses; so that he may revolve around himself as his real sun. Religion is only the illusory sun which revolves around man as long as he does not revolve around himself.' Man was Marx' god.

Of idylls and idols

However, we cannot leave the matter of Marx' criticism of religion there; it requires further examination. While his own faith was in a self-sufficient humanity, Marx levelled some damning accusations at the enemy of faith in mankind – Christianity. These, taken up more fully by Engels and in practical politics by Lenin, have led to the association of Communism with anti-Christian belligerence. Thus, in the late twentieth century, many believers (Protestant, Catholic, Orthodox and Jew) have been denied human rights, persecuted and killed for refusing total allegiance to party or state in China, the USSR and Eastern Europe. And while it is true that Catholics in Italy and Latin America especially have begun to co-operate with Marxists, it is not inappropriate to ask, on whose terms? Marx certainly left wide open the likelihood that his followers would regard Christianity as inimical to communism.

His primary intention, however, was to demonstrate the character of religion – as an idyllic illusion, a projection of the imagination – and then to get on with the real task of human liberation. His attack was valid, in so far as it related to the kind of Christianity, unsupported by the Bible, which is simply other-worldly, dividing 'nature' from 'grace'. He wanted to show *how* religion masked real human interests. When Marx later added the notion of religion as a class ideology, a distorted account of things-as-they-are, he completed his analysis of religion as a means of keeping society as it was. At the same time, he said, it gave people a vehicle to express their suffering.

Girardi, a Catholic contributor to the Christian–Marxist dialogue, affirms that historical events have made this a reality: 'Whenever the working class expressed its aspirations and demands, the Church stood with the opposition, against the workers. The workers grew up, therefore, considering the Church as their class enemy.'[3] (Girardi, however, misses the point that it has also sometimes been the association of workers' demands with threats of violent insurrection which has alienated the church from workers.)

But it is probably not so much opposition as sheer ignorance of the working class by the church which has produced such a gap between Christianity and the proletariat. E. R. Wickham, who studied an English industrial city in depth, concluded that the estrangement of the working class from the church has profoundly social and historic origins. Church buildings were not constructed with them in mind (in terms of location or space), but beyond that,

Poverty and wretchedness of material conditions as well as their own positive way of life bound them into a pattern of life that made them as foreigners in the midst of more stable townsmen . . . This, coupled with the economic rise of a middle class that was increasingly religious in its habit, led to a social stratification in which denominational lines ran parallel to the economic ones . . .[4]

It is true that, by default, the Christian church has neglected to sympathize with the real plight of workers under capitalism; it is also true that there have been some outstanding examples of Christian concern for the proletarian condition since the advent of industrialism. The evangelical Shaftesbury, for example, though he retained a paternalism characteristic of the nineteenth century, still showed great compassion towards the victims of the English factory system. He identified regularly with those 'slaves', making it his life's work to follow Christ's defence of the poor and powerless. Doubtless, Marxists would scorn his mere 'reformism', but curiously enough, Marx himself approved the results of some of his endeavours.

Missionary activity abroad has often been attacked as merely providing a foothold for the (more important) trading conerns of the rich nations. But it ought to be noted that while there has been a link between Christian mission and the vanguard of colonial imperialism in some Third World countries, which should be a source of acute discomfort to Christians, there have been many exceptions to that as well.

But as Míguez Bonino has indicated, Christians certainly have little cause for self-congratulation on these matters: much idolatrous manipulation of God's gifts has taken place in the name of Christ. And Jesus himself denounced religion used as a cloak for exploitation. The scribes who walked sanctimoniously around in long robes were the very 'ones who devour widows' houses, and for appearance' sake offer long prayers'. Jesus also 'broke the sabbath' in order to show how this gift of a day for worship and rest had been turned from its purpose and against human need. God really 'desired mercy and not sacrifice'. The institution had become so magnified as to obscure the human condition for which God cared: it was an idol.

As Míguez Bonino says, there is a striking resemblance between this double deception of idolatry and Marx' description of man-made religion.[5] 'On the one hand, (man) empties religion of its power to redeem and restore; on the other, he creates for himself a false assurance within the circle of unredeemed and alienated life.' Christians dare not deny their guilt here. They have all too often allowed the establishment to use Christian ideas to their ends. One need only mention the horrific crusades, the squire–parson connections and the 'Christian' justification of accumulated wealth in private hands by some Christians, to make a damning point.

Marx' mistake was *not* to say that men make their own religions. The biblical witness confirms, with anger and regret, that this idolatry is a continual process. Marx' error was to imagine that he was not making a religion himself.

But Marx moved on from the exposé of the 'opium of the people'. Once 'the holy form of human self-alienation has been discovered', continued Marx, the task is to 'discover self-alienation in its non-religious forms. The criticism of heaven is thus transformed into the criticism of earth, the criticism of religion into the criticism of law, and the criticism of theology into the criticism of politics.' Bauer's problem was that he had never come down to earth: he was lost in philosophy. But Marx wanted to introduce a dialectic between the real and the ideal. Philosophy does not exist on its own – it needs practical expression.

From critique to praxis

Though writing in France, Marx had Germany in mind and asked about the practical expression of philosophy thus: 'Can Germany achieve a *praxis* that will be equal to her principles, i.e. can she achieve a revolution that will not only raise her to the official level of modern peoples, but to the human level which is the immediate future of these peoples?' His answer was affirmative: 'The criticism of religion ends with the doctrine that man is for himself the highest being – that is, with the categorical imperative to overthrow all systems in which man is humiliated, enslaved, abandoned, and despised.' The means to that overthrow, more precisely, would be a combination of proletarian action with philosophical reflection.

Here is that vital link between anti-religion and revolution. Religion diverts and distracts attention from real people with real needs. Something (or someone) comes between people and their liberation. Get rid of religion and you can announce that 'we can free ourselves, by ourselves'. In particular those who understand things (theorists like Marx himself) and those who are most thoroughly stripped of humanity (the wage-labouring proletariat) may participate in the emancipation.

Marx was concerned that the French Revolution had never been completed. The task of completing it, of solving the social problem as well as the political, was constantly in the back of his mind at this time. In the French Revolution, as he saw it, one class (the new bourgeois class of industrialists and business-people) liberated society politically. But they did so assuming that what was good for them was good for everyone and that all class interests were identical. Here lay their error, accused Marx. Now a new class was needed for total human liberation, a 'class with radical chains' – the proletariat.

Because the French Revolution was his model, Marx saw the proletariat as the bourgeoisie of 1789. But there is a difficulty here which Marx never noticed. In his enthusiasm at discovering, as he thought, a class with radical chains, whose interests could authentically be the *general* interest, and thus bring about a classless society, he missed something vital. He failed to analyse more deeply the relationship between the bourgeois class of the French Revolution and the new proletariat. The bourgeoisie were carriers of a new mode of production. They introduced mills, factories, machinery: a whole new manufacturing technology.

Marx indicated that, in the flow of history, the new proletarian class would rise to power just as the bourgeoisie had done before: he simply substituted one class for the other. But he neglected that crucial *economic* role which belonged to the bourgeoisie. In what sense did the proletariat have an innovating economic role? What new feature do the industrial working classes bring into industry? The bourgeoisie had a solid base for their revolution: a new mode of production. The proletariat have no such base. They have never taken successful action without help from the intelligentsia. As we shall see, this poses huge problems in the understanding of revolutionary activity today.

However, what Marx did say, rather than what he did not, has been historically effective in stirring hearts to revolutionary agitation. As he continued with the proletariat/philosophy connection:

> As philosophy finds its material weapons in the proletariat, so the proletariat finds its intellectual weapons in philosophy, and as soon as the lightening of thought has struck deep into the virgin soil of the people, the emancipation of Germans into men will be completed.

But the sign was to come from France: 'When all internal conditions are fulfilled, the day of German resurrection will be heralded by the crowing of the Gallic cock.' Marx' conclusion, then, was that 'philosophy is the head of this emancipation, and the proletariat is its heart'.

However, even in those magnificent-sounding words was a tension which remained in the rest of Marx' writing. Philosophy is the revealer, but it is powerless without proletarian force. But proletarian force is useless without direction from the head. How exactly was this to work out in practice? Marx did not say, but bequeathed it as one of the contradictions typical of his post-Christian humanism.

Parisian seedbed

The months in Paris were crucial for Marx' thought-development. What he wrote in 1843—44 shows the link between his Romantic and Idealist (Hegelian) thinking and his political and economic social thought. Though he certainly was to change his mind on some details, the leading threads of the distinctive cloth he was weaving remained in the same place throughout. We have already noted the impact made on him by seeing industrial workers *en masse* in Paris and the general enthusiasm that working with other socialists gave him.

But all the while he developed a perspective which was uniquely his own. It was, for one thing, more communist. In fact, this led to his doctrinal split with Ruge, which was paralleled by disagreements over life-style. Ruge thoroughly disapproved of Marx' somewhat bohemian and apparently irresponsible life (he and Jenny had, for example, given away much precious money during their honeymoon). Ruge also found Marx' arrogance rather overbearing. But to Marx, Ruge now appeared too mild. When Ruge blamed the lack of political consciousness for the mal-handling of a Silesian weavers' revolt, Marx replied scathingly in another article. It was not the consciousness of the state which was problematic, he fulminated but the state itself. The state must go!

Marx had been looking for an opportunity to get some thoughts more systematically on paper and the chance came when his first daughter, Jenny, was born in May 1844. She was so sickly that she was taken by her mother to Trier for two months in a more stable atmosphere and where her old doctor could advise. Marx had grandiose schemes for writing monographs about law, politics and morals, but he only actually produced the one on politics.

Intended as a draft for what later became *Capital*, the so-called *Economic and Philosophical Manuscripts* came to be viewed as highly significant in their own right after their eventual publication in the early 1930s. Because they depict Marx' ideal person as an all-round, whole being and show why people are alienated and internally-broken, they have also been the focus of much discussion in the 'Christian–Marxist dialogue'. (This 'dialogue' was especially strong in the 1960s, in Eastern and Western Europe. Several major conferences were held, usually in academic settings, to discuss possible 'common ground' between theologians and Marxist thinkers.)

Marx' view of the person is surprisingly close yet fatally opposed to the Christian one. Man, for Marx, is *homo faber* – a maker. It is human character to work and to be a self-creator. People develop through transforming the world of nature in co-operation with each other. People take the initiative, making themselves, and constructing their world, through work. Marx, as we have seen, did not want a creator, upon whom men and women would be dependent and to whom they would be answerable. The self-creation of mankind, a humanity answerable only to itself, this was Marx' starting-point. If people make themselves, they can also liberate themselves.

But while there is this deep crevasse between Marx and the Christian outlook, there is, apparently, the bridge of 'conscious work' on which the Christian–Marxist dialogue rests. Christians often seem to have forgotten that work is crucially important to human life. Yet scripture maintains that people are to be working stewards of the world God created. Marxists, on the other hand, sometimes forget the nature of Marx' 'materialism'. It was Engels who preached the doctrine that 'matter is all there is', not Marx. It was Engels who saw spirit as a mere biological by-product of matter and it is often his interpretation of Marx which has been accepted as 'Marxism'.

But Marx' 'materialism' was to see the 'material base' of life as conscious activity. The 'economic factor' achieved its prominence simply because the person is seen as *homo faber* – the maker. In *The German Ideology*, things are summed up thus: people 'begin to distinguish themselves from animals as soon as they begin to *produce* their means of subsistence, a step which is conditioned by their physical organization. By producing their means of subsistence men are actually producing their actual material life.'

It is important to understand Marx' view of the person as a working self-creator, as this theme reappears in his mature work (*Grundrisse* and *Capital*). But it is also important because, unless human nature is understood, the character of the human condition cannot be understood either. Just as the Christian wishes to show that people forfeited a close and life-embracing relationship with God by rejecting or ignoring his directives, so Marx had to demonstrate the deleterious effects of the division of labour and capitalism in general. A person's essential humanity is lost, said Marx, when he loses control of his destiny. In religion, God takes the initiative and thus denies humanity. In economics, money pushes people around and determines relationships. Contemporary economics justified the treatment of people as mere commodities, instead of seeing purposive work and recreational leisure as part of the whole being of the person. (There were some exceptions to this, including a Christian economist, Sismondi, from whose insights Marx was to benefit.) The product of work, which would be an expression of human essence, is instead treated as a separate thing, an 'object' which appears to be over against the worker. Thus people are *alienated* from the objects of production.

But this was not all. Marx warmed to his theme of alienation by further describing and deprecating its effects. The very act of producing, said Marx, is alienating. The labour was forced and was done for another. Thus 'the activity of the worker is not his own spontaneous activity. It belongs to another and is the loss of himself.' In this way people were made animals, for they could not enjoy what made them distinctively human: work. Eating, drinking and procreating, activities shared in common with animals, were all that was left.

Taken further, this meant that man was alienated from his 'species-being'. The human species, according to Marx, is alone in being able to produce freely from any part of nature, but this freedom is inhibited when people do not produce *for the species,* that is, in a *social* way. This results in the final alienation: person from person. 'In general, the statement that man is alienated from his species-being means that one man is alienated from another as each of them is alienated from the human essence.' That both work and the product of work were alien from the worker meant that another now had to control both product and work. That was the ultimate inhumanity.

Marx' notebooks make it clear that he saw the practical manifestation of alienation especially in money and private property. That money was a social bond and that property and credit represented alienating social relationships only served to deepen the dehumanization process. To highlight the difference, Marx expressed his vision of future communist society. There, work would be intrinsically enjoyable and at the same time mutually satisfying the needs of others.

As he wrote in *The German Ideology*, under communism, 'society regulates the general production and thus makes it possible for me to do one thing today and another tomorrow, to hunt in the morning, fish in the afternoon, rear cattle in the evening, criticize after dinner, just as I have a mind'. (Quite how *all* members of society would manage to engage in such an idyllic round of activities, he did not explain!) 'Work would then be genuine, active property.' By contrast, 'Presupposing private property, my individuality is so far externalized that I hate my activity: it is a torment to me and only the appearance of an activity and thus also merely a forced activity that is laid upon me through an external, arbitrary need – not an inner and necessary one.'

But basic weaknesses run like geological faults through this view of alienation. Above all, if alienation results from class exploitation, then all alienation must be understood this way. But Marx was inconsistent here. Also, alienation, apparently, is ended by removal of those external conditions which foster it. As we shall see, although certain alienations may be reduced by a change of conditions, fundamental alienations still remain.

All the time, Marx claimed that his was a scientific analysis: '... my results have been obtained through a completely empirical analysis founded on a conscientious and critical study of political economy'. Critics of Marx point to the use of emotive words like 'alienation', saying that these are value-judgements inappropriate to science. But Marx, in common with Christians, would never have countenanced the suggestion that science could be separate from evaluation. He did not believe in neutral facts. What he meant was that given his 'material basis' (conscious human activity) his analysis was consistent and open to scrutiny. However, he firmly believed that his science was the only true description of reality.

From this, it is clear that any 'dialogue' which might occur between Christians and Marxists cannot take place on some 'common ground' of science even though there may be broad 'empirical' agreement. Any dialogue must acknowledge different starting-points for the Marxist and Christian analysis of the human condition. The Christian has to admit that worker/product, worker/self and worker/fellow alienations do occur. He cannot deny that at times Marx came embarrassingly close to a biblical understanding of co-operative, satisfying and unalienated work. But the Christian can never concede Marx' devastating disclaimer – his rejection of the Creator. For the Christian conception of the person, as Marx well knew, begins with God, not people.

Work in perspective

In the Bible, work and the making of one's world is certainly seen as a clue to human identity. But it is not *the* clue. Rather, work is seen in the wider context of the creature's response to the Creator. People are clearly distinguished from animals but in a far more radical way than merely by work. In Genesis 1:27 we are told: 'And God created man in his own image, in the image of God he created him; male and female He created them.' This points to the distinctiveness. People, as God's representatives on earth, are to subdue it and have responsible dominion over all other creatures.

Though finite, people are in many ways like God, sharing some of his characteristics. An important example is that, like God, we can communicate by speech. We may even communicate with him. But people are also fundamentally *un*like God. There is a basic distinction between Creator and creature which must always be maintained. Implicit in this is human dependence upon God. Whether we like it or not (and Marx hated the idea) we rely upon God to sustain and keep together the world he has made.

To say that people are dependent, however, does not mean that we are robots or zombies. People were placed on earth to be, literally, its caretakers, responding to God by living within the frameworks for freedom which he had made. People are in partnership with God to look after the earth. Friends of God are friends of the earth. The situation in Eden sums it up. Adam and Eve were given the task of responding to God by cultivating their plot, domesticating animals, building their mutual relationship with each other and raising a family.

These were their 'frameworks for freedom', and as Adam and Eve represent humanity, they are ours too. How is labour, or work, a framework for freedom? By 'framework for freedom' we mean that general structure of human life, given by God, within which there is freedom to respond to God's call to develop the creation. Labour is a necessary part of human life. But it must be integrated with the whole, which includes rest, play, eating, sex, buying, singing and so on.

But work itself also has many dimensions. It certainly is economic activity but it is more than just that. It involves trust, as one is obliged to work for family or community. It has a political aspect, as it relates to the common good. Work is also social – biblically, something which is done co-operatively whenever possible. It is something which even relates to worship, as God may be honoured through human work. Labour is far from being tied down to a narrow definition of drudgery. True, the human declaration of independence from God resulted in work becoming more difficult and frustrating but work's real meaning is still that of a framework for freedom. It is rooted in God's own character as Creator: the 'image of God' works in God's world. In a word, then, life is more than labour. And labour is more than economic activity.

But while Marx made work autonomous, giving meaning in itself, the Bible sees work as something to which God has given meaning. Notions of stewardship and service are intrinsic to the biblical view, as is the emphasis on work as a social activity. Thus the Christian would not only share some of Marx' misgivings about alienation but would want to penetrate much deeper into the distortions which have arisen in the world of work through neglect of service and stewardship. For as the Christian perspective links the meaning of work to a relationship with God and his ways, so the break in that relationship meant something damaging for work. Work became toil, work relationships became strained, exploitative and mutually destructive: this was the 'fall'.

But again, this was only a part of a wider picture of the human dis-integration which followed the first announcement of independence in the world. All meanings and purposes were twisted when the Creator/creature relationship of trust and obedience was shattered. But even in that moment of bitter tragedy for mankind, there was a shaft of light: a descendant of the woman would one day strike at the roots of alienation and human evil. The light dawned in the moment that Christ disabled the powers of evil at the crucifixion. For Christ's death was no martyr's moment. That death provides personal release from moral guilt stemming from rebellion against God. It provides for the renewal of relationship between creature and Creator and calls humanity back to the original frameworks for freedom within Christ's new kingdom.

But this, of course, was not the solution of the *Economic and Philosophical Manuscripts* to the misery of the alienated worker. Communism, 'the positive expression of the overcoming of private property' was Marx' proposal for *human* society. His model was the reciprocity between the sexes: 'The relation of man to woman is the *most natural* relation of human being to human being ... It shows ... to what extent he is in his individual existence a social being.' (This was the reason why he, and especially Engels, were to attack the bourgeois family so violently.) The male-female relationship showed a willing other-orientation, a feeling of solidarity with and concern for the partner. Marx was still tirading workers about their lack of solidarity and lack of mutual interdependence twenty years later.

Even over a hundred years on, in countries whose leaders claim to follow Marx, the problem of producing this 'new man' remains un-solved. Marx was in line with the biblical view when he saw the rela-tion between man and woman as the ideal for social life, for woman was made to complement man in a relationship of mutual trust and dependence: it was 'not good for man to be alone'. But biblically, social relationships are not only horizontal. The mutuality and har-mony of social relationships depend on a right response to the loving demands of God – to his frameworks for freedom.

The marriage relationship, another of God's 'frameworks', was in-tended to be characterized by particular kinds of responses. The response is best summed by the old English word 'troth'. This, a variant of 'truth', encompasses in one word the idea of faithfulness, honesty, openness, humility and love – all of which are necessary to marriage. Without the trothful framework, the marriage will have a tendency to imbalance, unfreedom and fragility. The response to God's direction is the 'vertical' relationship which makes the 'horizontal' truly meaningful.

Marx, ruling out that possibility by definition, continued with his dream of a harmonious society. Communism is not only the abolition of private property but 'the real reappropriation of the human essence by and for man ... It is the genuine resolution of the antagonism between man and nature and between man and man ... It is the solution to the riddle of history and knows itself to be this solution'. Later, in more Hegelian mood, Marx allowed that there would be a stage even beyond communism, when egoism would finally be abolished – a stage of truly human society.

Hegel had 'alienation' as a central theme in his philosophy but Marx' quarrel with Hegel was that alienation was never related to practical material life. The overcoming of alienation, however, was a common feature of their work. But whereas Hegel would see the end of alienation practically expressed in the appropriation of property by all, Marx argued that property was the utter negation of personality.

For Marx, the very notion of property meant that some have and others have not. Under capitalism, the right of each to dispose of what he has as he wills is proclaimed but this only has advantages for some. The wage-labourer may only dispose of his labour-power – which is the one thing he can call his own. The capitalist, on the other hand, has no obligation to dispose of his wealth for the community but is the arbitrary lord of his capital. The alienations inherent in property-relations, said Marx, may only be overcome by the abolition of the property-relations themselves.

Again, Marx had uncovered something about which Christians have often been confused, whereas the biblical scriptures are eloquent and clear. And, as before, he penetratingly discerned that a certain relationship – to property – was the cause of problems. But instead of seeing the *distortion* of property relations as the basic difficulty, he thought that property itself was wrong.

This topic rightly belongs in the next chapter but a comment is necessary here. Biblically, as we have seen, people are stewards of the creation and therefore should be willing to share for the common good. At the same time, each person and each family has particular needs which must be fufilled in order to achieve a balanced and wholesome life. Income and consumption should be worked out in relation to those needs.

The distortion of this state of affairs occurs when people either become unwilling to contribute what they have to the common good, or when they accumulate possessions beyond their needs (or both!). This will always be to someone else's disadvantage – which brings us back to Marx. But seen in this light, Marx had mistaken the symptom for the disease. The disease is not property as such but its misuse and misappropriation. And that has even deeper roots.

But while Marx was right to spotlight the unharmonious results of property-relations, the question still remains as to whether human alienation would be overcome by their removal (however that might come about). Having put God out of the picture, Marx was obliged to find a remedy for social evils within society itself. He was unwilling to acknowledge that the God he had banished might have a way for his creatures, a way that involved a meaning for work within the whole spectrum of human existence.

So alienation is the weeping sore of the human condition under capitalism. It affects the whole of life, according to Marx, vitiating our very humanity. It is the partner of religion, as both contribute to an upside-down consciousness of the world. Abolition of religion will reduce alienation: the end of alienation will be the beginning-of-the-end of religion.

Under capitalism, according to Marx, alienation has three ugly faces. People are alienated from nature, from themselves and from society. Self-creation through labour – the Marxian purpose of human life – is rendered impossible when the man-shaped world looms over the person, determining his conditions of life.

Alienation, however, presupposes an unalienated condition. Marx believed that in primitive communities, before the advent of money (rather than barter) and profit-seeking, there was no alienation. However his belief has no historical evidence to support it. It is a romantic myth. Hardly an unshakeable foundation for a science of society or a political theory. Even if such idyllic communities ever did exist, who got the idea of money and profit? How, in the best of all possible worlds, did oppression and exploitation creep in? As Andrew Kirk succinctly notes:

> The Bible also speaks constantly of sin in terms of man's oppression of man. At the same time it gives a satisfactory account of the reason for this sin: namely, that man's basic alienation is derived from the fact that on desiring to arrogate himself to the role of God he loses his true humanity.[6]

Here is a tragic irony. The very act which Marx sees as yielding humanity (persons becoming their own god, revolving round themselves) the Bible sees as denying humanity and leading to all other alienations.

This is why even the hopeful 'socialist humanism' of some contemporary Eastern European Marxists is bound ultimately to crumble. Between 1964 and 1975 (when it was suppressed by the authorities) a Yugoslav journal, *Praxis*, called communists back to the vision of the 'early Marx'. They were Marxist heretics in a socialist society, applying Marx' comments about the criticism of religion to the dogma of orthodox Marxism. They could see all too clearly how the Marxism of the party was a kind of religious faith.

Theoretically, someone like Petrović tried to reinstate alienation as a basic Marxian tool: 'The theory of alienation is not only the central theme of Marx' "early writings"; it is also the guiding idea of all his "later" works.'[7] This concept made the *Praxis* intelligentsia highly critical of dogma – especially of Stalinism. Marković crystallized their aim. Praxis is 'conscious, goal-oriented social activity in which man realizes the *optimal* potentialities of his being, and which is therefore an end in itself'.[8]

Practically, they endorsed Tito's efforts to make workers' self-management universal, because they saw this as the only way of avoiding the crippling bureaucracy which had enmeshed the Soviet Union. This was seen as the only radical negation of capitalism *or* fossilized Marxism – the only road away from the alienated dead-end. Unfortunately, this creative criticism was crushed in 1975 and the journal dissolved. Tito seems to be consolidating Yugoslavia in preparation for his own departure: he is now a very old man.

While the alienation of bureaucracy is a palpable evil of modern times and the *Praxis* efforts to combat it were highly laudable, they were nevertheless working on an ultimately false basis. That very same un-Christian humanism which fuelled Marx' faith in self-redemption is present also in the optimism of the *Praxis* group. A more radical understanding of alienation, which sees its roots in terms opposite to those of Marx, is the only basis for a true realism and even optimism. For the same God from whom humanity is fundamentally estranged has provided a way of reconciliation in Jesus Christ. Not only that, in his 'Word', the Bible, truly human frameworks for free and satisfying human activity are, at least in principle, spelt out. From this perspective, experiments with cooperative work may be tried but without the illusion that some fundamental human condition has thus been altered.

This is one of Marx' deepest failures – to plumb the depths of alienation. While he critically and perceptively analyses some of the symptoms, the cancer continues to wreak its deadly toll. As we have seen, even in the surprising (and encouraging) situation where there has been some internal criticism in a state-socialist society, continued adherence to Marx' un-radical concept of alienation has simply left the memory of the *Praxis* group as a sad monument to self-redemption.

Into partnership

With the *Economic and Philosophical Manuscripts* complete, the baby better and Jenny back in Paris, Marx plunged into more work. But there was a new element: he had just met Friedrich Engels. They hit it off immediately, recognizing that they had already developed many interests in common.

Engels was the son of a rich German industrialist who had a cotton-spinning factory in Manchester and he met Marx while returning from there to Germany via Paris. In Manchester Engels had been gathering material for his important *The Condition of the Working Classes in England in 1844* which was to give concrete reality to Marx' more abstract acquaintance with the industrial worker. He actually lived amid the Lancashire cotton mills for twenty years. He was a kind of fifth columnist in the firm, as he spent his whole life in bitter opposition to his father's Protestant pietism and to his capitalist principles. Both he and Marx were to depend on the business for their income, however, for the rest of their lives.

The Marx family delighted in nicknames. Because of Engels' military expertise (he wrote many articles on war as correspondent of more than one newspaper), and soldier-like bearing, they called him 'the general'. Marx himself, who was occasionally referred to as 'Old Nick', answered more frequently to 'Moor'. His darkish complexion seems to account for this.

Within the first few days of their meeting they decided to collaborate on the writing of an attack on Bruno Bauer, ironically entitled *The Holy Family*. But this was a minor work compared to the project which took all the winter months of 1945–46 to complete, in which the material concept of history was worked out in relation to their view of personhood and socialism. For the next forty years they were to work together mainly through correspondence but they were always in close touch with each other. They were deep friends, for whom a quarrel was extremely rare. For a long time Engels was Marx' sole intellectual audience; few others really understood him. And since Marx' death, the most influential interpretation of his work has been that of Engels – it was he who bore the brunt of the tedious manuscript editing.

But Marx was no longer welcome in Paris. The Prussian government against whom many of his comments were directed, was riled
by his journalism and the Parisian authorities felt that the time had
come for the 'German philosophers' (including Heine and Ruge) to
depart. Marx, followed soon after by Jenny, left for Brussels. There,
they had more freedom of expression and the company of other German *émigrés*. Life was fairly comfortable, due to the generosity of
Engels and the sale of furniture from their Paris house. Marx made a
bee-line for the municipal library, there slowly digesting material to
help him understand bourgeois society, all the while encouraged by
impatient letters from publishers and supporters to get down to some
more writing.

Theory and practice

It was during those months that Marx developed the major
characteristics of what was to become famous as 'Marxism'. Distinctive arguments were forged and final breaks with one-time influences
were made – especially with the Young Hegelians. Feuerbach in particular was the subject of much invective, despite the huge impact his
work had on them.

In the short *Theses on Feuerbach*, which Marx wrote during 1845,
he declared his belief in the unity of theory and practice: 'The question of whether objective truth can be achieved by human thinking is
not a question of theory but is a practical question.' What Feuerbach
failed to grasp, he said, was that changing circumstances produce
changing ideas. He had not finally accounted for (and thus dismissed)
religion. Theory had to extend into practical activity: religion would
not automatically disappear. Until now, 'The philosophers have only
interpreted the world in various ways; the point is to change it.'

Here again, we must sift the kernel of near-truth from the chaff of
activism. For the Christian is also concerned that mere doctrine be
transcended in practice; Jesus likened the person who heard *and
acted on* his words to a wise builder using rock-foundations for his
house. John the Baptist scorched his desert audience with the denunciation of mere mental repentance – fruits in keeping with their
change of heart had also to be produced. Faith without works is quite
dead. The specific fruits mentioned by the Baptist, listed in Luke
3:10–14, include the sharing of clothes and food, fairness in tax-
collecting, not extorting or slandering and contentment with
adequate pay.

All this is biblically rooted in the character of God and in man's
relationship with God. To know God, according to Jeremiah, is to
'judge the cause of the poor and needy', for God is like this. The same

prophet (Jeremiah 9:23), says that God is not impressed by human riches: 'but let him who boasts boast in this that he understands and knows me, that I am the Lord who exercises lovingkindness, justice, and righteousness on earth; for I delight in these things.' What happened in Israel (and it is not without significance that Marx and Engels do not seem to have considered this case) was that there had been a forsaking of social equality with the institution of the monarchy.

When Palestine was first conquered by Joshua there was considerable evidence of a common standard of living throughout the different tribes. But, as Samuel warned in 1 Samuel 8:11–18 and 10:17–19, when the lordship of God over people and land is rejected and a human king instated, exploitation, accumulation of wealth and social inequality would result. In the places where God's lordship had once been acknowledged, resulting in widespread similarity of living standards, the rich houses became bigger and better built and in a different quarter from where the poor houses were huddled together.[9]

Thus the prophets had repeatedly to denounce the wealthy and exploiting minority who, as Isaiah 5:8 has it, 'join house to house and add field to field'. In the previous verse, this primitive accumulation is put in context: 'For the vineyard of the Lord of hosts is the house of Israel, and the men of Judah his delightful plant. Thus he looked for justice, but behold, bloodshed; for righteousness, but behold, a cry of distress.' Here, the criterion of truth, the standard for change, is not revolutionary practice but the knowledge of and responsibility to the God in whom justice and concern are perfectly and practically displayed.

The *Theses on Feuerbach* were a prelude to their fuller exposition in *The German Ideology*. After a six-week summer trip to England, in which important contacts (especially with the 'League of the Just') were made for the future, Marx and Engels set to work on this definitive statement of their break with Feuerbach and other Young Hegelians. Marx later wrote that in *The German Ideology* he and Engels had finally settled accounts with their 'erstwhile philosophical consciousness'. Here is found the key notion of people making themselves through labour – historical materialism – worked out in a striking manner.

Marx was especially annoyed with the latest craze from the Young Hegelian stable: Max Stirner's anarcho-existentialism. Marx attacked Stirner's notion that oppressive forces were illusory and that to realize himself, man had to abandon himself to sheer conscious egoism. This, fumed Marx, was but one manifestation of that peculiar German trait of experiencing massive revolutions – in the mind. Ideas must no longer be regarded as *the* realm of reality.

Ideas, announced *The German Ideology*, are always the product of social-economic circumstances. 'As individuals express their life, so they are. What they are, therefore, coincides with their production, both with *what* they produce and *how* they produce. The nature of individuals thus depends on the material conditions determining their production.' How, then, does this social location of ideas work itself out? To this question Marx had a rather involved answer.

Firstly, as people first developed tools, so division of labour increased. It became possible for one to make cart-wheels while another wove cloth and yet another ground flour. But for convenience sake this meant that some occupations were placed in towns and others remained in the countryside. Along with these rifts might come others – such as that between commercial and industrial interests – and with them different forms of ownership. The land to be farmed might be owned by one person and let out to others. Another person might own several factories in one city.

Thus the division of labour eventually leads, according to Marx and Engels, to class struggle. This is because some are owners of the means of producing things, while others are not. Some people are producing goods under conditions which they never willed or wished. Thus Yorkshire and Lancashire 'Luddites' might break machines or burn a factory when direct action seemed the only way to express bitter grievances to callous owners.

But those early nineteenth-century Luddites knew that their insurrection could easily lead to the scaffold. This illustrates Marx' next point – that some sort of political structures are needed to curb class conflict. But even those political structures, in the form of the state, cannot contain the egoism of its citizens. Ironically, that egoism has been sanctified by state ideology, which encourages and protects the pursuit of individual self-interest.

Thus, said Marx, nearing the end of his argument:

> Out of this very contradiction between the interest of the individual and that of the community that later takes an independent form as the *state*, divorced from the real interests of individual and community . . . the struggles within the state . . . the struggles for the franchise, etc., are merely the illusory forms in which the real struggles of the different classes are fought out among one another.

The point is that when a political group makes a manifesto point of widening the franchise, one may be certain that this is not the real issue. Understood in terms of its *social location*, it is seen as a cover for *class* interests. It is 'ideology'.

Such a doctrine, that ideas are always related to particular social and economic circumstances, has important consequences. On the one hand, genuine understanding is enhanced by seeing where an idea originates. Take another Marxian example: the 'rights of man'. One can appreciate the French Revolutionary enthusiasm for such noble-sounding ideals when their singular appropriateness for defending the revolutionaries' interests is noticed! Looked at carefully, those 'rights of man' were the rights of *propertied males* to legal and political equality. The non-propertied automatically had fewer 'rights'.

On the other hand, to place some set of ideas in their social setting is not necessarily to say anything about their *truth*, or their contribution to the cause of justice. The person who realizes that he is being hoodwinked by some constitutional 'rights' which in fact only apply to his boss may make it his business simply to counteract this with another deception.

This is where the Christian concept of truth is so refreshingly liberating. Jesus Christ, who lived a life of authentic truth and justice, himself claimed to be *the* Truth. Here alone is a standard – personal, not clinically abstract – which is both external to the human context and yet vitally connected with it. Though the two are linked, the social location of ideas is one thing, the test of their truth is another.

But for Marx and Engels, no ideas have any external or objective validity. They are always the ideas of the people at the top. 'The ideas of the ruling class are in every epoch the ruling ideas.' Those ruling ideas might include the notion of a 'career' as 'lawyer' or 'businessman', but these ideas, by pigeon-holing free people, thwart their human capacity for self-directed variety in productive activity. The proletariat, having been classified as 'labour' must oppose the condition in which the ruling class have put them:

> If the proletarians are to assert themselves as individuals, they will have to abolish the very condition of their existence hitherto (which has, moreover, been that of all society up to the present), namely, labour. Thus they find themselves directly opposed to the form in which, hitherto, the individuals of which society consists have given themselves collective expression, that is, the State. In order therefore to assert themselves as individuals, they must overthrow the State.

To descend from the clouds of German idealism is to confront the state with revolutionary practice.

Even the German socialists, lamented Marx and Engels, made the mistake of over-emphasizing ideas. They exalted altruism as the means of getting people to live and work together harmoniously. But as far as Marx was concerned, nonsense-phrases about the universal love of mankind could never match the scientific logic of revolutionary enthusiasm as the only way ahead. This was the outworking of the third thesis on Feuerbach, that people are not only the products of their circumstances but the potential changers of those circumstances. 'The coincidence of the changing of circumstances and of human activity or self-changing can be conceived and rationally understood only as *revolutionary practice*.'

Marx and Engels were ruthlessly opposing all previous conceptions of history, philosophy and politics, on the basis that they were 'ideological' or false, but on what grounds? To say something is illusory and misleading is to imply that something else is not. But how did they imagine that they had escaped the 'ideology' trap themselves? How was theirs not also an upside-down world? Their answer was this: 'Where speculation ends – in real life—there real, positive science begins: the representation of the practical process of development of men.' That is, a science of society is the only non-ideological observation-point possible. In Christian terms, this is where religion fully supersedes theory in Marx. He places himself beyond discussion by his faith in the historic role of the working class.

This is difficult to swallow. A contemporary French Marxist, Louis Althusser, has taken up this theme and argues that true Marxism only began when Marx forsook everything preceding *The German Ideology*. The 'humanistic' writing belongs to a mere enthusiastic youth – science started after he had discarded metaphysics. But Althusser cannot convincingly account for the continuation of the 'alienation' theme throughout Marx' writings and neither can he deny the part played by indignation and compassion in all attempts to bring Marx home in practice. How do these relate to 'science'?

The answer to that question lies in the twin-impulse in all of Marx' work: to accurately describe *and* to catalyse action. Historical materialism corrects and explains all other ideological views, calling the moral bluffs of mankind by showing how moral outlooks depend on class interests. But, as practice is inextricably yoked to theory, it also provides the practical solution to all human difficulties. As a combination of science-of-society and revolutionary ideology, Marxism is the only way. This is the quintessence of the Marxist faith.

This faith became somewhat obscured by the heavy hand of Bolshevism in Russia in the inter-war years of the twentieth century. German descendants of Marx sometimes despaired of ever finding an outlet for their beliefs. The choice was either to throw in their lot with what was already becoming a cumbersome neo-Catholic jugger-naut, or dilute their ideas by mixing them with the moderate socialism of the new Weimar Republic.

In fact, some of them chose a third way (to continue the ecclesiastical analogy) of reformation. They rediscovered that quintessence of Marxist faith as they examined the original foun-dations of his thought – especially his softer, Hegelian side. *Praxis*, the notion derived from several of his early writings, was revived by a group of high-powered intellectuals who came to be known collective-ly as the 'Frankfurt school'. (The amazing continuity of this group, who moved to the USA under the Nazi threat and later *returned* to Frankfurt, is related elsewhere.[10]) The emphasis on praxis led to their work being described as 'critical theory'.

Members such as Erich Fromm and Herbert Marcuse were in-fluenced by the discovery and publication early in the 1930s, of the *Economic and Philosophical Manuscripts*. They wove the Marxist notion of alienation into their anthropology in bold form. From the outset they were united in their opposition to the arid fact-science ap-proach of 'positivism', opting rather for the quest of adequate knowledge yoked to human emancipation. This applies to their most important director, Max Horkheimer, to Theodor Adorno and their latter-day disciple, Jurgen Habermas. They continue to exert a deep influence on many who search for a human orientation (as opposed to the sometimes irrelevantly statistical and cold approaches) in contem-porary sociology.

Ironically, however, one of the most trenchant criticisms levelled at critical theory is that while criticism is certainly abundant, theory is strikingly absent. True, they have produced plenty of useful insights, and someone like Marcuse has become world-famous for his in-novative style within the New Left but there is no full-blown theory of society. They are searching for a place to stand, from which vantage-point they can observe the whole social set-up of industrial capitalism in genuinely critical perspective.

My contention, however, is that no matter how much orthodox Marxist dogma (as interpreted by Engels and company) is softened, made critical, or whatever, until a biblical perspective is radically in-troduced, the picture will continue to be lopsided. It is the lens of the scriptures alone which enables the religious roots of industrial capitalism (or any other system) to be exposed. When that dimension is probed and industrial capitalism and socialism are located within the biblical drama, then truely critical theory begins. The model of social analysis which is attuned to human purposes, so central to the vision of the Frankfurt school, may well yet bear fruit. But until those human purposes are understood to be in the creature-Creator framework, the fruit will continue to be bitter, or at best, simply unsatisfying.

Marx the master

From Brussels, Marx continued to write and to attempt to forge links between French, German and English socialists. He not only wanted them to keep in touch with each other but also wished to remedy their abysmal lack of theory. At one point Marx invited the French atheistic socialist Proudhon to be a member of the Paris corresponding committee but he changed his mind when he discovered Proudhon's beliefs.

Marx was disgusted to find that, totally failing to grasp (his view of) the historical development of humanity, Proudhon fell back on 'eternal concepts' such as reason and justice. He demolished Proudhon in *The Poverty of Philosophy*, the title of which inverted Proudhon's own mention of Marx – 'The philosophy of poverty'. (Karl Popper was to take up the gauntlet a hundred years later, when he attacked Marx' alleged historicism in *The Poverty of Historicism*.) Moving from the argument about human self-creation in work, Marx hinted at theories of class which were soon to figure prominently in his writings. With the victory of the proletariat, class struggle would cease. The bloody conflict would bring social rebirth.

It is instructive to see why Proudhon was uneasy about Marx himself, before this exchange ever took place. In his reply to Marx' initial invitation to join the committee, he wrote:

> ... let us not – simply because we are at the head of a movement – make ourselves the leaders of a new intolerance, let us not pose as the apostles of a new religion, even if it be the religion of logic, the religion of reason. Let us gather together and encourage all dissent, let us outlaw all exclusiveness, all mysticism; let us never regard a question as exhausted, and when we have used our last argument, let us if necessary begin again – with eloquence and irony. On these conditions, I will gladly enter into your association. Otherwise – no![11]

Were Proudhon's fears justified? The following glimpse of Marx in action at these early workers' meetings is a clue.

> Marx himself was the type of man who is made up of energy, will and unshakeable conviction. He was most remarkable in his appearance. He had a shock of deep black hair and hairy hands

and his coat was buttoned wrong; but he looked like a man with the right and power to demand respect, no matter how he appeared before you and no matter what he did. His movements were clumsy but confident and self-reliant, his ways defied the usual conventions in human relations, but they were dignified and somewhat disdainful; his sharp metallic voice was wonderfully adapted to the radical judgements that he passed on persons and things. He always spoke in imperative words that would brook no contradiction and were made all the sharper by the almost painful impression of the tone which ran through everything he said. This tone expressed the firm conviction of his mission to dominate men's minds and prescribe them their laws. Before me stood the embodiment of a democratic dictator such as one might imagine in a day dream.[12]

Marx had indeed become the self-styled prophet of a new religion. But the power of this faith could be seen in its closeness to Christianity. It was an impressive counterfeit, using many Christian themes and often echoing biblical philippics against the love of money, exploitation and injustice. Marx uncovered the seamy side of industrial capitalism – to which the church has so often turned a blinkered eye – with a searing moral indictment.

But in trying to understand human nature, Marx put humanity in the centre of the universe. Thus alienation was seen in merely human terms, Marx' eye always being on the human relationship to nature and fellow-creature. What he observed was often tragically true-to-life but his remedy, lacking the creational perspective, never transcended the creaturely autonomy and rebellion against God which had produced the original alienation.

Notes and references

1 David McLellan, *Karl Marx: The Early Texts*, Oxford University Press, 1971, p. 82.

2 Johan van der Hoeven, *Karl Marx: The Roots of His Thought*, Wedge Publishing Foundation, 1976, p. 35.

3 G. Girardi, quoted in José Miguez Bonino, *Christians and Marxists*, Hodder and Stoughton and Eerdmans, 1976, p. 60.

4 E. R. Wickham, *Church and People in an Industrial City*, Lutterworth, 1957, p. 215.

5 José Míguez Bonino, 1976, p. 68f.

6 Andrew Kirk, 'The Meaning of Man in the debate between Christianity and Marxism', *Themelios*, 1976, vol. 1, 3, p. 88. Kirk refers to most of the material on Marx' concept of personhood in his notes. The position I adopt here is similar to that of P. Walton and Andrew Gamble, *From Alienation to Surplus Value*, Sheed and Ward, 1972. Theirs is a self-consciously Marxian position, but the more critical Shlomo Avineri makes much the same point in *The Social and Political Thought of Karl Marx*, Cambridge University Press 1968, p. 65f. Further useful material is in the survey by Robert Banks, 'The Search for Man in the Christian-Marxist Dialogue', in *Theology*, LXXVII, March 1974.

7 Quoted in Gerson S. Sher, *Praxis: Marxist criticism and dissent in Socialist Yugoslavia*, Indiana University Press, 1977, p. 70.

8 Gerson S. Sher, 1977, p. 73.

9 Roland de Vaux, *Ancient Israel, Its Life and Institutions*, McGraw-Hill, 1961, Darton, Longman and Todd, 1965.

10 Martin Jay, *The Dialectical Imagination: A History of the Frankfurt School and the Institute of Social Research 1923–50*, Heinemann, 1973.

11 David McLellan, *Karl Marx: His Life and Thought*, Macmillan, 1973, Harper and Row, 1974, p. 159.

12 David McLellan, *Marx*, Fontana Modern Masters, 1975, Penguin Modern Masters, 1976, p. 15.

The 1848 Chartist meeting on Kennington Common, London

CHAPTER 3

Revolutionary years

Like the early Christians awaiting the Second Coming,
they regarded their present life as of little importance
compared to the great event that was to come.
David McLellan

1848 was a crucial year in European history – and in the work of
Marx. In that year revolutions swept across the European continent,
putting fear and dread into kings and confidence into the surprised
and successful Romantic revolutionaries. Utopian socialist ideas
enjoyed a widespread popularity in Europe and it seemed for an
excited moment that the economic crises, the harvest failure and
numerous local revolts would be the occasion to turn those ideas into
reality.

France, during those years, was the test-case for the rest of Europe
and Marx followed closely events which took place there. Although
the revolutionary fires were as quickly quenched as they had been lit,
they nevertheless gave him great hopes for his developing theory of
class struggle. For, just before the revolutions broke out, Marx, with
Engels, completed the first compact version of his current beliefs:
The Communist Manifesto. And two years later he tried his hand at
writing contemporary history, testing out those new ideas in *The
Class Struggles in France*.

Although Marx had only visited England once, he and Engels
placed their highest hopes in the activities of a group of German
workers in London. If working-class politics were to succeed
anywhere, they thought, it would be in England. They kept in close
contact with their London compatriots, whose avowed aim was to
'overthrow the old bourgeois society' of England. Marx was also
enthusiastic about the Chartist movement of English workers
(though there was less chance of influencing them), for he saw in
them a genuine possibility of revolutionary action. While it is true
that France was a test-case in those revolutionary years, being less
industrialized than Britain, it was also less likely to provide from its

peasants, artisans and shopkeepers the revolutionary fuel that Marx required.

Marx had higher hopes for the Chartists, as they represented much more the urban working class. The main platform of this otherwise diverse movement was universal suffrage: obtaining for all the right to vote. They had been disappointed by the failure to achieve a wider vote in 1832 (it was limited to '£10 householders'), and angered by the insensitivity of the 1834 Poor Law. This, in its provisions for those who were out of work, used what amounted to worker-imprisonment and forced labour. Thus unemployment – which in fact was largely the result of the industrial factory system – was 'counteracted'. A spokesman of workers threatened by this Act's provisions, Oastler, described it as 'damnable ... infernal anti-Christian, unsocial ... the catechism of Hell ... the Devil's own Book!' Passions thus aroused erupted in riots in Oldham, Huddersfield and Bradford in 1837 and 1838.

But such passions were quickly channelled into Chartism, the leaders of which felt that once the have-nots obtained a significant political voice, a social revolution would ensue, bringing a fairer deal to all. In the event, things happened at a much slower pace and Chartism was to be decimated after the confused demonstration on Kennington Common, London, in 1848.

Despite this, Marx still felt that England was an appropriate place to enlarge upon his ideas, which was why he was keen to pay London another visit. Even in 1849 he could imagine a situation where, given a world war to spark things off, the Chartists could rise 'against their gigantic oppressors' and 'head the English government'. In the end, however, his actual contact with a far more industrialized society than Germany or even France forced him to withdraw from *practice*. He was to remain a marginal figure, as far as British workers were concerned, to the end of his days.

However, if he was to come to England and form a closer alliance with the German workers, he made it quite clear that he would come only on his terms. He suggested that they call a congress at which his ideas would be expounded. The group, which became known as the Communist League, did eventually hold a congress in November 1847 and he was the main speaker.

Eager to refute those who favoured impulsive revolutionism, he put a strong emphasis on the education of workers in socialist principles – so much so that Bakunin complained, when Marx was back in Brussels, that he was 'spoiling the workers by making logic-choppers of them'. But Marx, unperturbed, made his mark, as shown by this observer's description of those London meetings.

Marx was a born leader of the people. His speech was brief, convincing, and compelling in its logic. He never said a superfluous word; every sentence contained an idea and every idea was an essential link in the chain of his argument. Marx had nothing of the dreamer about him ... Marx represented the manhood of socialist thought.[1]

As it turned out, the most significant outcome of that congress was the decision to produce a manifesto of communist aims. Those involved in its production revealed their deep trust in it by referring to it as a 'confession of faith', and by wording its first drafts like a catechism. Though Engels influenced its drafting, in fact its final sole author was Marx: his persuasive style prevailed.

The Communist Manifesto

Marx had little faith in the intelligence of the average working man, so he wrote *The Communist Manifesto* as simply and as cogently as he could. He wanted it to be a rallying-call for communists in all European countries and a clear statement of communist aims which would show their governments that communism was more than a 'spectre haunting Europe'. Marx began by proclaiming: 'The history of all hitherto existing society is the history of class struggles.' He then attempted to give evidence for that and for the necessity of continued struggle against the ruling class and its objections to communism. He closed with the resounding battle cry: 'Workers of all countries, unite!'

In the manifesto, Marx produced an amazingly compelling case for workers' action and proletarian revolt. It flows like a poem, powerfully presenting a series of arguments designed once and for all to silence the sceptic, though its strength lies as much in the triumphalist style as in the argument. As Berlin remarks, 'its effect upon succeeding generations is unparalleled outside religious history'. Here Marx spelt out briefly the ideas upon which he staked his life. It is these words of this 28-year-old social prophet which above all have been taken up by the multitudes of his followers.

Marx, from his reading of the French socialist, Saint-Simon, had seen the historical importance of conflict between social classes. And this fitted well with the Hegelian notion, which he also accepted, of *Aufhebung*. It is important to use the German word here, as there is no direct English equivalent. It means abolition, transcendence and preservation. This was used as an interpretive key for unlocking history's secrets. Marx expected to find in history a process of abolition (or 'negation') and transcendence, as one kind of society was replaced by another.

But there is a major difficulty. Philosophers have for many centuries tried to unlock history's secrets and find hope for the future in what the past reveals. But there is no hope within historical processes. No recipe for human contentment can be discerned in the patterns of the past. What hope is there in an unknown future which will supposedly follow the negation of the present?

Genuine hope may only be found in the continuity of a creation which is being gradually *restored* and renewed by God. It is in a person who is at once outside and yet working within history (pre-eminently in the cross on which Christ died) that there can be hope. What is now will be made better, not simply abolished and transcended. Paul the apostle says that the whole creation groans in childbirth until the time when it 'will be set free from its slavery to corruption into the freedom of the glory of the children of God' (Romans 8:21). This, insists Paul, is worth waiting and hoping for. What God once began, he will complete. Here is the crux of historical certainty and hope.

Marx was to build his case on the notion of class antagonism. History, it was said, was not made by great individuals but was a process whereby one social class gained dominance, only to be succeeded by another:

> Freeman and slave, patrician and plebeian, lord and serf, guild-master and journeyman, in a word, oppressor and oppressed, stood in constant opposition to one another, carried on an uninterrupted, now hidden, now open, fight, a fight that each time ended, either in a revolutionary reconstitution of society at large, or in the common ruin of the contending classes ...
>
> The modern bourgeois society that has sprouted from the ruins of feudal society has not done away with class antagonisms. It has but established new classes, new conditions of oppression, new forms of struggle in place of the old ones.
>
> Our epoch, the epoch of the bourgeoisie, possesses, however, this distinctive feature: it has simplified the class antagonisms. Society as a whole is more and more splitting up into two great hostile camps, into two great classes directly facing each other: Bourgeoisie and Proletariat.

How had this come about? Marx showed that each stage of discovery and invention since feudal times had produced new forms of social organization and government. Since manufacturing and industrial enterprises had taken over from the old small-scale production plants with their guilds, so the modern state had become dominated by these new interests. The bourgeoisie, that class of traders, industrial entrepreneurs and employers, had a powerful ally in the state, which Marx described as a committee for managing their affairs.

Once upon a time, the bourgeoisie themselves were revolutionary, destroying the old master-serf relationships of feudalism. But instead of bringing about just social relationships, they had 'left remaining no other nexus between man and man than naked self-interest, than callous "cash payment"'. Human dignity had been reduced to exchange value and in place of the traditional, chartered freedoms, the bourgeoisie offered free trade, in which there is no hindrance to exploitative relationships.

But the bourgeoisie, the owners of the means of production, had also created another class of people, at once dependent on them but also with different interests from them. While the bourgeoisie destroyed the old aristocracy and the old system of production, Marx argued, it could not destroy the proletariat, for it is necessary to its existence. The industrial set-up relies upon the army of workers who sell their labour-power to the bourgeoisie. But it also depends upon the *expansion* of the proletariat, as markets grow and as production increases.

However, the proletariat cannot remain passive forever. An old life-style had been brutally shattered and people had been transformed into machine appendages. Given the new situation, it is futile to try to return to the idyll of the Middle Ages: the proletariat will soon find themselves with the upper hand, as capitalism exhausts itself in economic crises. Thus Marx reasoned that what the bourgeoisie produce above all is their own grave-diggers: 'its fall and the victory of the proletariat are equally inevitable'.

That dialectical process which brought capitalism into existence cannot be stopped: it will move people before it until capitalism itself becomes part of history. Marx' belief in the flow of history came out strongly at this point and showed itself as an unintentional secular parody of the Christian belief in the providence of God. Moreover, just as the knowledge of God's control over history goes hand-in-hand with the belief that people are still fully responsible to God, so Marx also stressed that the proletariat had a task to perform.

For communism is a description of relationships – and relationships must be transformed. Private property, which makes for an unequal relationship between owners and non-owners, must be abolished. The bourgeois family, now also centred upon the cash-nexus, must go, and along with it the idea that women are simply child-producers. Lastly, nationality must be abolished and an international community of workers be brought into being, the vanguard of peaceful co-operation between countries. Yes, affirmed Marx to the horror of the bourgeoisie, 'Communism abolishes eternal truths, it abolishes all religion, and all morality, instead of constituting them on a new basis; it therefore acts in contradiction to all past historical experience.'

The proletariat should temporarily become the ruling class, and thus eventually put an end to all class antagonism. Taxes should be increased, landed property abolished, factories state-owned and education should be free for all. In the end, Marx assures us, 'In place of the old bourgeois society, with its classes and class antagonisms, we shall have an association in which the free development of each is the condition for the free development of all.'

In the final sections of the manifesto, Marx outlined his objections to other, inadequate forms of socialism. There were the attempts by the church to show a common interest with workers, such as Christian Socialism. But this, said Marx was 'nothing but the holy water with which the priest consecrates the heart-burnings of the aristocrat'. Christian social concern was a mere façade behind which lurked the passionate desire to maintain the *status quo*. Then others like Proudhon seemed to want all the advantages of modern conveniences brought to all without a deep struggle, and without radical changes in the capitalist-worker relationship: this was insufficient and unsatisfactory.

Lastly, Marx objected to the attempts at small-scale experiments with co-operatives and worker-centred communities, such as those of Fourier and Owen. (He did not distinguish, however, between those which were mere ideas and those which had been successfully tried out.) No, wrote Marx, none of these will do. There is only one way and we must be plain:

> The Communists disdain to conceal their views and aims. They openly declare that their ends can only be attained by the forcible overthrow of all existing social conditions. Let the ruling classes tremble at a Communistic revolution. The proletarians have nothing to lose but their chains.
>
> They have a world to win.
>
> WORKING MEN OF ALL COUNTRIES, UNITE!

The revolution was not only historically inevitable, it was the only logical next step for the proletariat.

Unpacking the Manifesto

Only the proletariat, according to Marx, could achieve the 'redemption of humanity' through revolution. But were all his assumptions correct? Were there any flaws in the fine phrases? While there is much to be said in favour of parts of Marx' analysis, we shall question what he wrote in terms of *prophecy, property* and *people*, as this leads us to further doubt regarding his proposed solutions.

First, there is the question of whether what he said about the past and the future was true. Is it true that the history of society is propelled by class struggles? Unfortunately for Marx, there are many historical examples of class co-operation – activity which crosses class boundaries. In Marx' own time, for instance, improvements in factory workers' conditions in England was brought about by a coalition of Tory and Radical forces. In the present day, voting patterns often defy all popular expectations, with working-class votes being cast for conservative parties and middle-class votes for labour and radical parties.

But even in the 1840s, Marx was on slippery ground when he condemned the rule of the bourgeoisie and predicted the triumph of the proletariat. For in Germany (the possible location of early revolution, according to *The Communist Manifesto*) the proletariat numbered only 5 per cent of the population and even in England, the most advanced industrial country, the bourgeoisie were far from being in control.

Marx cannot be blamed for failing to foresee the future but later developments do decrease the credibility of his work. He failed to see that classes are not always equally important (compare Britain and the United States, for example!) and that they are seldom homogeneous or cohesive. Since Marx, welfare provisions for all classes have increased beyond his wildest dreams, in all advanced capitalist and socialist countries. Moreover, labour and trade unions have also increased their power and influence, although they tend to spend their energies in obtaining better deals rather than 'changing the system'.

Again, in Marx' time, yet without his full recognition, nationalism was becoming a tremendous force. That the strength of nationalism was greater than that of class was demonstrated in 1914. The labour parties, rather than maintaining an international solidarity by voting against war-credits, sold out to war and began the systematic slaughter of their comrades. Nowadays, there are few revolutions which are not at the very least tinged by nationalism: most are thoroughly shot through with this deeply emotive ideology.

Lastly, Marx did not perceive the phenomenon which Lenin was to make central to his doctrine – the exportation of the class struggle and poverty through imperialism. Marx was simply not aware of the extent of the impact of capitalist expansion on the colonial territories, especially in the way an 'external proletariat' can be created. As we shall see, there is much to be said for Lenin's theory, especially as it is exemplified in the contemporary Third World. But Lenin's understanding considerably modified Marx' view of the class struggle, which is weaker without it.

The central problem, perhaps, is that Marx allowed the idea of class (along with its negation and transcendence) to become a key belief in his system. His followers have adhered, often with fanatical obsession, to the 'class' category, at the expense of other equally important explanatory categories. While his analysis of class deserves study, it nevertheless blinded him to other important historical and human realities.

Property: a third way

Secondly, we may see why his analysis of class deserves study, by glancing at the notion of 'property'. In Marx' analysis, private property ownership is related to class position. Especially important is the connection between ownership and non-ownership of the means of production. Here is the basic class antagonism, between bourgeoisie and proletariat. Moreover, the triumph of the latter was guaranteed by the activities of the former. For as the bourgeoisie expanded their industries, so they increasingly brought workers together, who could then form revolutionary associations. Thus Marx saw the bourgeois class digging its own grave.

So, he insisted, communist ideas were not just 'invented'. Rather, they expressed actual relationships arising from the class struggle. They could be summed up in a phrase: abolition of private property. 'But just a moment,' he expected his critics to say, 'Do you mean to abolish the right to the fruit of one's own labour?' His reply was that such an idea was a mere myth of the bourgeoisie anyway. The proletariat certainly did not have any property, small farmers and artisans were rapidly losing theirs to big capital and capital itself, being something produced collectively, should be owned collectively.

But from a Christian perspective, such answers are not enough. It is true that the biblical scriptures give no justification of a human 'right' to dispose of goods at personal will and whim. The only glorification of ownership in the Bible is God's; Psalm 24 : 1 says 'The earth is the Lord's and all it contains'. This does not mean that God's creatures may have nothing! The Bible does not teach that people 'own' even their labour-power, but it does repeatedly emphasize the obligation of employers to give a fair wage, related if necessary to need, for an honest day's work.

A Christian understanding of this is that people are trustees in God's world, stewards of resources for the common good. Labour and 'dominion' should include contributing resources (including one's labour-power and abilities) to the common good. As far as consumption goes, however, there are limits. John Taylor has called this the 'theology of enough'.[2] God faithfully provides for his creatures sufficient for all their needs. But when, for example, Israel was fed manna in the wilderness and some tried to collect beyond their immediate needs, the stuff rotted and stank. Consuming beyond need by some may also result in the deprivation of others, so that God's faithful provision is misappropriated.

The Bible goes further than Saint-Simon but not as far as Marx in its limiting of property. The Saint-Simonians, while they (rightly) vigorously opposed laws of inheritance which produced gross inequalities of wealth, still maintained that each person had the right to the fruit of his or her own labour. This is fine up to a point. But while the Bible does not always condemn the *controlling* of certain resources by one person, it roundly condemns the *consumption* of all those resources by one person. Jesus' parable of the rich man who kept up a luxurious standard of living – the original bloated plutocrat – while Lazarus, a poor man covered with sores, starved at his gate, is a searing exposé of such a distortion.

In fact, one Christian economist, Donald Hay, has argued that a solution may lie in the separation of stewardship and consumption.[3] The building-site labourer may contribute muscle-power and a steady eye to the economic activity of the community, while a teacher may contribute her intellectual and communication skills. That is one thing. Quite another is the matter of the consumption of the product. This depends upon the principle of each having a right to share in God's provision, the principle of 'enough', and not assuming that resource-control means resource-consumption. The above-average turnover of the store-owner does not bestow the right to dispose of all the profit at will. There are principles for economic life.

But 'capitalism' depends upon a notion of private property, and on the right of everyone to dispose of resources and labour-power to their best personal advantage. This idea was given great ideological backing by English philosopher John Locke. He argued that property-ownership should be unrestricted and socially unconditional. The idea of property-owning (in this sense) is obviously more prevalent than 'trusteeship' in capitalist societies. Not surprising, then, that Marx observed a link between class struggle, property-owning and selfishness.

Having frequently used the term 'capitalism', perhaps some definition ought to be attempted at this stage. Because Marx believed that communism would eventually grow out of capitalism (it is its *Aufhebung* – dialectical abolition) he passed his days analysing the dynamics of capitalist society. Communism, he believed, would both negate capitalism, transcend it and yet preserve its potential for producing abundance for all and humanizing the world. For example, he described the joint-stock company as 'the transcendence of the capitalist mode of production within the capitalist mode of production', seeing it as a more *social* process for economic life.

But private property is capitalism's big contradiction, according to Marx. Its implications will be spelt out further in the next chapter. But the assumptions of capitalism include the idea that the distribution of resources is automatically just: this is taken for granted. Another basic assumption is the necessity of competition. This is the dynamic which keeps the capitalist machine running. All efforts are combined to obtain maximum money profit on capital in a competitive struggle with other entrepreneurs.

This is linked with the market mechanism, which regulates the flow of goods and resources. Capitalism tends to be geared to market criteria for determining value and profits. People are said to choose freely between alternatives such as pattern of occupation and consumption. One result of this, which became more evident in the 1970s, is the rampant exploitation of the natural world. Commercialism justified the rape of the earth.

Although no 'pure' capitalist economy exists, it is not unwarranted to talk of 'capitalism' or even 'capitalist society' when referring to the Western countries of Europe and North America. Some refer to 'neo-capitalism' to describe the situation where the state intervenes radically in economic life, as it has tended to do since the aftermath of the Depression in the 1930s. But capitalism is still the basis of 'mixed economies' such as Britain, where the private sector still accounts for more than 75 per cent of total employment.

However it is defined, class structure is a feature of all modern societies and has much to do with economic inequalities. While a widespread blurring of class differences has taken place this century, falsifying Marx' prediction of the polarization of the two major classes, it is still true that a small minority of people in capitalist countries own by far the greatest share of wealth. There are still large numbers of working-class people whose standard of living remains well below what the majority would consider to be minimal.

Class theorists since Marx have pointed out his failure to see other dimensions of class apart from the economic – particularly those having to do with social esteem and power. But few have gone further, to examine the impact of what Christians regard as sinful responses to God in the development of class conflict. Marx said that class originated in the economic conditions and the mode of producing commodities which seemed to him to develop inexorably through history: he had little to say about wrong motivations and attitudes.

The 'people-problem'

Thus, thirdly, we look at people – those who make up classes and whose habitualized attitudes form the contrasting beliefs of contemporary society. Once Marx had lighted upon the historical destiny of the proletariat, he concentrated on making them conscious of it, oblivious to the fact that they were made up of the same human stuff as the bourgeoisie. His view was that the evils of capitalism were all exhibited in the bourgeoisie but rather than seeing that acquisitiveness itself was wrong, he maintained that the proletariat should be allowed to have what the bourgeoisie already possessed. If the bourgeoisie was selfish, this was bad but if the proletariat demanded the same as them, this, apparently, was good. His ethic was one which favoured the proletariat and which lacked any external standard. What was good for the proletariat was good for humanity and vice versa. That envy and coveteousness might be important features of the outlook of both classes was something he never considered.

He would have been shocked, moreover, at the war-like nationalism of European workers in 1914, for he believed, with many others of his day, that the age of war was finally over. In short, he looked at the proletariat through rose-coloured spectacles. Biblically, for example in James 4:1–2, the origin of conflict is rooted in misdirected hearts – informed by those crucial attitudes of envy and frustration at the failure to obtain what is desired. No wonder Marx had to write off the efforts of Christian social concern, Utopian Socialism and the small-scale experimental worker-communities. By definition, if they did not spring from the proletariat alone, they were doomed to failure by their association with capitalism.

Unless, as he contradictorily maintained, the bourgeois intelligentsia had somehow managed to transcend their mental blockages. He had to find a place for himself!

But Marx had good reason, given his philosophical background, for believing that what is good for the proletariat is good for humanity. He reckoned that all the suffering and alienation of humanity at large is summed up in the proletarian condition. When the worker comes home, tired from a frustrating day minding a machine which has no particular purpose that he can see, nor any tangible product, he represents the human situation under an alienating system. In short, Marx held up the proletariat as a 'universal class'. Understand their plight and you understand the universal human plight.

Why did he think this? Not, we may be sure, because of his 'observation' of class society. He simply inherited the notion of a 'universal class' from Hegel. As usual, the process also gave Marx the pleasure of turning Hegel over to put him 'on his feet'. For, though Hegel recognized the existence of a universal class, he was still benighted enough to imagine that it was in fact the bureaucracy. But there was no way that Marx could stomach that! The very idea that petty officials in their hierarchy of desks-and-stools should represent humanity itself was unthinkable.

Contrary to what many think, Marx did anticipate the growing power of the bureaucracy though only in a limited way.[4] In *Capital*, volume III, for example, he noted that the real government of the East India Company was 'a large staff of irresponsible secretaries, examiners and clerks at India House, of whom . . . only one individual has ever been in India, and he only by accident'. But though he saw its potential he also despaired of its role. For it just distorted and perverted true social relationships. (Though he did not say that it simply reflected social-economic forces.) Bureaucrats, in order to justify themselves, must imagine that theirs is a real world and that their pen-pushing enterprise achieves concrete results. It is the essence of alienation!

This is why, as Avineri points out, Marx never spent much energy analysing the state apparatus. Why bother peering at the distorted glass when it is possible to explore the real world behind it?

As we have seen, biblically, the state apparatus may well be distorted in the interests of a ruling class, to the gross disadvantage of an underclass. And God's concern is consistently for the underclass. He cares especially for the helpless: as Psalm 68:5 says, 'he is the father of the fatherless and defender of the widow's cause'. There are no evils that God is quicker to condemn and punish than the mistreatment of minorities and the oppression of the powerless. But it does not follow that because the state may be twisted that the best thing for it is its abolition. No, it may also be untwisted.

That the state has a special sphere of responsibility in the social world is made clear in numerous biblical passages. Its task is justice and the common good. Though the state may function in relation to all manner of creation's aspects – such as economic life or education – its functions are for justice. The state is not competent to educate or to engage in economic activity. These are tasks for which others have responsibility and competence. Thus, in so far as the state is warped by its relationship to any other aspect of social life, including class interest, it needs to be untwisted and recalled to its task of justice for all.

Returning to class, then, we can see why Marx, though thoroughly non-proletarian himself, presumed to speak on behalf of that class. Its social role is fundamental, universal. So much so that class division virtually came to separate right from wrong. Marx' proletarian-coloured spectacles prevented him from seeing that they might have as many vices as the bourgeoisie.

The Christian understanding of persons is that all are equally prone to self-centredness and injustice, for all share in the same universal alienation from God. Theodor Geiger makes an apposite comment about Marx' fixation with the proletariat. At this point, he says, 'the proper analysis of the interest-structure of social class ends – religious mania alone speaks here'.[5] Marx' stance had its source in his religiously-rooted world-view.

The Communist Manifesto, Marx admitted, was not wholly original but he believed that what was new would stand the test of time. In 1852 he wrote in a letter:

> What I did new was to prove: (1) that the existence of classes is only bound up with particular historical phases in the development of production; (2) that the class struggle necessarily leads to the dictatorship of the proletariat; (3) that this dictatorship itself only constitutes the transition to the abolition of all classes and to the classless society.

In fact, by the time he wrote the preface to the 1872 edition, he would probably have modified parts of it but for the fact that, as he put it, it 'had become a historical document'. In the same preface, he and Engels reaffirmed their basic commitment to its tenets, saying that the general principles were 'as correct as ever'.

The partisan pen

Scared by the news of revolutionary movements fanning out towards Brussels from Switzerland, the Belgian king offered to abdicate in February 1848. However, when the strength of government forces was soberly reassessed, he decided instead to rid the country of troublemakers – and the author of *The Communist Manifesto* headed the list. Following some last-minute bureaucratic skirmishes, Marx left Brussels in March for a jubilant welcome in revolutionary Paris. Immediately, he threw himself into the activities of the Society of the Rights of Man, one of the 147 political clubs then flourishing in the French capital.

But his eye was still on Germany, for which he still maintained the highest revolutionary hopes. He wished to encourage internal revolt (rather than to force revolution from outside), and thus snatched the opportunity to return to his homeland when the repressive state chancellor Metternich was overthrown. He and Engels chose the obvious base of Cologne, the third biggest industrial city in Prussia, where fast-growing socialist groups were already active. Factory workers were far from being in a majority however, even there, and it was into a liberal climate, sceptical of 'class struggle' ideas, that Marx spoke. The medium he chose, suiting his unique talents, was radical journalism.

Marx managed to persuade a group of liberal industrialists and communist sympathizers to found a successor to the previously-suppressed journal: the *Neue Rheinische Zeitung*. It was to be a big success until its 'dictator' (thus Engels described Marx as editor) overstepped himself with the advocacy of violence. This new left-wing journal was unique for its clarity, and for its adherence to particular policies.

In the *Neue Rheinische Zeitung* Marx advocated firstly the formation of a single German democratic republic and secondly a struggle with Russia for Polish liberation. He brought the accumulated opinions of the past few years to bear upon these issues, illustrating practical politics with thought-out policies.

According to Marx, Prussia was still politically feudal and had only achieved revolution of thought, with no truly socialist consequences. The workers ought to form a conditional alliance with the radical wing of the bourgeoisie to bring about wider suffrage, direct elections, the abolition of feudal dues, a state banking system and state responsibility for unemployment. Because of the pattern of history, in which the bourgeois revolution precedes the proletarian, Marx felt it was important to stress this temporary association, which could later be broken when the working-class forces were dominant. Only once, before the final issues of the journal, did Marx give vent to the belief that the only ultimate solution would be revolutionary terrorism.

Marx was always confronted by – and seemed to thrive on – opposition both from the authorities, and other socialists. Gotteschalk, the organizer of the Workers' Association, was especially bitter about Marx' opportunism, denouncing him roundly:

> You are not serious about the liberation of the oppressed. For you the misery of the worker, the hunger of the poor has only a scientific and doctrinaire interest ... you do not believe in the revolt of the working people ...[6]

There was something in this, as we have seen. After all, his view of the proletariat as universal class came more from Hegel's model than from compassion for the workers.

The subscribers and owners of the *Neue Rheinische Zeitung*, moreover, were highly volatile. After one dispute, the owners pulled out, leaving Marx as the sole proprietor and subscriber numbers diminished each time a controversial issue appeared. On one memorable occasion, Marx was prosecuted for agreeing that the Prussian taxation system was illegal and advocating the obstruction of tax-collection. In court, he defended himself so convincingly that he was not only acquitted but the foreman of the jury thanked him for his instructive speech. He had argued that the law 'was not worth the paper it was written on' because it was the creation of a past age and thus not in step with the laws of history.

In the end, events in France were to catalyse the dissolution of the journal and Marx finally despaired of the bourgeois revolution, turning his attention to the workers alone. Conservative forces were rallying themselves in Paris and socialists fought them in the streets for three days in June 1848. Marx angrily defied those who were horrified at the bloodshed by complaining against the honours accorded the government's soldiers:

> The State will take due care of the orphans and widows of these men. They will be honoured in decrees: they will be given a splendid public funeral: the official press will declare their memories immortal ... but the plebeians, tormented by hunger, reviled in the newspapers ... their wives and their children plunged into greater misery than ever, the best among the survivors transported – surely the democratic press may claim the right to crown with laurel their grim and sombre brow?

Marx was ordered to leave the country forthwith. He produced one more issue of the *Neue Rheinische Zeitung* in red print, insisting (against the evidence) that he had only ever supported working-class emancipation. 20,000 copies were sold and soon resold on the black market as curiosities. He left for Paris, still expecting the imminent socialist triumph. He lived there briefly with his family, under the pseudonym of M. Ramboz. But they were in miserable poverty and Marx was soon made unwelcome and thrown out of the capital. Rather than move to what he scathingly described as 'the pontine marshes of Brittany', he left for England on 24 August 1849.

While Marx imagined that he would only have to stay in England for a few weeks or months, for then would come the revolution, he was in fact to make London his home for the rest of his days. In comparison with his apocalyptic hope, domestic details took on a secondary, *ad hoc* importance. Jenny and the children had to put up with much hardship over the ensuing years, for the expected revolution never came.

Marx spent most of his time with fellow-Germans, in the German Workers' Educational Association and in the Communist League. He gave careful, methodical lectures on 'bourgeois property' and other topics which were immensely worrying to the German authorities when they got to know of them, but which appeared not to perturb the English hosts at all.

As usual, Marx had one eye on Germany itself. Though he worked with the Communist League in London (which, as he dominated it, he referred to as 'my party') he also kept up his contact with German socialists. He urged them to oppose democratic parties and hasten the proletarian revolution. A new journal would have answered his needs most perfectly, and for a short time another resuscitation appeared from Hamburg rejoicing in the title of the *Neue Rheinische Zeitung*, subtitled: *Politische-Oekonomische Revue*. But it was generally rejected for its intellectuality and because Marx was in a minority as someone still enthusiastic about the events of 1848–49.

Marx learned other lessons through its failure, however, most significant of which was the realization of his relative ignorance of English economics. The British Museum was to be the location of his making good this deficiency in the years which lay ahead. Nevertheless, he did produce some creative writing during this time, in which he analysed recent events in terms of the 'materialist conception of history' and of class struggle. Both were written as journal articles and make lively reading.

The first of these sets of articles was originally destined for the ill-fated *Revue* but appeared in 1850 as *The Class Struggles in France*. It was an attempt to capture the spirit of those stormy years and interpret them as a series of class-based contests of economic interest. Why had the revolution failed?

> With the exception of only a few chapters, every more important part of the annals of the revolution from 1848 to 1849 carries the heading: *Defeat the Revolution!* ...
>
> In a word: the revolution made progress, forged ahead, not by its immediate tragicomic achievements, but, on the contrary, by a powerful, united counter-revolution, by the creation of an opponent in combat with whom, only, the party of overthrow ripened into a truly revolutionary party.

The workers had no chance of victory while in alliance with the bourgeoisie but their defeat was not the end:

> ... the June defeat has created all the conditions under which France can seize the initiative in the European revolution. Only after being dipped in the blood of the June insurgents did the tricolour become the flag of the European revolution – the red flag!
>
> And we exclaim: *The revolution is dead! – Long live the revolution!*

Rather than seeing the revolutionary upheavals as the work of a few key figures alone, Marx tried to show how each figure represented a class. The true understanding of this period, according to the materialist conception of history, was that economic class interests were the crucial backdrop to the political events.

The second article appeared in a New York journal, entitled *The 18th Brumaire of Louis Bonaparte*. This took further the themes of the *Class Struggles*, indicating the role of class in bringing Louis Napoleon to power as emperor in the conservative reaction following 1848. Later on, Marx said that he wished to demonstrate 'how the *class struggle* in France created circumstances and relationships that made it possible for a grotesque mediocrity to play a hero's part'. The word-play of the title hinted that Louis Napoleon's *coup* was a repeat performance of Napoleon Bonaparte's of 1779. The first was a tragedy, the second a farce. Things happen thus:

> Men make their own history, but they do not make it just as they please; they do not make it under circumstances chosen by themselves, but under circumstances directly encountered, given and transmitted from the past. The tradition of all the dead generations weighs like a nightmare upon the minds of the living. And just when they seem engaged in revolutionizing themselves and things, in creating something which has never yet existed, precisely in such periods of revolutionary crisis they anxiously conjure up the spirits of the past to their service and borrow from them names, battle cries and costumes in order to present the new scene of world history in this time-honoured disguise and this borrowed language.

Marx illustrated this further using the example of Cromwell who, with the English people, had

> borrowed speech, passion, and illusions from the Old Testament for their bourgeois revolution. When the real aim had been achieved, when the bourgeois transformation of English society had been accomplished, Locke supplanted Habakkuk.

Here is the materialist conception of history at its baldest – and most misleading. For while we cannot hide the fact that some have used ideology – 'the poetry of the past' – to cover self-interest, this interpretation simply tars all with the same bourgeois brush, in this case casting damaging doubt upon any genuine Christian convictions of Cromwell's people.

Yet Marx himself disliked the bourgeoisie for making similar sweeping statements about the proletariat:

> During the June days all classes and parties had united in a *party of order* against the proletarian class as the *party of anarchism*, of socialism and communism. They had 'saved' society from the 'enemies of society'. They had given out the watchwords of the old society, *'Property, family, religion, order ...'*

But the bourgeoisie could not arrest the spread of those very freedoms for which they had once stood – in their own interest. When the proletariat cry out for education and votes they are (dirty word) 'socialistic'. Thus 'the sword that is to safeguard it must at the same time be hung over its own head as the sword of Damocles'.

Marx then documented the rise of the state as an independent power to safeguard bourgeois interests, from the time of the first Napoleon (when it was only a means of preparing for the class rule of the bourgeoisie) to the second (when it seems to have made itself independent). Yet this power is not suspended 'in mid-air': 'Bonaparte represents a class, and the most numerous of French society at that, the *small-holding peasants.*'

The peasants, Marx pointed out, being scattered, could not represent themselves, thus Louis Napoleon would speak for them. He would protect their small-holdings but at the same time levy heavy taxes from them, and man the army from them. Thus he enslaved them, in fact, to capital: 'Bonaparte would like to appear as the patriarchal benefactor of all classes. But he cannot give to one without taking from another.' So, concluded Marx, Louis Napoleon depended upon the 'lumpenproletariat' (casual, socially-marginal workers) to maintain bourgeois rule. The revolutions had ended in a fiasco.

An historical lens

Almost by-the-way Marx had revealed his view of history through historical writing. It relates directly to his conception of persons. Labour, we saw, is the instrument of human self-creation. People make themselves and their environment through work. The way in which labour is organized, especially under capitalism, gives rise to distinct class divisions. The ensuing class struggles are the motor of history.

History, for Marx, is no accident, neither is it shaped by divine providence. Moreover, Marx had no time for the 'great man' theory of history – that Caesars, Napoleons or Hitlers are its ultimate directors. It is the creation of labouring people and exhibits certain predictable tendencies.

The Christian must agree that history is made by people. Indeed, humans have the task of opening up the creation in accordance with God's frameworks for freedom. But it is no more made by the proletarian class than by great men. All contribute, taking their God-given responsibilities more or less seriously, to the pattern of historical events. And sometimes the contribution is via some other thing, such as technological innovation, the media or some political election.

We have quoted Marx' celebrated phrase: 'Men make their own history, but they do not make it just as they please; they do not make it under circumstances chosen by themselves, but under circumstances directly encountered, given, and transmitted from the past.' One always meets with this dialectical swing of the subjective and objective: we create ourselves (subjective), but within certain social and historical limitations (objective). This 'dialectic of labour' will reappear when we examine Marx on unionism.

But some nagging contradictions remain. On the one hand Marx arrives at his understanding of the 'universal class' through purely abstract Hegelian reasoning. This is an interpretation of history from outside history itself (though worked out from 'autonomous' philosophy). But on the other hand he gives the theory credibility and bite by referring to tangible human suffering. If Marx could overcome this tension, he could conclusively marry his doctrine of human self-creation with that of human self-redemption. As it is, there will always be an ambivalence. Should we strive (as Gotteschalk required) for workers' revolt against the system of suffering? Or should we simply allow the *Aufhebung* to work itself out over our heads?

The Christian may never confront Marx with a pat answer. Interpreting history rightly, so that one may act rightly and consistently, is ever a complicated and precarious business. Christians do not even pretend to *possess* a radical and integrated programme for human redemption and restoration. The Christian approach to history begins with the honest admission: we do not know. No self-spun philosophy and no identification with the oppressed gives a right perspective on our situation. It has to be revealed to us.

As van der Hoeven pointedly remarks:

> Mankind, society, and history are in even worse straits than Marx
> felt them to be. The suffering and cross of Christ tell us how much
> worse. Moreover, all our desperate attempts at self-recognition
> and self-redemption are deceptions and illusions ... Self-denial is
> the reverse side of radical belief in and radical surrender to Jesus
> Christ. That self-denial involves the radical denial of our own
> power to self-recognition and self-redemption and also of our own
> ability to establish what is given, whether through thought or
> suffering.[7]

The embers of revolution

By the time Marx had written *The Class Struggles in France* in 1850,
the only truly revolutionary chapter in his life had closed. The embers
were to be fanned sporadically in later years but never again would he
expect revolution with quite the certainty and eagerness of the years
around 1848. The spectre haunting Europe had become flesh,
fleetingly triumphant, before finally succumbing to the strength of
restored regimes. Both the hope of an imminent revolution leading
to a socialist utopia and the potato famine and bad harvests which
had given hope its chance, were over – for the present at least. By
now the dread fear of Chartism had waned in England and everyone
prepared feverishly for the demonstration of 1851: the Great Exhibition in the Crystal Palace, when Britain would parade her industrial
might over all lesser offerings from other countries. Outside England,
the biggest hope for many lay on the far side of the newly-united
States of America. The Californian gold rush was still magnetizing its
multitudes.

Having established his theory of persons, religion and history and
having now permanently woven in the notion of class struggle, Marx
was ready to spend the following years working on economic theory,
the prelude to his projected work of synthesis. But despite his
numerous perceptive insights into the machinery of capitalist society,
despite his great faith in himself and despite the fact that others
followed him as a charismatic and commanding figure, it is not out of
place to express some uneasiness about the man and his endeavours.

The fateful ambivalence which characterizes all his compositions
has had more illustrations here. There is the historical issue: abstract
philosophical interpretation or partisan study of the oppressed underdog? Then there is the issue of the state. It is an evil contraption
designed to camouflage real human relationships and may be

operated in favour of one class. But what, we may well ask, did Marx intend by the 'dictatorship of the proletariat'? With hindsight, we have even more cause to consider it a menacing phrase.

Though he had still to expand on the theme of the accumulation of private property, Marx was already convinced of its evil nature. He correctly observed how its owners became enslaved to it ('the property of property'); he was more ambiguous on how it should be socialized. Lastly, class interest, at once detested (if bourgeois) yet represented (if proletarian) by Marx becomes the lens through which history is viewed. Thus the possibility of sincere action is ignored and the notion of any abiding standards of judgement becomes redundant.

At these sensitive points the Christian must think carefully. For while class interest is a palpable feature of urban industrial capitalist (and socialist) society, it cannot be divorced from the collective refusal to follow the way of God. Although, for example, the character of the state has changed considerably since biblical times, the principles for government derived from the scriptures still form a coherent framework for freedom for today. Whatever the particular features of a modern government may be, justice is still its primary task. This may better be served by decentralization, or any number of possible modifications, but the central task remains the same.[8]

Justice is not class-partial, for the simple reason that it originates in the very character of God. That it may become class-partial is also a fully biblical supposition. Amos frequently warned against exploitation by the ruling class. But the state is accountable to God, and it is part of the Christian message to insist upon this. It is not accountable primarily to any 'universal class' or interest group.

Lastly, we must place a further question mark next to Karl Marx himself. Behind the prophetic aura which now surrounds his name – what was he really like? We have had some glimpses into his personality already: he was a man who *had* to be right and only admitted error long after he had estranged himself from any who had had the audacity to disagree with him. He spoke for proletarians but had a most condescending attitude towards them. He wrote of free, communal, purposive activity but never himself managed to get along with anyone in his life. He had a devoted wife in Jenny and a trustworthy friend in Engels but can these compensate for a life of social self-isolation in the one whom so many thousands have followed?

There is a strong contrast here with Jesus, the carpenter of Nazareth. He both spoke for, and mixed with, the underclasses of his day. His actions were so beautifully consistent with his words that he is the only person worthy of the kind of allegiance which so many have misplaced in Marx.

But Marx was often oblivious to these ironies: he was, after all, a stranger in a strange land. What that meant for his family and for his days and nights of intense study of economics, we must now examine.

Notes and references

1 F. Lessner, 'Before 1848 and after', in *Reminiscences of Marx and Engels,* quoted in McLellan, *Karl Marx: His Life and Thought,* Macmillan, 1973, Harper and Row, 1974, p. 177.

2 John V. Taylor, *Enough is Enough,* SCM Press, 1975, Augsburg, 1977.

3 See D. Hay, *A Christian Critique of Capitalism,* Grove Booklets, 1975.

4 Marx' comments on Napoleon III's France, the dictatorial state, was the nearest he came to a study of the state, and that did not amount to much. Trotsky's work on Fascism was more thorough, but did not deal with the entity known as the 'capitalist state' such as Britain. Ralph Miliband's *The State in Capitalist Society,* Quartet, 1969, is a modern, systematic, Marxist analysis of the state.

5 T. Geiger, quoted and translated by R. Dahrendorf, *Class and Class Conflict in Industrial Society,* Routledge and Kegan Paul and Stanford University Press, 1959, p. 175.

6 Quoted in McLellan, 1973, p. 217.

7 Johan van der Hoeven, *Karl Marx: The Roots of His Thought,* Wedge Publishing Foundation, 1976, pp. 90–91. Although van der Hoeven concentrates only on an analysis of the early Marx texts, his perspective is illuminating for Marxism in general.

8 Although there is yet no Christian equivalent to a Miliband-type of analysis, insights which might contribute to a framework for study may be found in H. Dooyeweerd, *The Christian Idea of the State,* Craig Press, 1968, and Alan Storkey's forthcoming *A Christian Social Perspective,* Inter-Varsity Press. But there is also something very attractive in the recent Anabaptist contribution to discussion of Christian attitudes to the state. See John H. Yoder's *The Christian Witness to the State,* Newton, Kansas, 1964 for an early statement. Yoder ought to be read in conjunction with Richard J. Mouw, *Politics and the Biblical Drama,* Eerdmans 1976, which comments helpfully both on the state and Yoder's attitude to it.

Manchester cotton mills

CHAPTER 4

Labour and capital

*Now listen, you rich people, weep and wail because of the
misery that is coming upon you ... You have hoarded
wealth in the last days. Look! The wages that you failed
to pay the workmen who mowed your fields are crying out
against you. The cries of the harvesters have reached the
ears of the Lord All-powerful.*
The apostle James

Marx' mother once complained, 'If only Karl had *made* capital, in-
stead of just *writing* about it'. These words were ruefully recalled by
Marx on his fiftieth birthday, not long after the publication of
Capital. For, as Jenny wrote in a letter at the time:

> You can believe me that seldom has a book been written under
> more difficult circumstances, and I could write a secret history
> that would uncover an infinite amount of worry, trouble, and
> anxiety. If the workers had an inkling of the sacrifice that was
> necessary to complete this work, written only for them and in
> their interests, they would perhaps show a bit more interest.

Marx expended an amazing amount of energy in the writing of his
'Economics', while the entire family underwent severe privations of
poverty and illness. This was his labour for *Capital*. The major
themes of capital and its relation to labour, central to Marx' lifework,
were expounded under unimaginable stresses and continual setbacks.
The causes of trouble were not unconnected with Marx' singleness of
vision (in which priority was given to analysing capitalism before the
revolution broke out), and his total inability to handle (as opposed to
writing about) capital. Before we examine the contradictions of
capitalism, then, we must look at the context in which Marx studied
and wrote: the contradictions between his professed view of the
world and his actual life-style in it.

We have already noted Marx' arrival in London in August 1849
and his anticipation of imminent revolution. His work to assist Ger-
man refugees, his attempt to reorganize the Communist League in
Germany and to revive the *Neue Rheinische Zeitung* as a 'Review of
Political Economy' took up much of his time during the early days in
England. The refugee work was fairly successful in providing a hostel

and recreation facilities – not to mention the opportunity for Marx to deliver lectures on bourgeois property! A short-lived 'Universal Society of Communist Revolutionaries' was set up in 1850, temporarily linking European communists but this lost its impetus as the enthusiasm of 1848 waned. Lastly, the journal, which did actually appear in a few numbers, gave posterity *The Class Struggles in France*. But study was to be the keynote of the London years, culminating in the *Grundrisse* of 1857 and *Capital*, which was as complete as it ever would be by 1867.

A friend noted that 'Marx lives a very retired life, his only friends are John Stuart Mill and Lloyd and when you visit him you are greeted with economic categories instead of compliments.' He had very exact ideas about the right approach to any question and woe betide any so bold as to cross his path! That he had to be the central figure of any group is borne out by the nicknames given to one of the discussion groups meeting in Soho pubs: the 'Marx Society' or the 'Synagogue'.

All refugee politics in London was riddled with feuds and intrigues, in which Marx seemed to delight to take part. Ideas worked out in the study determined the quality of his relationships with others. Leaders of the only English political group with which Marx felt at home, the Chartists, were divided by Marx. George Harney, who wanted a broad front between chartism and the trade unions and co-operatives, pressing for a better deal against Parliament, was contemptuously written off as a 'very impressionable plebeian'. Ernest Jones, however, who believed in the class struggle above and beyond mere improved conditions within capitalism, Marx found much more congenial.

But Marx' study and his political squabbles, took place against the backdrop of poverty, illness, creditors' demands and begging letters. The family had hardly been in London a year when they were evicted from their flat. Their new baby, Guido, who only lived ten months, was not sleeping well and Jenny had 'terrible pains in the breast' as she fed him. One day, while she was trying to feed Guido the landlady (who was sub-letting their flat and in debt to *her* landlord) marched in demanding £5. Bailiffs came and began carrying out what few possessions and toys were there, with Laura and Jenny crying helplessly by the door. No one seemed willing to take in a family with young children and in any case, the furniture had all gone to pay off debtors who crowded in as soon as the bailiffs arrived. Eventually, with the help of friends, they obtained two rooms in a German hotel, where, to quote Jenny, 'For £5 per week we were given a humane reception.'

Things reached an all-time low around 1852, when Marx wrote:

> My wife is ill, my little Jenny is ill, Lenchen has a sort of nervous
> fever. I cannot and could not call the doctor because I have no
> money for medicine. For 8–10 days I have fed the family on bread
> and potatoes of which it is still questionable whether I can rustle
> up any today. I did not write any article for Dana, because I did
> not have a penny to go and read the newspapers ... The best and
> most desirable thing that could happen would be that the landlady
> throw me out of the house. At least then I would be quit of the
> sum of £22. But I can scarcely trust her to be so obliging. Also
> baker, milkman, the man with the tea, greengrocer, old butcher's
> bills. How can I get clear of all this hellish muck?

Engels often received letters like this and in fact supplied nearly all
the Marx family's needs for many years, sharing his income from the
Ermen and Engels firm in Manchester. The Marxes were frequent
visitors to the pawnshop, where winter coats lay in summertime, to
pay for paper and postage as well as food.

The root problem, it seems, was not lack of money, so much as inability to handle it. The Marxes always had to keep up appearances.
For a lower-middle-class family, living in mid-century London, £150
per year was a sufficient income and the Marxes often had more.
When Marx was made London correspondent of the *New York Daily
Tribune*, some regular payment came – but when Jenny visited Trier
in 1854, she had to travel with several outfits of new clothes! In the
early 1860s, things were no different. Marx, who had been friendly
with Lassalle in 1848, was lavishly entertained by him in Berlin and
was then obliged, when Lassalle came to London, to reciprocate: 'In
order to preserve a certain façade', Marx wrote to Engels, 'my wife
had to take to the pawnbrokers everything that was not actually
nailed down.'

A birth and another death were added blows to their miserable
family life. Their housekeeper, Hélène Demuth, gave birth to a son by
Marx, who they named Frederick. Engels got the family out of a tight
spot once again by accepting paternity. The death from consumption
of their own eight-year-old son Edgar, left scars that probably never
healed. But there were also short-lived moments of relief. On one
level, there were frequent picnics on Hampstead Heath, while the
family was still at Dean Street, and late-night pub-crawls with Engels
when he came to visit them from Manchester. (These sometimes
ended with pranks learned in student days, such as smashing gas-
lamps with bricks.)

At another level, two legacies made life easier in the early 1860s and provided Marx with support for work on *Capital*. But even then, after he had gained £400 on the American Stock Market, another begging letter went to Engels in 1867. He prefaced his remarks with the comment that they were partners in a 'combined task', in which Marx dealt with the theory and party-politics. He confessed to living too expensively, but excused himself on the grounds that the children needed to 'make connections and relationships that can assure them a future'. He continued frankly: '. . . a purely proletarian set-up would be unsuitable here, however fine it might have been when my wife and I were alone or the children were young.'

It was Jenny who probably suffered more than any from their difficulties. Marx hated to see her plight which she once described in a letter to him in Manchester: 'Meanwhile I sit here and go to pieces. Karl, it is now at its worst pitch . . . I sit here and almost weep my eyes out and can find no help.' Yet Jenny seemed willing to go through it for Karl. She acted as his secretary, copying out his almost illegible manuscripts and writing all the begging letters. Marx described her as 'mercurial' but in fact she became more and more miserable and irritable as she grew older. Every time she had bad news she sank into despair and seemed to have quite lost her senses in 1860 when she contracted smallpox. Marx managed to retain *his* sanity only by feverishly studying differential calculus!

But he himself was very ill for several years during the writing of *Capital*. He had boils which plagued him night and day and which he tried to treat with such bizarre remedies as arsenic, creosote, opium and cold baths. He even gave up smoking his pipe for a while. He was sometimes heard to wish that the boils could have been given to a Christian, who might have 'turned them to good account', and on other occasions he expressed his pleasure at suffering from such a 'truly proletarian disease'. But it did not help his work in any way, though it gave him more of which to complain to Engels in their twice-weekly London–Manchester correspondence.

Women : weals and woes

The early sixties saw the only quarrel between Marx and Engels. It arose because Marx failed to sympathize over the death of Engels' common-law wife, factory-girl Mary Burns. Marx had simply bemoaned his own situation. But he also partly blamed Jenny for the upset: 'I repeatedly told my wife that nothing in the whole mess was important to me compared with the fact that, owing to our lousy bourgeois situation and her eccentric excitement, I was not in a position to comfort you at the time, but only to burden you with my own private needs. . . . Women are funny creatures – even those endowed with much intelligence.'

It would not be exaggeration to say that Marx was fanatical about his project. He certainly seemed to be obsessed with his study, as this quotation reveals. His resolve was to 'pursue my aim through thick and thin and not let bourgeois society turn me into a money-making machine'. But it meant that he came perilously close to the objects of his own condemnation – the bourgeois family. There, according to *The German Ideology*, 'the wife and the family are the slaves of the husband'.

And his view of women cannot have pleased the feminists of his day, for he allowed Jenny's interests to become absorbed in his, without, it would appear, giving anything in return. Even if one makes allowances for the difficulties of *émigré* life in mid-Victorian London, social and sexual equality did not feature highly on Marx' personal list of priorities. He not only looked down on workers less intelligent than he but seemed to have taken advantage of the patience of his wife, who, fortunately for him, shared his revolutionary faith. 'Women', said Marx 'need to be controlled.'

Needless to say, this opinion did not tally with Marx' theoretical opposition to the bourgeois family, which he saw as an institution which had been modified to protect and support capitalism. But what did he mean by this assertion? It is worth pausing at this point to consider the position of the family – and women in particular – in relation to Marx' and Engels' work. The charge is often laid at the church's door that it buttresses the oppression of women and though sadly this has sometimes been true, the opposite has often been the case. One of Marx' contemporaries, Catherine Booth, refused to marry William Booth, founder of the Salvation Army, until he recognized her Christian feminist principles as fully biblical![1] What then *did* Marx and Engels say and how does this relate to contemporary socialist-feminism and Christian commitment?

In fact, as with the state, Marx never wrote anything systematic on women and the family, so that today's socialist feminists have to raid a variety of his texts in order to make anything coherent. The association of the monogamous nuclear family with the rise of capitalism rests on a dubious historical argument that the 'oppressive state', private property and the family emerged more or less simultaneously. Contemporary historical sociologists at Cambridge University, England, have grave doubts about the romantic image of the contented, integrated and extended families of our pre-industrial past. But the property/family connection is not without foundation.

The other family/capitalism link is made via the idea of two modes of production. The capitalist mode of production is said to depend on the capitalist mode of reproduction. Later in this chapter, we see how Marx shared the opinion of English economists of his day that value is determined by the amount of labour invested in the product. Labour and labourers are always needed in the capitalist system to maintain profit. It is thus imperative that labourers who die or are sick be efficiently replaced. This is the task of the family, in its monogamous, patriarchal form.

But it is Engels', rather than Marx' writing on the family which is receiving renewed attention in the wake of feminism and women's liberation movements of the late twentieth century. Engels' *The Origin of the Family, Private Property and the State* is often quoted as a starting-point for sociological and anthropological discussions of the family – despite the fact that the evolutionary basis on which it rests is disputed and often discounted by others in the field. Engels, in fact, depended heavily upon the work of an anthropologist, Lewis Morgan, as he tried to reveal the historical roots of the social institutions of the family, private property and the state.

The basic contention is that the oppression of women – their being treated as inferior people – is an historical, not a biological, problem. According to him, class exploitation and sexual oppression of women together served the interests of the private property system. It *is* hard to deny that the advent of capitalism brought with it numerous laws relating to property-rights for men and massive utilization of women for 'domestic' (and other) work but always at far lower rates than their male counterparts.

While the Christian is likely to disagree with Engels' analysis on some points, he or she will be much happier with other assertions than with contemporary socialist-feminism. Engels felt that oppression of women was stronger among the bourgeoisie than the proletariat and that there ought to be greater mutuality between husband and wife and greater freedom to choose a partner for love. But he did assume monogamy and the 'rightness of husbands and wives'. Contemporary liberationists have travelled far beyond Engels to the demand for free abortion and contraception and legalized homosexuality.

Engels also assumed the division of labour between men and women, with bread-winning on one side and child-rearing on the other. The Christian, however, would question this arrangement on biblical grounds: the work given in Eden was never restricted to man as maker, but to man as male-and-female. Moreover, child-rearing is seen, biblically, as the joint duty of man and woman; a reciprocal arrangement, though one which, admittedly, may involve the woman more intensely in the first few months of a child's life.

There is no biblical justification for the chaining of women to the kitchen sink – whatever present-day liberationists might say to the contrary! Current studies of the economic importance of 'domestic work' may have a far-reaching effect on future male-female relationships. But while the women range themselves against men, or the capitalist system as the root of oppression and sexism, they will be fighting the wrong enemy. Male domination and the oppressive tendencies of capitalism have deeper roots in the inner life of humanity. Made for reciprocity and equal responsibility before God, men and women clashed with each other, exchanging mutual interdependence for domination and false subjection when they rejected the Creator's framework for freedom. It is in the book of Genesis that we must look for the tragic descent into what was to become, in the nineteenth century, the bourgeois family.

Christians have misgivings about the sexual equality movement, not because they believe the pernicious nonsense about the innate superiority of males but because to focus on 'equality' and 'rights' is to bark up the wrong tree. (This is not, of course, to deny that Christians have been guilty of sexist behaviour. That is a matter of shame, not rejoicing.) Made by God, male and female stand together as persons – different yet complementary to each other but never superior or inferior.

But Christians should be unembarrassed about the biblical emphasis on submission and subjection. For sexual complementarity finds particular fulfillment in marriage, where it is seen as *mutual* submission of both partners. It is Paul, saddled as he is with the unjust charge of misogyny, who in Ephesians 5:21 offers the kernel of his sexual theology: 'Submit to one another out of reverence for Christ.' Christians, while doing all possible to imitate God's own concern for the 'low estate of his handmaidens', should be marked by their self-denying *mutual* submission and subjection, rather than demands for their sexual rights.

This emphasis on mutual submission, though there at the beginning, was soon distorted in Eden. Part of the curse on humanity was that men would rule over women. But the curse is not the framework for freedom. The perennial Christian task is to oppose the curse – as Christ opposed the curse of death in the resurrection – and to announce to the world by consistent practice that neither domination nor the demand for rights is God's way of freedom.

Sadly, Marx missed all this. His doctrines have no place for joy and love. He never appreciated the connection between the curse-denying resurrection and man-women relationships. One hears yearning pleas for closeness, intimacy and mutuality, which never surface in his theories. He once wrote to Jenny, while working on *Capital*, that, buried in her arms and awoken by her kisses, 'the Brahmins and Pythagoreans can keep their doctrine of reincarnation and Christianity its doctrine of resurrection'.[2]

From alienation to surplus-value

Amazingly, out of the 'hellish mess' of Marx' domestic circumstances came some of his most creative and insightful writing. The expected economic crisis did occur in 1857, so Marx was frantically scribbling his notes in order to finish before the (equally expected) revolution. In the winter of 1857–58, the outline of his major work was completed. Even he spoke with a tone of achievement about it. He announced in the Preface to *A Critique of Political Economy* (1859) that he had here spelt out his views both comprehensively and scientifically. The Preface promised a whole world-view, including the understanding of history in all its sociological, economic and political dimensions. But the published chapters of *A Critique of Political Economy* are disappointingly devoid of any such comprehensive statement. So what could Marx be talking about? Why be proud of some abstruse and incomplete manuscript?

Until 1939, this mystery remained unsolved. For not until then was the *Grundrisse* disinterred by the Marx-Engels-Lenin Institute in Moscow. This was the outline which Marx spoke of as an achievement. Though only an outline, the *Grundrisse der Kritik der Politische Oekonomie* (as it is cumbersomely entitled in full) runs to over 800 pages, ranging widely through many topics.

Marx expressed his satisfaction with it, not because it is coherent – far from it! – but because it contains a complete understanding of capitalism. As it turned out, it is the only complete view that Marx would ever present. It is a description of capitalism from its genesis to its dissolution. Marx explains why the present system of social-economic organization must collapse through the strain of its internal conflicts, to be replaced (*Aufhebung* again) by a higher form of civilization.

The first, shorter section is on money and how the value of things is determined. The second section, subdivided into three parts, is on capital. Marx wished to show how they were connected and in antagonism with each other. Above all, perhaps, Marx stressed that they could not be treated abstractly but only as social relationships. He was emphasizing the importance of ethics and sociology for economics.

The *Grundrisse* was the outline for a longer work (which was never completed), and provides a vital link between his earlier (1840s) and later (1860s) writing. The influence of Hegel is still very clear (though Marx insisted that he was 'stripping the mystical shell off the rational core') in the ideas of objectification, appropriation and the social nature of man. But he was now more economically sophisticated, foreshadowing the much denser style of *Capital*. On money, he pointed out that

> The economists themselves say that men accord to the object (money) a trust that they would not accord to each other as persons ... Money can only possess a social property because individuals have alienated their own social relationships by embodying them in a thing.

In other words, different processes go on beneath the surface-phenomenon of money: one can discuss money without ever realizing that as payment it can represent less than the worker is worth and as exchange it can hide unfree buying and selling relationships. Marx also shifted from his previous emphasis on exchange, to production. He now argued that men *create* value by their work – workers sell their *labour-power*. In fact, when he works for his capitalist employers, the worker is selling 'the right of disposition' of his labour, for the capitalist then disposes of it in *his* way. The capitalist uses labour-power for *more than* its exchange-value, thus creating what Marx triumphantly termed *'surplus-value'*.

Thus, if the worker was paid a certain fixed sum of money for a day's work, Marx would argue that in fact he had created more value in the time but that the capitalist took the difference as profit. Here he followed Malthus' idea, summed up in Lassalle's 'Iron Law of Wages', that wages could never rise permanently above subsistence level. There are hours in the day when the worker is not paid for his labour power, and this is the surplus-value that he has created for the capitalist. 'Surplus-value' therefore is the same as 'profit', which may also be seen as the indicator of exploitation.

It is really the worker's surrender of control over his creative power which Marx calls exploitation. Even though, according to the apparently fair wage-contract, the capitalist may have paid the worker enough to enable him to continue living and working, it is the very idea of exchange which is lopsided. For the worker has sold a unique commodity when he sells his labour-power: the capitalist, for his part, simply hands over some money. But in return for money the capitalist purchases control over the worker's creative power. The worker has sold that which makes him human. This, the *legal slavery* of the worker, is the contradiction which Marx said would lead to the breakdown of capitalism.

Whatever Marx exactly meant by value – and this is still the subject of hot debate, as is the labour theory of value – the theory of exploitation known as surplus-value has a palpable power. It holds an obvious appeal to workers, who can clearly perceive that they belong to a class which produces more wealth than it consumes. They can also see that the owners of resources, machinery, transport and so on, which the workers need for their jobs, may easily compel them to work on their terms. Surplus-value was a highly appropriate idea for much Victorian manufacture. Things have become more complex since, and surplus-value rather over-simplifies matters.

Big assumptions are needed to support the surplus-value theory. Capital and management must be relegated to being thought of as non-producers of value: capital itself being regarded as 'dead', stored-up wealth. But the idea has its convincing exponents today, among them the editor of the Belgian weekly *La Gauche*, economist Ernest Mandel. He presses for the continued use of Marx' argument in the present day. For him, only an anti-capitalist policy designed to move through a few short-termed structural reforms, could lead to the construction of a socialist democracy free from all exploitation.[3]

Whatever the status of the assumptions behind the surplus-value theory, it draws our attention to important matters for Christian reflection. It is no accident that the biblical account of economic life never extols the virtue of hiring labour. Quite the opposite. Economic independence (not to be confused with pretended autonomy in relation to God, or with *laissez-faire* notions of economic 'freedom', or even with non-communal work) is a deeply biblical principle.

The Old Testament law made explicit and repeated provision for those who had the misfortune to be economically dependent: hired labourers and servants. There should be no delay in the payment of wages, or any other discriminatory treatment according to Leviticus 19:13 and 25:14. Above all, those who were slaves in Israel were to be freed every seventh year according to the 'jubilee' principle (Deuteronomy 15:12–18). Not only that, but they were to be given the means of getting economically on their feet again.

Why all this special provision in the God-given Israelite law, if there was not a particular risk of exploitation where hired labour was concerned? And why bother to reinstate the slave-labourer as an economically free and independent person if there is nothing intrinsically worthwhile about using one's own creative abilities? How these principles are to be implemented in today's socio-economic structures, or how those structures ought to be modified to accommodate them, is another issue. But the principles cry out for realization.

And as we shall see in our discussion of labour unions, the business enterprise should be above all co-operative. Neither capital nor labour has the right to claim special access to the results of *corporate* effort.

Capitalism, technology and the wages of leisure

Several fascinating byways fill the pages of the *Grundrisse*. One striking feature is the ambiguity of capitalism: it is not all evil. The *Aufhebung* idea comes into its own again: there is both abolition and preservation in the dialectical process. Marx took further the notion of capitalism as liberator of technological forces leading to tremendous increases in production but argued that it was wrong to imagine that the apex of history had been reached with capitalism. For though freedom for capitalist entrepreneurs was important for its development, it is absurd, said Marx, to 'consider free competition as being the final development of human liberty, and the negation of free competition as being the negation of individual liberty'. The *moving* structure underneath capitalism must be understood (here he followed Hegel's questioning the reality of what the senses at first perceive) – even the apparently fixed presuppositions must be seen in motion – always flowing (here he went beyond Hegel).

Marx is caught on the horns of a dilemma here. Having accepted the notion of 'progress' from his Enlightenment forebears, he had to assume that, in general, history revealed increasing improvements to the human condition. Mechanization, a more-or-less inevitable development in this scheme, cannot therefore be criticized in a truly radical manner.

But machines bring debilitating disadvantages. Hegel had already bemoaned their effect on the worker's role: from master to cog, from participant to observer. Marx introduced some comments on *time*, which he believed to be an important, though neglected category.

Time created this ambiguity. The profits of capitalism are made in surplus time; yet capitalism frees men from manual labour, by the use of machinery, thus giving workers more free time. But if profits *do* come from surplus time, then capitalism will face huge crises with the advent of increased automation. Capitalism is both creative and self-destructive, according to Marx – it is bound to be transcended. He also argued that machines themselves would become an alienating force. Machines once providing the potential liberation of the social individual, with the advent of automation, could take over from workers and control them.

Science thus appears, in the machine, as something alien and exterior to the worker; and living labour is subsumed under objectified labour which acts independently. The worker appears to be superfluous insofar as his action is not determined by the needs of capital.

Throughout the *Grundrisse* there is a tension between what is and what could be, between capitalism and communist society, where the 'universal individual' could develop in freedom and harmony. But there is also a tension between the use of machinery and so on, in capitalist and future society. Marx wove into his vision many features of the world around him – feeling that they could be harnessed in the cause of human liberation. In this dream, the social individual, above all, would be in control of nature, working in community rather than in competition with others and having more and more free time due to automation for personal development.

Marx' view of work, which was already evident in the *Economic and Philosophical Manuscripts* of 1844, reappears in the *Grundrisse*. This makes the claim, that the 'dialectics of labour' is the central argument of all Marx' work, seem the more convincing, especially as those 'dialectics', though in a more 'earthed' context, are worked out further in *Capital*. But it is important to note that his view involved a misunderstanding of the biblical position. He wrote:

> In the sweat of thy face shalt thou labour was Jehovah's curse, which he gave to Adam. And it is thus as curse that A(dam) Smith regards labour. 'Rest' appears as the adequate condition, as identical with 'freedom' and 'happiness' ... But ... the overcoming of obstacles is self-realisation, objectification of the subject, therefore concrete freedom, whose action is precisely work.

The Bible, with Marx, sees work not as an imposition, but as the human task in the world. That it has *become* an imposition, because of human rebellion, does not mean that the *effects* of the curse are not to be reversed. Christ came to annul the consequences of the curse, including work. The original divine mandate to 'have dominion' and to 'subdue the earth' is still in force. Made more difficult by the fall, (that is, the creature/creator rebellion) as we approach the twenty-first century we may see how far work has become an easier thing through technological advance.

There is cause for uneasiness over Marx' understanding of work and technology here in the *Grundrisse*. On the one hand, as we have seen, there is a linear movement between human self-creation and self-redemption. But at the same time, Marx almost seems to slide into Adam Smith's association of happiness with leisure. Maybe *homo faber* really prefers the *homo ludens* (man-at-play) role to the *homo laborans* (working man) role. Maybe it is more important to make time for strumming the lute and mountain-walking than it is to be at the coal-face, desk or kitchen sink. For Marx mentally salivates at the thought of automation yielding more leisure-time.

Work, in itself, is not liberating. Neither is leisure. Work has its own freedom-framework and remains (ideally) as a satisfying aspect of full-orbed human life. To be a whole person, in the biblical sense, one may no more forsake work for leisure than abandon sleep for a 24-hour waking day.

Moreover, the curse is still in force, infecting work with frustration and sweat. This also means that every technological advance brings with it some disadvantage to be overcome, whether it be conveyor belts and boredom or test-tube babies and human engineering. But technology, conceived within the right framework, may be used to reduce the frustration and sweat of the curse. It can be part of the opening-up of creation's potential. It need not, as Egbert Schuurman has said, lead either to the stagnation and entropy of technocratic culture, or to the vortex of the ideology of revolution. According to him,

> The disruptions we are experiencing in our culture only arise when the ethos of men is wrongly directed, so that in all their technological doings they myopically focus on something within created reality, absolutizing and asphyxiating it, instead of offering themselves and all their deeds as living sacrifices in the service of God, who in Christ rules over creation.[4]

Likewise, only when work itself is seen in the context of God's work and purpose in the world will it become part of total human liberation. Marx was mistaken in his suggestion that the dialectic of labour – or leisure – is the ultimate context of human life. But his notion of communal, co-operative, free work does come somewhere near the biblical ideal.

Explosive capitalism: total Marx

Curiously enough, at least for those who imagine Marx to be obsessed with the idea of bloody revolution, the *Grundrisse* makes no mention of the violent cataclysm. Instead Marx soberly assesses capitalism's chances of survival and argues that, sooner or later, it must break down. What Marx failed to foresee was the ability of capitalism to take measures against collapse and especially the rise of the Welfare State (unless one thinks of the 'bourgeois socialism' section of *The Communist Manifesto* as an anticipation of Welfare Statism). We shall return to these later.

Of lasting value, perhaps, is the insistence, as McLellan has put it, that 'there are other alienations than those based on sweated labour'. There is an insidious process behind the cheated worker. That is, that capitalism *itself* is questionable from an ethical standpoint. Marx is right here, but his alternative is rooted in the same humanist soil as capitalism. There is a split between what Marx calls 'productive forces' and 'social relations' under capitalism, when both are aspects of the social individual's development. The worker, remember, has sold his humanity for a living wage. The capitalist views the worker's creative energy only as a means to capital growth and profit. 'In fact,' warns Marx, 'these are the material conditions to blow this basis sky-high.'

Thus the *Grundrisse* straddles Marx' life-work; he had been working on it for fifteen years and *Capital*, 'the application of a small part of the outline', was to appear ten years later. But the *Grundrisse* was not published until 1939 (English 1973) and has since sparked off a spate of reinterpretation. Simply put, those who thought they had found a 'break' between the 'old' and the 'young' Marx have a difficult problem in sustaining their case now. The orthodox view in Stalinist Russia, a variant of which is held by Louis Althusser,[5] was that the writing of the 1840s was mere juvenilia and the later work in *Capital* was Marx' lasting contribution.

As we have seen, the connection between the *Grundrisse* and both Marx' past and future work are legion, suggesting that there is a real continuity between the two. By the *Grundrisse* period, he talks more of *production* in his economics, and relies far more on statistical data. (He made pioneering social scientific use of government 'blue books'.) Like most people, he clarified his ideas as he grew older and read and experienced more, weaving other men's theories into his. But there is a convincing case to be made that he was *clarifying* rather than finding new starting-points. If that is so, then the 'total Marx' is one always concerned with human nature, alienation and liberation in terms of the dialectics of labour. He is a profoundly humanistic and ethical thinker who deserves to be evaluated as such. His work requires a truly radical critique.

The eternal student

Marx was a fanatical scholar, with all the bohemian and other-worldly connotations which that term might have. A Prussian government spy once described him thus:

> In private life he is an extremely disorderly, cynical human being, and a bad host. He leads a real gypsy existence. Washing, grooming and changing his linen are all things he does rarely, and

he is often drunk. Though he is often idle for days on end, he will work day and night with tireless endurance when he has a great deal of work to do. He has no fixed time for going to sleep and waking up. He often stays up all night, and then lays down fully clothed on the sofa at midday and sleeps till evening, untroubled by the whole world coming and going through the room.

For many years Marx studied in the British Museum (he read classical economics, plus mountains of previously unused government blue books) and wrote up his notes at home. Jenny converted his scribble into legible script, ready for publishers, as no one else could do. (Once in desperation, Marx applied for a job with a railway office but was rejected after interview on account of his atrocious handwriting. Thus he was preserved from bourgeois society's only attempt to make him into a money-making machine!) After the realization of the two legacies in the early sixties, the family moved into superior accommodation, where Marx had his own study.

It was on the first floor, flooded by light from a broad window that looked out onto the park. Opposite the window and on either side of the fireplace the walls were lined with bookcases filled with books and stacked up to the ceiling with newspapers and manuscripts. Opposite the mantelpiece and on one side of the window were two tables piled up with papers, books and newspapers; in the middle of the room, well in the light, stood a small, plain desk (three foot by two) and a wooden armchair; between the armchair and the bookcase, opposite the window, was a leather sofa on which Marx used to lie down for a rest from time to time. On the mantelpiece were more books, cigars, matches, tobacco boxes, paperweights and photographs of Marx's daughters and wife, Wilhelm Wolff and Frederick Engels.

Throughout those years, Marx had a large output. First came *Theories of Surplus-Value*, which revealed again his great debt to English classical economics. It was later published by Kautsky as a sort of fourth volume of *Capital*. It was followed by the three volumes of *Capital* itself, though Marx only saw one volume through to publication in his lifetime. He also wrote numerous articles for German periodicals. It is hardly surprising that he felt himself to be 'a machine, condemned to devour books and then throw them, in a changed form, on the dunghill of history'!

Every beginning is difficult
No sentence in Marx is more true than this: 'Every beginning is

difficult.' It comes in the preface to *Capital* volume I, written in 1865–66 and published one year later. He referred to the extremely abstract first nine chapters of the one book which everyone associates with the name of Karl Marx, in German: *Das Kapital.*

Despite the boils and despite his miserable remark that '*Capital* will not even pay for the cigars I smoked while writing it', he decided for safety's sake to deliver it by hand to his Hamburg publishers. Having received a strong hint regarding travel costs from Marx, Engels obligingly posted by return the halves of seven £5 notes. On being notified by telegraph that they had arrived *chez Marx*, he slipped the remaining halves in the mail.

Marx was delighted when at long last the thing was in print. Others, who have never waded out of the first nine chapters, might wonder who he expected to buy it. But after that 'difficult beginning', there are passages which vividly describe the birth of capitalism, illustrated with a wealth of contemporary detail. Others, such as this one in the 1867 Preface, show Marx at his most caustic. Political economy, he says, arouses more wrath than other sciences because of its sensitive subject-matter. It summons

> the most violent, mean, and malignant passions of the human breast, the Furies of private interest. The English Established Church, e.g., will more readily pardon an attack on 38 of its 39 articles than on 1/30 of its income. Nowadays atheism itself is *culpa levis* [minor fault], as compared with criticism of existing property relations.

However, he goes on, referring to an English blue book and corroborating it with a speech of US Vice-president Wade, the establishment is getting worried about changes in labour/capital relations:

> These are signs of the times, not to be hidden by purple mantles or black cassocks. They do not signify that tomorrow a miracle will happen. They show that, within the ruling classes themselves, a foreboding is dawning, that the present society is no solid crystal, but an organism capable of change, and is constantly changing.

The later part of volume I is peppered with passages like this. His old journalistic style refuses to be repressed. Historical materialism comes to life, in actual social-economic analysis.

The familiar themes of labour, surplus-value and so on fill the early part of volume I. The Hegelian mode (even though 'turned right side up') befogs things somewhat, as does Marx' dialogue with economists long since regarded as defunct curiosities. Marx wanted to discuss production-modes and how they lead to capitalism's downfall: economists since him have begun by assuming capitalism as 'given', and analysed that.

Volume II, very technical, is about capital circulation and economic crises. Volume III deals with value and prices and also discusses the falling rate of profit. It breaks off, tantalizingly, during a section on class. *Capital* has none of the comprehensiveness of the *Grundrisse*, of which it was a mere 'subsection'. But it more than compensates for the *Grundrisse's* lack of completeness in detail – especially in the first volume. It is as damning a picture of nineteenth-century England as Engels' *Condition of the Working Class in England* (1844), only now yoked with a sophisticated economic theory both of how things got that way and how they must change.

The most important feature of Marx' *Capital* is his stubborn refusal to take capitalism for granted. His critique of capitalism is radical. Unlike other economists of his day (and ours) who began with capitalism and proceeded to discuss its effects, Marx wishes to analyse 'the birth, life and death of a given social organism and its replacement by another superior order'. In this unique fusion of economics, sociology and history, he sought to discover 'the economic law of motion of modern society'. Capitalism had to be unmasked. He agreed with the British economist, Ricardo, that the exchange-value of an object was the amount of labour embodied in its production but gave the idea an historical twist by adding to it the key notion of surplus-value. This term had been used, but not elaborated, by Adam Smith.

The difference between the value of the labour-products and the labourer's subsistence is the surplus accruing to the capitalist from the objects produced after the worker had been paid for the job. This was the central bone of contention in the struggle between capitalist and worker. But even though this profit-production was the capitalist's strength, while it worked, it would eventually lead to crisis. For, according to Marx, surplus-value comes from labour, not from fixed capital and so as machinery took over from labour, less surplus-value (profit), at least in Victorian capitalism, would be made. Though increased production and expansion of colonial markets might temporarily offset this, collapse was bound to come in the end.

Though, in its early phases, capitalism had some advantages as far as production was concerned, Marx believed that once it had reached the stage of mid-nineteenth-century English capitalism, it could only increase the misery of the worker. The capitalist is obsessed with the accumulation of capital – the pursuit of wealth – and must therefore keep a reserve army of unemployed workers to serve the oscillation of the market. This is the ultimate evil:

> We saw, when analysing the production of relative surplus-value: within the capitalist system all methods for raising the social productiveness of labour are brought about at the cost of the individual labourer; all means for the development of production transform themselves into means of domination over, and exploitation of, the producers; they mutilate the labourer into a fragment of a man, degrade him to the level of an appendage of a machine, destroy every remnant of charm in his work and turn it into a hated toil; they estrange from him the intellectual potentialities of the labour-process in the same proportion as science is incorporated in it as an independent power; they distort the conditions under which he works, subject him during the labour-process to a despotism the more hateful for its meanness; they transform his life-time into working-time, and drag his wife and child beneath the wheels of the Juggernaut of capital.

Marx went on to demonstrate the connection between surplus-value, accumulation and unemployment. As the worker provides surplus-value for the capitalist, the latter increases his accumulation of capital. The labourer's lot, whether or not he is well-paid, will grow worse. Marx believed there is an economic law which ensured an ever-present surplus-population, an industrial reserve army of unemployed, which 'rivets the labourer to capital more firmly than the wedges of Vulcan did Prometheus to the rock'.

The unemployed capital-less worker is *dependent* upon the capitalist for work. The capitalist, for his part, may always regulate his production, according to how business is going, by hiring or firing labour. The argument does not lack contemporary relevance. Marx concludes:

> It establishes an accumulation of misery, corresponding with accumulation of capital. Accumulation of wealth at one pole is, therefore, at the same time accumulation of misery, agony of toil, slavery, ignorance, brutality, mental degradation, at the opposite pole, i.e. on the side of the class that produces its own product in the form of capital.

Marx also delved back into pre-capitalist times to try to explain how the whole business began. He argued that 'Primitive Accumulation plays in Political Economy about the same part as original sin in theology'. That is, it may be used to justify the existing, unequal state of affairs. From the historical materialist standpoint however, it began with the inability of each person to create the means of production for his own use, which brought about the division of labour. This in turn led to one group using the labour power of another and accumulating wealth thereby.

But this must also be seen as a crucial example of the weakness of Marx' analysis, for he refused to see beyond this limited mode of explanation. Other possible alternatives do exist. Why could primitive accumulation not have produced a social wealth which was equally shared between members of that society? If capitalism was the only line of development possible, Marx is deterministic and even if communism was bound to emerge in the end — what of those condemned to live before its inauguration? Lastly, Marx gives no reason why primitive accumulation should not develop again in the projected society of the future.

These questions deserve further exploration. In early Israelite society, to which reference has already been made, primitive accumulation seems to have produced an equally-shared social wealth. Marx might not have believed it but it was to work like this. Israel was constituted by covenant with God. He made certain promises to Israel, while Israelites agreed to recognize his ultimate sovereignty. Thus he was regarded as the rightful owner of all his creation ('and all it contains'), and Israelites held their land in communal trust on his behalf. (In fact, actual common ownership was usually within the extended family.)

The very name of God disclosed at the time of the exodus-liberation from slavery in totalitarian Egypt — Yahweh — indicated God's promise-keeping character. He who had seen oppression and had liberated his people would keep his word. He would take them to the land of promise and ensure that they settled there in opposite circumstances to the built-in exploitation and injustices of the repressive Egyptian economic machine.

The covenant-terms included the 'jubilee' principle and a sabbatical year. Both militated directly against private accumulation. The radical jubilee principle of Leviticus 25 returned all land (the 'capital' means of production of an agrarian economy) to its original (family) trustee every fifty years. In the sabbatical year not only were slaves freed but the land was to lie fallow and *all debts were to be cancelled* every seventh year.

There were no loopholes, either. The law said that no loans were to be refused to the poor person in the sixth year, just because the creditor knew that he would lose his money in the following year! Here was concern for the disadvantaged — and a check against private accumulation. Disobedient Israel may not have observed these crucially important principles but that is no ground for discounting them. Yahweh gave them and even in the present day their potential application would be a real threat to the insidious principles which underlie capitalism in its 'purest' form.

Unlike the Marxist thesis, which argues that accumulated wealth develops alongside the division of labour, the biblical testimony says more about the ruling class and accumulation. There may well be something in the Marxian idea but the biblical one also bears reflection. The covenant laws of Israel's theocracy made accumulation in private hands virtually impossible. But after the monarchy was established (the classic passage is 1 Samuel 8) the prophetic castigation of exploitation and oppression became louder and louder. In Isaiah 5:7–8 God 'looks for justice, but behold, bloodshed; for righteousness, but behold, a cry of distress'. In stark contrast to the time of original settlement of Canaan, when property was parcelled out equally, Isaiah pronounced 'Woe unto you who add house to house and join field to field'.

Eventually, in Mary's joyful song about the boy-child she will bear, we read of God:

He has brought down rulers from their thrones
And has exalted those who were humble.
He has filled the hungry with good things,
And sent the rich away empty-handed.

Throughout the teaching of Jesus it is clear that *private* accumulation is not the Christian way, not the mode of the kingdom of God. Andrew Kirk has made a careful study of this,[6] and refers especially to parables, sermons and encounters which Jesus had – all of which confirm the point. He sent away disappointed an earnest would-be disciple because he knew that his wealth was an insurmountable obstacle to his true allegiance to Jesus Christ. And Zacchaeus, the over-charging tax-gatherer, showed the genuineness of his desire to follow Jesus by giving half his extorted wealth to the poor and the interest on the other half back to those whom he had defrauded.

The history of the early church shows that accumulation is to be used for the good of all, as in Acts 2:45. And injunctions against the attachment to wealth continue, being summed up in Paul's famous (and notoriously misquoted) phrase: 'The *love* of money is the root of all evils.' Towards the end of the New Testament, in James's denunciation quoted at the beginning of this chapter, we come across the doom pronounced on accumulation of a kind of surplus-value which, but for the reference to the 'Lord All-powerful', could have been written by Marx himself.

But to return to our questions. It is not obvious, given *this* framework, why accumulation should not produce shared social wealth. It does not lead automatically to capitalism, in principle at least. The other questions remain and must be answered by Marxists. It must be said that, with regard to those living *now*, that the biblical God has a concern even for those living *before* the revolution. And, if the revolution comes and with it the 'withering away of the state' (Engels' phrase; Marx inevitably used the less biological word *Aufhebung*), who or what then will ensure that private accumulation will not again begin to rear its heinous head?

Critical economics

With history ever pressing towards the breakdown of capitalism, Marx had no time for questions like these. The third volume of *Capital* revolves around the idea of the falling rate of profit. Because profit depends on surplus-value, which is produced by labour (which declines) as opposed to capital (which is fixed and, according to Marx, unproductive), the average rate of profit will tend to decline also. But the capitalist drive for accumulation cannot be halted, so new technology must be developed, or new markets opened up. Eventually, however, capitalism's contradictions are bound to catch up with it.

This further indication of capitalism's self-destructive tendencies (which is more plausible than certain aspects of the surplus-value theory on which it partially rests) is linked to the phenomenon of capitalist over-production. Indeed, if production is for capital, rather than for the common good, as Marx insists with some justification, it is not surprising to find capitalism in a crisis of over-production. Many economists believe that world capitalism since the mid-1960s has entered a new deep structural crisis of accumulation, analogous to that of the inter-war period. One response to this has been Eurocommunism, which has tried in Europe to combat the crisis without actually combatting capitalism itself – which, if he had been around, would not have pleased Marx.

Marx did make some perceptive comments, for his time, on the debilitating effects of the capitalist exploitation of agriculture. He understood that the earth is precious and almost stumbled on the idea that mankind is its steward. But within his framework, not fundamentally different from the equally humanistic capitalists, economic growth, science and technology (properly organized) were still the basis of a good society. Stewardship has no place within that framework.

But the main message of *Capital* is that capitalism, as seen most vividly in England, is doomed to collapse. Surplus-value, created by the exploitation of workers, could only decrease (as the profit-rate) with the mechanization of everything. The lust for lucre would lead to monopolization and the concentration of economic power in fewer and fewer hands – but also to the growth of worker-power. But 'centralisation of the means of production and socialisation of labour at last reach a point where they become incompatible with their capitalist integument. This integument is burst asunder. The expropriators are expropriated.'

Marx' *Capital* was to become tremendously important as the intellectual foundation of international socialism but it received precious little attention at first. Marx offered to dedicate it to Darwin, who politely declined the honour, probably because he wished not to be associated with Marx' atheistic opinions. It got a brief mention in the English *Saturday Review* and Engels managed to get no less than seven reviews of it published in German periodicals!

Marx' work was a new departure for economics. He wished to 'produce a precise analysis of the concept of capital, since it is the basic concept of modern economics just as capital itself, which is its abstract reflection, is the basis of bourgeois society'. Seeing capitalistic economic activity as the clue to modern social relationships, however, was both the strength and the weakness of *Capital*. Positively, Marx produced a damning analysis of one aspect of nineteenth-century England, using economic concepts which contained within them an almost moral critique. He bitterly attacked English capitalist society – reserving just about his only expression of praise for the factory inspectors, whose reports of the shocking conditions and exposure of law-avoiding factory owners were its only redeeming features.

But it is his *mode* of analysis which is perhaps more important, as it is this which contemporary Marxists assert to be his abiding contribution. His was a critical economics, one which probed below supply and demand curves to the supposed essence of things. He recognized that the categories of economic analysis may never be divorced from social and personal realities. Those who made economics a science of inanimate objects, ruled by pseudo-objective laws of supply and demand, Marx scathingly denounced as having succumbed to the 'fetishism of commodities'. The Christian must agree with this emphasis (on economics as a 'personal' science), even while disagreeing with Marx' own misunderstanding of what it is to be a 'person'. The theory of surplus-value, for Marx the very heart of capitalist society, is profoundly critical in content. But, though critical, as it comes out of a human-centred world-view, this economics cannot be truly purposive. Its 'principles' are tied *within* the creation. Only an economics whose principles derive from *outside*, from the Creator, can be truly purposive and radically critical. Naturally 'surplus-value' is discarded by contemporary commodity fetishists, who maintain that the market-price is the only gauge of value. It is in their interests to do so. Marx' theory of surplus-value is a loaded critique – a testable means of exploring the inner workings of capitalism, which takes into account people with motives and conflicting interest-groups. It is on this level that it must be judged.

A long tradition of Marx criticism has maintained that history simply has not vindicated his theories or assertions. Some modern Marxists, however, maintain that the theories of surplus-value, for example, are still relevant. Curiously enough, arguments now used against Marx, were often anticipated by him, both in *Capital* and in the *Grundrisse*. For example, he foresaw the growth of the middle class, which has taken place in the twentieth century, but still maintained that capitalism's internal contradictions would lead to crisis. He also prophesied the rise of monopoly capitalism, though he underestimated the capacity of the state to intervene in this and curb its power.

In fact, though in a sense he saw the hints of what was to become, in the mid-twentieth century, the Welfare State, he did not realize its potential as a weapon against his own ideas. Nevertheless, there is a cause for unease whenever one hears economists still vaunting the 'scientificity' of their beloved supply and demand curves, or justifying the existence of a pool of unemployed labour. Has modern economics really superseded Marx, as it claims, or is capitalism still vulnerable? But if there is a possibility that Marx was right about some aspects of the nature of capitalism, might he also be right about future society – after the expropriation of the expropriators?

The answer must be that neither capitalism nor socialism are inevitable events in human history. Marx, consistent to his view of the person as *homo faber* and his understanding of history as the dialectics of labour, blinded himself to certain deeper facets of human experience when he rejected all idealism (and, as he imagined, all religion). Within the wider biblical framework, some of Marx' assertions come near Christian understanding; wrenched out of it, they are dangerous distortions of the socio-economic realities of late capitalism. What will happen to capitalist society will depend partly on the out-working of the contradictions of which Marx wrote, and partly on a multitude of other factors, including world trade, organized labour, exchange-rates and so on. It will also depend upon the valuing and decision-making of the people comprising it.

Marx was right to say that unfettered capitalism will collapse through over-production and industrial concentration but had no grounds for believing that a new harmony would grow phoenix-like from the wreckage. What has happened, however, is that while monopoly capitalism *has* come into being, there are still certain checks to its growth.

The most worrying feature, perhaps, is the role of the state. This power, which *could* curb that of monopoly capitalism, all too often appears as its servant. Indeed, the state itself may sometimes resemble a monopoly capitalist operation. A contemporary Marxist, Ralph Miliband, argued that capitalist societies are 'regimes in which an economically dominant class rules *through* democratic institutions, rather than by way of dictatorship'.[7] That is, the 'pluralism' of Western societies is a chimera: all is subordinated to capitalistic priorities. Moreover, if Marx is right about the human past being the history of man's pursuit of material advantage, coupled with lust for power, then there is nothing to stop the West sliding down the slope towards a managerial totalitarianism, which sociologist Andreski has called 'the direction of least resistance under the circumstances created by contemporary technology'.[8] It is worth remembering, too, that the same lust for power and desire to dominate, which is evident in monopoly capitalism, is also a key to the understanding of the bureaucratic totalitarianism of the Soviet Union and her satellites.

Industrialism or capitalism?

It is important to remember that an alternative conception of social development and transformation has grown up alongside Marxism in the twentieth century. In a word, this is the 'industrial society' theory. Because it has no one originator and has a multitude of variant forms, it is not always recognized as a coherent alternative. This understanding of Western social change is built on a contrast between 'pre-industrial' (or 'traditional') and 'industrial' society.

Rather than treating capitalism as a particular kind of society (Marx was at pains to demonstrate in *Capital* that he was writing about *social* arrangements on an economic base), it is relegated to the status of a phase within the wider process of industrialization. Class conflict thus becomes, not something inherent within capitalism as such, but a temporary strain in the transition to the higher stage of industrial society. And a notion like 'classlessness' becomes a matter of *distributive* rather than *productive* equality. So-called equality of opportunity is a goal of 'classless' industrial society theorists, whereas it is the co-operative and communal control of the means of production which is the Marxist ideal.

In some respects the work of early twentieth-century sociologist Max Weber may be seen to cut across the Marxism/industrial society divide. But Weber's emphasis on the growth of bureaucracy and the rationalization of technology and economic life has significantly in-fluenced several industrial society theorists. Some believe that capitalist and socialist societies are becoming more alike because of their common base. (Marxists, however, would retort that state socialists are degenerating back into capitalist consumerism.)

Today, the idea of 'post-industrial' society is gaining some curren-cy. In essence, it is argued that the same sort of evolutionary process which is the focus of industrial society theories has lifted some Western countries (with the USA in the lead) out of one phase into a 'service society'. In such a set-up, an élite of experts (especially scien-tists and technologists) rule. But this view (essentially a variant on the industrial society theme) tends to neglect the very features which Marx specifically pointed out: conflict between social groups whose interests are incompatible.

Anyone wishing to pursue a realistic analysis of contemporary societies must consider *both* the insidious worship of technique which, as an aspect of industrialism, is prevalent in Western societies (and sometimes obscured in industrial society theories) and the Marxian exposure of class-conflict.[9] Industrial society theories tend to neglect or underplay structural inequality and injustice. Marx, on the other hand, as even his sympathizers admit,[10] failed to devote adequate attention to the rise of the bureaucratic state.

One other matter, which will also be touched on in chapter seven, is that of dependency. Marx was bound by his Europeanism and never did justice to the *international* state system which accom-panied the rise of capitalism. Both industrial society theorists and Marxists must take dependency relationships into account. 'Internal' development hardly ever takes place today without an 'external' domination or dependency relationship. In today's global village, the classical question asked of Jesus – who is my neighbour? – has huge implications for international justice.[11]

Beyond Marx

But although our title-verse sounds familiar in relation to Marx' writing, *Capital* was written by someone who had rejected the 'Lord All-powerful', and who imagined that the solution to human problems lay in human hands alone. But he had no grounds for saying that evil was inevitably manifest in the form of primitive accumulation, or that good would be manifest in the future, communist society. While he went far in showing how capitalism works via exploitative surplus-value relationships, he failed to root his analysis in the wider context of 'sin' and 'redemption' – imagining that these categories were associated only with the false consciousness of social realities. From a biblical standpoint, it must be argued that sin, the turning against the human-welfare-oriented Creator to artificial and ultimately futile patterns of living, is *prior to* private accumulation and its associated evils.

Aspects of the Marxist analysis of structural inequality must be held alongside the basic truth that sin is the root of exploitation and domination and that the only hope of escape from that is through Jesus Christ. The struggle for liberation and justice will continue, but never at the expense of life now, nor with the false hope of earthly harmony through the reorganization of the relations of production which ever recedes before the eyes into a misty future. The hope is in the God who has directed his people to be frugal, generous, living in contrast to the dominant economic power-holders of the age. For the same Yahweh rescues not merely from exploitation but from its root cause, sin, and constantly helps his followers to put labour, capital, leisure and technology into the context of his scenario of present salvation and eternal life.

Notes and references

1 See Donald Dayton, *Discovering an Evangelical Heritage,* Harper and Row, 1976.

2 David McLellan, *Karl Marx: His Life and Thought*, Macmillan, 1973, Harper and Row, 1974, p. 11.

3 Ernest Mandel, *An Introduction to Marxist Economic Theory*, Pathfinder Press, 1970.

4 Egbert Schuurman, *Reflections on the Technological Society*, Wedge Publishing Foundation, 1977.

5 Louis Althusser, *For Marx*, Allen Lane Press, 1970.

6 Andrew Kirk, 'The Origin of Accumulated Wealth: The Marxist thesis and a hermeneutical reflection', Shaftesbury Project Paper, 1976. See also Martin Hengel, *Property and Riches in the Early Church*, Fortress Press and SCM Press, 1974. Unfortunately, Hengel's conclusion is not as helpful as the data he marshalls together here. Against him it must be argued that there *is* a coherent biblical perspective on property, and that it is highly appropriate to apply this to each generation. See further Peter Davids, 'The Poor Man's Gospel', in *Themelios*, vol. 1, 2, Spring 1976, and Dick France, 'Serving God or Mammon?', in *Third Way* vol. 2, 10, 1978.

7 Ralph Miliband, *The State in Capitalist Society*, Quartet, 1969, p. 21.
8 Stanislav Andreski, *The Elements of Comparative Sociology*, Weidenfeld and Nicholson, 1964, University of California Press, 1964, p. 363.
9 Compare this with the deeper perspective on class conflict presented by Alan Storkey in *A Christian Social Perspective*, Inter-Varsity Press (Leicester), 1979.
10 Perry Anderson, *Considerations on Western Marxism*, New Left Books, 1976, p. 114. This is a very honest and searching account, from a Marxian perspective, of Western Marxism's failures and inadequacies.
11 For Christian reflection on this, see James W. Skillen, 'International Justice: Is it possible?' in *International Reformed Bulletin*, 1975, no. 62/3. See also Ronald Sider, *Rich Christians in an Age of Hunger* Inter-Varsity Press, 1977, and Hodder and Stoughton, 1978, for a biblical treatment of the problem of world hunger, which includes a structural analysis of poverty, world trade, and wealth. José Miranda also pursues the theme of wealth, oppressive structures, and God's concern for the underdog in *Marx and the Bible*, Orbis Books, 1974, and SCM Press, 1977. While Miranda's effort to bring together biblical material is laudable (he makes a strong case), he diverts attention from sin as rebellion against God by limiting its scope to injustice among people.

The peasants' revolt in Russia

CHAPTER 5

Schools of socialism

*Trade Unions are the schools of socialism. It is in Trade
Unions that workers educate themselves and become
socialists, because under their very eyes and every day the
struggle with capital is taking place.*
Marx, Hanover, 1869

For nearly ten years (1864–1872) Marx threw himself enthusiastically
into working with trade unions, as the schoolmaster of international
socialism. Now forty-six years old, his prematurely-white hair and
beard flowed over his contrasting black suit as his commanding figure
dominated the London-based General Council of the International
Workingmen's Association. The energetic Marx of *The Communist
Manifesto* resurfaced to write its vigorous sequel, an inaugural address to the International. 'The emancipation of the working class
must be conquered by the working class themselves', he declared.

Marx entered the maelstrom of European socialism, each brand of
which had its distinctive trademark, determined to convince all of
their inadequacy in contrast to his. None understood fully the nature
and necessity of proletarian revolution. In *The Communist Manifesto*,
Marx had criticized reactionary, bourgeois and utopian socialism. He
now opposed them again in their union guise.

The 'reactionaries' were the 'feudal' and 'Christian' socialists who,
Marx believed, wished to join hands with anyone who would be their
allies against the newly-ascendant bourgeoisie. Christian Socialism
was just one of the many socialisms available in Victorian England:
in this chapter we shall look at its modern counterpart.

The 'bourgeois socialists' had a fair grasp of the contradictions of
capitalist production but were not revolutionary. They wished rather
to restore movements like the old 'guilds' in manufacture. Though
Marx knew first of the French version of this (often associated with
Christian economist Sismondi), guild socialism was also an important strand of British socialism. Lastly, Marx despised the utopian
socialists for their appeal, not to social analysis, but to mere
metaphysical concepts such as 'freedom' and 'justice'.

But although other socialisms were deficient for their lack of historical understanding or social 'earthing', Marx still depended heavily upon others' formulations of socialism. His originality lay in his unique synthesis of others' ideas. A clearer idea of his intentions and his vision of future society emerge from a look at the middle course he steered between the anarchism of Russian-born Bakunin, the limited reformism of the French Proudhonists and the government-courting Lassalleans from Germany.

It was within the 'schools of socialism' – the trade unions – that the major conflicts between reformists and revolutionaries were to be played out. This ambivalence of the unions (whether to go for gradual or cataclysmic change) is still with us today. However, the question of 'reform or revolution' cannot be settled by a simple appeal to Marxian orthodoxy: Marx' own position left the options wide open (at least to a choice between short-term structural reforms and sudden, total transformation). But as always, whatever the method employed, capitalism had to go!

After the revolutionary outbreaks of the late 1840s, there were years of reaction and government repression which lasted until the early 1860s. By then, authorities were becoming more lenient towards workers' combinations and meetings, thus leaving greater space for union activities. In Napoleon III's France, for example, unions were permitted under police surveillance, partly because the government wished to play off the workers against the financial aristocracy. In Germany, Bismarck tried hard to give the impression that he sympathized with the workers by introducing policies aimed against the bourgeoisie. Union membership and activity were growing on the Continent and in England and this, together with increased mutual aid (French-English strike fund contributions for example) made for a rising spirit of internationalism.

But that is not to say that an international association was planned, even less that Karl Marx had a part in its original formation. It happened almost coincidentally. French workers had crossed the channel, as tourists or semi-official visitors, to see the Great Exhibition of Modern Industry in 1863. They had met with English workers to discuss the effects of the recent abortive Polish uprising and, having found things in common, determined to meet again. Various other radicals attached themselves to the group, including Italian Mazzinists, Proudhonists, neo-Jacobins and Blanquists.

About 2,000 workers attended the arranged meeting in St Martin's Hall, London, in 1864. Professor Edward Beesly, a genial radical positivist, who taught history at London University, chaired it. Thus an international federation of working men was formed to destroy the prevailing system of economic relationships – capitalism – and to press for workers' communal ownership. Marx had been invited only at the last minute and he joined the elected committee of thirty-four as secretary for German affairs. Odger, an English shoemaker and secretary of the London Trades Council, was made president.

Marx and unionism

But why should Marx be keen to join such a movement? How was this in keeping with his analysis of the human condition? Ever since the 1840s, Marx had shown his confidence in the role of workers' associations. But at the same time he could not place all his trust in them, as they were only indirectly involved, as instruments, in bringing about the new society. Yet their task was crucial and necessary.

Marx' life-task concerned the *quality* of human existence. He believed that free, conscious, self- and world-transforming activity constitutes human 'species-being' but that species-being is denied and vitiated under capitalism. Therefore the quality of life, for Marx, can never be fundamentally changed while capitalism remains. Yet he insisted that it was worthwhile to soften the most glaring atrocities of capitalism – inhuman hours of work, dangerous machinery and so on – and that trade unions were the only means of curbing the power of the owners of capital. Under certain circumstances, unions could also take direct action against capitalism.

So, given that trade union activity will never remake the world, or change the structure of society, what other benefits could come this way? Marx was ambivalent. On the one hand, he often despaired of the British unions during the 1860s. But he nevertheless retained his conviction that they could be the focus of authentic human social behaviour, where people co-operate in an other-directed fashion towards short-term goals. Improvements in working conditions could be achieved by communal action, people working with, rather than against each other. So proletarian associations are potentially what future society could look like, where being and consciousness are one. Thus, as Avineri puts it, workers' association 'does not have a narrowly political, nor a trades unionist significance: it is the real constructive effort to create the social texture of future human relations'.[1]

A noble sentiment, indeed. But is it possible in advanced industrial civilization? 'Liberty! Equality! Fraternity!' was the French Revolutionary slogan but did Marx really believe that the achievement of fraternity was yet a realistic aim beyond liberty and equality? Evidently, yes. He believed that the unions could embody the hope of universal fraternal relationships just as some Israelis believe that the kibbutzim hold the promise of future society and as Christians believe that the church is a foretaste of things to come.

The vision of fraternity (founded on equality) was recently reiterated in the BBC's 1977 Reith Lectures by Professor Halsey. According to him, the only alternative to the roads to tyranny in Britain is that 'we, once again, take our traditions of citizenship and democracy seriously in their infinite richness and inspiration. They offer the basis for a new fraternity without which neither liberty or equality is possible'.[2]

Such sentiments should not be belittled – either by saying that fraternity is unattainable in industrial society (for the church consists of 'brothers and sisters in Christ' and her existence is not in principle limited by any social arrangements), or by saying that fraternity may exist in the church but not in the work community (for the impact of the church-in-the-world includes the world of work: Ephesians 6:5–6).

The principles involved may again be deduced from God's directives to Israel on their arrival in Canaan (Numbers 26:52–56). Land (their 'means of production') was to be divided roughly equally between families and tribes and used for the common good of all. Work, as we have seen, was viewed as a *communal* activity, the Mosaic system striving against the possibility of 'hired servants', who owned no capital and, on the other hand, the accumulation of capital in the hands of a few. The prophets made it clear that if work was not done *together* and in *harmony*, peace and justice would give way to oppression, greed, subservience and unjust rewards.

There is therefore good reason for thinking that the firm or business enterprise as a human community called to responsible stewardship (of all its members) is a description which comports well with Christian commitment. So trade union activity could be seen as part of this *whole responsibility* of the industrial enterprise (with obvious allowances for the difference between an agrarian and an industrial economy) to stewardship before God. This is obviously very different from the idea that unions are in opposition to the business enterprise. Fraternity is thus bound to play a part. The gap between the possible ideal – either as conceived by Marx or by the Christian community – and the reality of industrial life in nineteenth- and twentieth-century Western countries is one which is amply illustrated by the history of the First International.

The International Workingmen's Association

The new organization needed a unifying declaration of principles and, true to character, this is where Marx stepped in. The association may not have been initiated by him but, seeing its potential for revolutionary change, Marx took it over. French and Italian delegates had drawn up a vague humanitarian set of statutes which Marx totally replaced, complete with an inaugural address composed for the occasion. Carefully worded to avoid offence (especially to the English workers), Marx avoided calls to revolutionary action, while simultaneously making it abundantly clear that the existing capitalist system had to be subverted and overthrown, where possible by worker-politicians entering democratic governments.

The burden of *The Inaugural Address* is that things will not improve while capitalism exists. England, as the leader of world industry, gave Marx his main examples. 'It is a great fact', he began, 'that the misery of the working classes has not diminished from 1848 to 1864, and yet this period is unrivalled for the development of industry and the growth of commerce.' Stark poverty existed amid vaunted abundance. No palliatives would be enough, he wrote, for, under capitalism the rich would be bound to get richer and the poor poorer:

> ... On the present false base, every fresh development of the productive powers of labour must tend to deepen social contrasts and point social antagonisms. Death of starvation rose almost to the rank of an institution, during this intoxicating epoch of economical progress, in the metropolis of the British Empire.

But he did not despair: there was some light for the workers amidst the gloom. The Ten Hours Act (limiting the working-time of textile operatives, the parliamentary success of the evangelical Shaftesbury) and the co-operative movement were also 'great facts' of which the unions ought to be proud. Both were symbolic victories, the Ten Hours Act being 'the first time in broad daylight the political economy of the middle class succumbed to the political economy of the working class'. The 'greater victory', though, was the co-operative movement. 'By deed, instead of argument, they have shown that production on a large scale and in accord with the behests of modern science, may be carried on without the existence of a class of masters employing a class of hands.'

Marx argued that the International should aim to establish close relationships between members from different countries, to inform each other of conditions, discuss questions of common interest and to have annual congresses arranged by a democratically-elected council. He deliberately left the constitution as elastic as possible to allow the maximum recruitment. Written into both constitution and inaugural was the clear warning that unless the economic structure was opposed and economic emancipation sought, misery, degradation and enslavement would continue. So, 'Proletarians of all countries, Unite!'

The International grew fairly rapidly, both in numbers and prestige. Other union organizations became affiliated to it, so that by the time of the first congress at Geneva in 1866, seventeen unions had joined and a further thirteen were negotiating membership. The organization was superior either to the Chartists or to the earlier Communist League. Marx, without a doubt, was the one who held it together with rigid discipline and authority. He discouraged independent activity, ever trying to guide the workers towards his solutions.

But there were problems. Marx had to weave a tricky course between the various national groups and influential leaders in order to retain his grip. The Italians, for example, never forgave him for his ruthless surgery on their draft constitution and deeply objected to his *class* analysis. Their removal was soon contrived. Germany was a constant embarrassment to Marx. He believed that there was considerable revolutionary potential there but had to exaggerate his reports of its rather weak and Bismarck-stuffed union activity. And the French, even though they had the longest history of socialistic activity, were split by ideological disputes. As we shall see, this was explicitly true of Proudhonism which provided a major challenge to Marx' position in the London General Council.

Between 1867 and 1869 the International reached its peak. Three congresses were held at Lausanne, Brussels and Basle. Although the Reform Act of 1867, which widened the English franchise, did focus more attention on the working classes, few new unions joined after that year and there was never any impact in the heavy industries. (This was due partly to the focus of activity being London, while the workers were concentrated in the more northern industrial areas of England.)

The real successes of the International were on the Continent and in the field of extensive strike-fund aid. And Marx' ideas were being accepted at each succeeding congress. At Brussels, for example, strikes were accepted as a legitimate weapon of the working class. It was agreed that machinery had potential for human welfare as well as alienation and, most important, collective ownership of land, railways, mines and forests was agreed as an aim. The significance of this last resolution cannot, however, be appreciated unless the nature of the opposition to such sentiments is made clear.

Between Proudhon and Bakunin

Marx' bugbears in the International could be divided into two main groups: Proudhonists, who were not political enough, and Bakuninists, who were anti-political. There was Proudhonist trouble from the start (even dividing the ranks of the French International supporters), and it was Bakunin's anarchism which was to provide the final internal threat to the International.

The Proudhonists wanted to build a purely working-class trade union movement and comprised mainly shopkeepers, peasants and artisans. They were keen on co-operatives and on protective tariffs, having little time for centralization or strike action. They wished to improve their lot by collective action but eschewed political activity as being irrelevant to their aims. Yet they represented a large number of French workers and Marx was obliged to include them in the International. Ironically, their French rivals, the Radical Republicans, who *did* believe in political action, were drawn mainly from the middle classes and were thus not the heirs of Marx' revolution at all.

Marx' big headache was the problem of Proudhonism: the un-revolutionary working class. He had to work with them (in the International) but against them (ideologically). If Marx was right (and there was never any question of that as far as he was concerned), capitalism could not be reformed: the economic structure had to be transformed out of all recognition. Capitalist governments had to be harassed and subverted by strikes and demonstrations and infiltrated by articulate representatives of the revolutionary working class. Thus one of the things that was to please Marx most during the history of the first International was the eclipse of Proudhonism and the accept-ance of his ideas. To persuade the delegates to vote for land nationalization (and thus against private property-accumulation), and to declare the strike a weapon of the proletariat: these were momen-tous events!

It was at Basle in 1869, with the International on the crest of the wave, that the major land nationalization vote was carried. At the same congress Bakunin emerged as a major threat to Marx. He wanted inheritance laws abolished and had been agitating for this in Italy and Switzerland. Marx made it clear that this was not a goal compatible with his vision for the International. It was far more strategic to abolish the economic system which *causes* inheritance laws than merely to get rid of the symptoms of the disease.

Though they tolerated each other for a while, the rift between them was to come to a head before the International finally fizzled out. Bakunin, an anarchist, objected to all state power and even resisted the centralization of the International. He felt that Marx held the reins too tightly and that he stood for 'authoritarian communism' which would never realize itself in true freedom. He declared:

> We revolutionary anarchists are the enemies of all forms of state and state organisation ... we think that all state rule, all governments, being by their very nature placed outside the mass of the people, must necessarily seek to subject it to customs and purposes entirely foreign to it.

He held that people with ideas like Marx' would 'destroy the present order only to erect their own rigid dictatorships upon its ruins'.[3] This was the real difference between them, though it was often veiled before the final struggle. Marx, though he was suspicious of Russians in any case, believed Bakunin's ideas to be erosive of true revolutionary potential. His was a hollow utopian heroism, unsuited to Marx' dream of a unified workers' alliance which soberly analysed conditions and waited for its historical moment. For Marx, the new society was being nurtured in the womb of the old, so there would be some continuity between capitalism and socialism. For Bakunin, total destruction had to precede the dawn of Utopia.

It would be misleading however, to give the impression that Marx' course was simply to steer between Bakuninism and Proudhonism. The Germans, whom Marx was supposed to represent, did not meet his requirements either. The General Union of German Workers (ADAV) had been led by Lassalle, who died just before the foundation of the International. His programme included the co-operation with bourgeois parties to achieve mutual goals. (Bakunin, of course, shared Marx' distaste for this attitude – this was one point on which they agreed.)

Lassalle was of the opinion that a socialist initiative could come from the Prussian government and thus encouraged workers to support Bismarck. Marx thought Bismarck embodied the antithesis of socialism, warning that 'the honour of the workers' party demands that it rejects such phantasms before it discovers their emptiness from experience. The working class is revolutionary or it is nothing'.[4] He refused to countenance the notion that 'compromise with the powers-that-be' would never achieve anything valuable for the proletariat.

Somehow the International held together after 1869 but it declined from then on. At its strongest (though the anxious bourgeois newspapers wildly exaggerated its strength) its membership could be measured in hundreds, though if the number was calculated from affiliations of unions, there were several thousand involved. Although there were probably in the region of 50,000 British affiliated workers, even they managed to think independently of Marx. As he himself admitted, he had failed to infuse them with 'socialist theory and revolutionary temper'. But in the end political events, not mere decline of fervour, spelled the end of the International. They erupted in 1870, when Napoleon III declared war on Germany.

The Paris Commune

The Franco-Prussian war of 1870 came as a complete surprise to Marx and Engels. However, they took it in their stride. The French socialists denounced the war, the Germans were divided in their response. Marx and Engels predicted revolution in France if the French lost the war but that present conditions would continue, though worsened, if Germany lost. In the event, the emperor was defeated at Sedan and a republic was proclaimed in France.

Marx wanted the International to plead for British recognition of the republic and Thiers, its president, and to discourage revolutionary activity by French Socialists which would easily be crushed by the Prussian army. He modified his views when the provisional government became more reactionary and the Paris National Guard declared themselves to be the true government. A commune was set up in March 1871 when Thiers and his officials left Paris for Versailles: the revolution was under way!

But the commune represented a huge variety of political persuasions, including a large proportion of old-style Jacobins alongside Proudhonists and Bakuninists. They were reformist, not socialist in any strong sense. As Berlin describes it:

> By a great effort the people had shaken off the nightmare fist of the Empire, then of the siege; they had hardly awoken yet when the spectres seemed to advance upon them once again: terrified they revolted. This common sense of horror before the resurgence of the past was almost the sole bond which united the Communards.[5]

In this atmosphere of horror and suspicion of all, the terror began. Executions followed unreasonable accusations and many innocent lives, including that of the Archbishop of Paris were taken. It was the turn of the rest of Europe to be horrified at the bloodshed and inhumanity of the Commune. Finally the horror took active form in the avenging forces of Prussia, who ruthlessly crushed the Commune, indiscriminately taking more lives in the atrocities of 'white terror'. The bloody suppression was considerably worse than the evil it was intended to eradicate. The Commune was finished.

Members of the International, not least in England, had been uncertain how to respond to the actions of the French communards – should they applaud or denounce? Few were willing to condone the violence and yet the Commune did exhibit some redeeming features. Marx, too, had no sympathy with the Jacobin violence but he settled the issue by coming out in general favour of the Commune. He confirmed the suspicion of many (which was in fact quite untrue) that the Commune had close links with the International. He wrote a pamphlet, on behalf of the International, which came out later in 1871 as *The Civil War in France*. This obituary note earned him the notorious title of the 'red terrorist doctor'; he was almost universally branded as a social incendiary.

In *The Civil War in France* Marx created a heroic legend of socialism, declaring it to be the first open class confrontation in history. Though he regarded it as a major tactical blunder, Marx lauded the Commune as a manifestation of what was possible: a working-class revolution. Unlike *The Communist Manifesto*, in which the proletariat was seen to seize the state machine and turn it to socialist ends, this document had far less centralist emphasis. The replacement of the bourgeois state by the Commune was the way through to Socialist Society. The Commune was exalted as a model for every town and village:

> Instead of deciding once in every three or six years which member of the ruling class was to misrepresent the people in parliament, universal suffrage was to serve the people, constituted in communes, as individual suffrage serves every other employer in the search for workmen and managers in his business.

Thus, despite his enthusiasm for movements such as land nationalization, Marx clearly indicated here that he did not envisage socialism as bureaucratic collectivism. The Soviet state-machine was no more anticipated by him than was the power of the Vatican by the apostle Paul. President Tito of Yugoslavia inaugurated 'workers' self-management' in 1950 along lines which would have appealed to Marx. The idea was to avoid bureaucratization at all costs.

Marx here tells us more of his vision for the future socialist society, for the communards were *not* unilaterally drawn from the proletariat and they had been far from single-minded in their pursuit of equality. Nevertheless Marx proclaimed them the 'direct antithesis' of the Empire and the 'positive form' of the 1848 Republic. Those who died were christened by Marx 'the martyrs of International Socialism'. They might have failed but their names would live on for the historical role they had enacted.

The Commune was a symbolic step forward for the emancipation of labour. But yet he counselled:

> The working class have no ready-made utopias to introduce . . . in
> order to work out their own emancipation, and along with it that
> higher form to which present society is irresistibly tending by its
> own economical agencies, they will have to pass through long
> struggles, through a series of historic processes, transforming cir-
> cumstances and men. They have no ideals to realise, but to set
> free the elements of the new society with which the old collapsing
> bourgeois society itself is pregnant. In the full consciousness of
> their historic mission, and with the historic resolve to act up to it,
> the working class can afford to smile at the coarse invective of the
> gentleman's gentleman with the pen and the inkhorn, and at the
> didactic patronage of the well-wishing bourgeois doctrinaires,
> pouring forth their ignorant platitudes and sectarian crotchets in
> the oracular tone of scientific infallibility.

Thus the Commune was hailed as the 'glorious harbinger of a new
society'. Class struggles would continue but the victory was already
won in principle: 'The martyrs are enshrined in the great heart of the
working class. Its exterminators history has already nailed to that
eternal pillory from which all the prayers of their priests will not avail
to redeem them.' In this document, oratory and rhetoric had a distinct edge over the social analysis of a work like *Capital*. Marx the
journalist had his last real fling.

The International was doomed. Marx may have retained his
revolutionary optimism (as he did for a year or so) but it was not
shared by the international workers. German support, which had at
length been won, now declined. British trade unionists began a ten-
tative alliance with the Liberals. And no hope of revolution remained
in the miserable wreckage of Paris. Only in Bakunin territory, Italy
and Spain, did any enthusiasm remain.

A London conference, which attracted a tiny and motley collection
of French refugees, two Swiss, two British and six Belgian workers,
ended in disagreement, especially between Marx' and Bakunin's
followers. Marx (for the first time) attended the final full meeting of
the International in the Hague in 1872. There he and Engels dropped
their bombshell: they suggested that the General Council move to
New York! This impractical idea had the desired effect of finally
breaking up the membership – the vote was split.

Despite this, the International died only slowly over the next few
years. Although Bakunin had at last been banned at the same
meeting, his followers staged a rival meeting after the Hague and
anti-Marxist anarchism was to reappear sporadically during the com-

ing months. The International was ultimately dissolved in Philadelphia in 1876.

Reform or revolution?

With Marx at the helm, the First International had been steered on a fairly revolutionary course – ending with Marx' vehement vindication of the Commune. By 1889, when the Second International was born, Marx had been dead six years. Though explicitly revolutionary, in practice the new association was more parliamentary, respectable, conciliatory and committed to a gradualism whereby capitalism was expected to evolve into socialism with mounting pressure from below. It was in the Second International that the famous conflict between Karl Kautsky and Eduard Bernstein – over the latter's so-called revisionism – was to occur.

Bernstein's revisionism, which became the ideology of 'gradualism', 'reformism', or 'evolutionary socialism', was developed against the backdrop of the perceived inadequacy of Marx' account of capitalism. Though he set out as an orthodox Marxist, he later questioned some of Marx' ideas. He held that the transition from capitalism to socialism could be piecemeal, not abrupt, and could come about through legislation. He also held that there should be some 'ideals' of the common good – of what ought to be (which Marx, though he implicitly did this, would have denounced as 'utopianism').

His own analysis of capitalist society led to his desire to 'revise' Marx, because capitalism seemed more resilient than Marx had been willing to admit. As he noted: 'Peasants do not sink, middle class does not disappear: crises do not grow even larger: misery and serfdom do not increase. There *is* increase in insecurity, dependence, social distance, social character of production, functional superfluity of property owners.'[6] As social science, with political implications, this was all very sensible, but as 'Marxism', it was quite unacceptable to Kautsky.

Kautsky, who accepted Engels' understanding of 'scientific socialism', opposed Bernstein on political grounds, wishing to maintain above all the revolutionary core (which was, of course, also derivable from Marx). It was ironic, though, that this dogmatic version should become orthodoxy, when the more 'scientific' procedure was surely that of Bernstein, who was willing to modify the theory when faced with the discrepant evidence.

But it was the Marxism of 'scientific socialism' which was to dominate the political scene in Europe, eventually also being backed by Lenin and the Bolsheviks in the Russian Revolution. 'Are we slandering the readers of *Worker's Cause* by calling them concealed Bernsteinians', asked Lenin in *What is to be Done?*, 'when they advance their thesis on the necessity of struggling for economic reforms? Revolutionary social Democracy has always included the struggle for reforms as part of its activities. But ... it subordinates the struggle for reforms, as the part to the whole, to the revolutionary struggle for freedom and for socialism.' Kautsky and Lenin took the dogmatic and revolutionary view that the struggle was inevitable. The tangible result in Russia was what Marx would have called 'crude communism'.

The question of 'reform or revolution' which vexed European socialism at the turn of the century, is still urgent today. For one thing, world citizens of the late twentieth century must grapple with the idea – and sometimes the reality – of revolution, for as Hannah Arendt predicts:

> Even if we should succeed in changing the physiognomy of this century to the point where it would no longer be a century of wars, it most certainly will remain a century of revolutions. In the contest that divides the world today and in which so much is at stake, those will probably win who understand revolution ...[7]

A contemporary example of the need to understand reformism-revolutionism dilemma is the phenomenon of Eurocommunism. This represents the gradual and parliamentary route to socialist society. Eurocommunists claim to seek a democratic socialist solution, and are not directly 'anti-capitalist' as such. Rather, they concentrate their energies on opposing monopoly-power above all. To reduce the insidious strength of monopolies, they believe, would make room for a peaceful 'transition-to-the-transition' to socialism. Monopolies are treated, not as a sign of the deeper cancer of capitalism but as benign tumours which can be cut out in the interests of social health.

(It ought to be mentioned that many are suspicious of the alleged 'democracy' of some Eurocommunists. British foreign secretary David Owen, for example, writing in the February 1978 issue of *NATO Review* bemoans the 'glaring discrepancy between the pluralist professions of all these Western communist parties and their continuing attachment to the principles of "democratic centralism" in their internal organization'.)

But those to the left of Eurocommunism despise its lack of frontal attack on capitalism itself and its anaemic reformism. The example of Chile is set up as a warning. There, the reformist Popular Unity government, by attempting a democratic transition to socialism, gave time for the mobilization of counter-revolutionary forces. Moreover, because it seemed that urgent economic problems were not dealt with quickly enough, there was a popular right-wing backlash.

There are also other questions which must be asked about the issue of reform or revolution. The first is this: in fairness to Marx, did he think that revolution was necessary *and* inevitable? Did he allow for the possibility of peaceful revolution? Was he more committed to struggle than to eventual freedom?

The last question relates strongly to the 'flowers and chains' issue. What is the relationship between Christianity, revolution and human freedom? Is there such a thing as a Christian origin to revolutionary thought, or a *Christian* revolutionary tradition? Does the Christian have to justify violent revolutionary activity in some version of Christian socialism in order to destroy the image of Christianity as pretty camouflage on the chains of bondage? Or does the practical Christian social witness demand another understanding of flowers, chains, and freedom: a third way?

The meaning of revolution[8]

'Without revolution, socialism cannot develop' affirmed Marx in 1844. Though it is patently clear that he believed in revolution, it is far from clear *how* he intended that revolutions should come about. In the next chapter we shall examine how some revolutions have in fact taken place in Marx' name but this only shows how widely his words may be construed, not what he intended. For Marx, revolution was the means of remaking the world: of reconstituting social structure on a new economic base. But both evolutionary socialism (gradual) *and* scientific socialism (cataclysmic in practice) are derivable from Marx.

The *meaning* Marx gave to revolution, however, was clearly a religious one. He glowingly described the Commune as 'the political form of social emancipation', the 'liberation of labour' and a social movement of 'the general regeneration of mankind'. It was not just a new social structure but new people, set free from the 'trammels of slavery' for classless 'harmonious national and international co-ordination'.

But what was to guarantee this? How exactly were the new people to arise? The answer depends entirely on Marx' unbounded confidence in what he called the 'spontaneous action of the laws of the social economy of free and associated labour'. He expected this to supersede the similar laws of capital and property. But, as we have already argued, it is futile to hope for the cessation of conflict between interest groups (class or any other) while the God-given freedom-frameworks are ignored and while people remain alienated from their Maker.

Marx, unwittingly, was groping for a more radically new society. Paul writes of it in 2 Corinthians 5:17: 'If anyone is in Christ, he is a new creation; the old is gone, the new has come!' (New International Version). And this process, as it grows by the power of God's Spirit, has a distinctively social dimension. Paul goes on: 'All this is from God, who reconciled us to himself through Christ and gave us the ministry of reconciliation.' This Christian 'ministry' goes beyond merely *announcing* the good news of reconciliation with God. As we shall see, it involves actively promoting the reconciliation between persons and groups which is made possible through Christ. The message is of paramount importance but it is hollow without its practical partner.

The Marxian shadow of the Christian reality may be understood in Christian terms. It follows logically from Marx' un-Christian desire to remake the world his way, to gain autonomy for humanity. It is part of a desire not to be ruled by the norms of the past, the handed-down traditions of previous generations. In fact, it is a plea for human independence from all rules and structures, to start afresh on our own.

In his desire to be non-utopian, offering no ready-made ideals, Marx wisely left open the question of what future society would be like, giving only the vaguest hints. They serve to tantalize rather than to direct. The Bible also leaves open some aspects of the future age. They are not spelt out in any detail. But the difference is this. Whereas Marx was writing within the horizon of human imagination only, the biblical message begins beyond that horizon. Christ, who in John's Revelation is described as the 'bright morning star', heralds a new dawn which is as certain as the first creation. It is no less sure simply because Christ is the creative agent of both the old world and the new. He brings both into existence.

So both Christians and Marxists live in eager expectation of the future and this spurs each to energetic action. But the hope of each is radically different. Christians have 'rebirth into a living hope' (1 Peter 1:3). Revolution, as a hope-object, is a desperate surrogate for this. Christian hope eschews violence. Marxist hope often includes violence as a more-or-less essential midwife. Above all, the pregnant present in which all participate (Romans 8:22) is one which will finally be delivered, not by revolution but by Christ himself. His rightful lordship, usurped and ignored for so long, will one day usher in the new society which Marx unwittingly hoped for . . . after the revolution. But Christ has already begun the work, now.

As van der Hoeven rightly cautions, this 'hope' 'is not so much a matter for clarification; much rather it is a matter of existentially experiencing and doing . . . more and more it will be in the crucible of living that it counts'.[9] Christians, because they see glimmers beyond the human horizon, have even more incentive to work out their hope than do Marxists. Tragically, because Christian social obedience has been at such a relatively low ebb for many years, the Marxist hope of revolution sometimes shines more brightly out of the chaotic and self-destructive culture of contemporary capitalist societies.

It is easy to say that Marx' belief in revolution was an expression of un-Christian autonomous self-creation, but what was he supposed to do with his vivid sense of what was wrong with the world? The more he examined the workings of capitalism, the more he found it rotten to the core. Marx saw that whereas people are taught that poverty is a natural phenomenon, it may be shown to be a political phenomenon – and thus subject to humanly-directed abolition. Poverty could then *help* people to break the shackles of oppression, for they had nothing to lose but their chains. Revolution had this further meaning for Marx. As Hannah Arendt succintly puts it:

> . . . the young Marx became convinced that the reason the French Revolution had failed to found freedom was that it had failed to solve the social question. From this he concluded that freedom and poverty were incompatible. His most explosive and indeed most original contribution to the cause of revolution was that he interpreted the compelling needs of poverty in political terms as an uprising, not for the sake of bread or wealth, but for the sake of freedom as well.[10]

Marx had a genuine social concern; he was no mere headstrong anarchist who wished to destroy for the joy of it.

Marx' idea of freedom is sub-Christian because it is founded on a self-sufficient concept of personhood. The freedom to make oneself is not Christian freedom. Christian freedom is to be remade like Christ within God's framework of life-patterns. In fact, it is freedom *from* pretended self-creation. It is liberation from the most radical human alienation, which in biblical terminology is 'sin'. And this explains why Marx' idea of the human plight is also sub-Christian.

For him, the cancer to be eradicated was the capitalist system of production. He was justified in his condemnation of a corrupt system, by default taking the Christian role of prophetic exposer. But he did not discern the depths of the cancer. Sin is truly radical, in all its dimensions and manifestations. Like Marx, Christians are sceptical of piecemeal social engineering and minor adjustments to the existing system. It is like spray-painting an automobile with a rusted subframe. While Marx placed his trust in revolutionary regeneration, Christians may work towards the radical reformation of social structures according to biblically-directed purposes. One of these, in this present context, is the aim of communal work, where the labour unions *and* the business enterprise co-operate at the expense of neither, and where service-to-neighbour is the shared understanding of their task. There is no reason why Christians should not be taking the lead here, initiating such co-operative endeavours.

For Marx, one of the major routes to revolution and the new society was unionism. Here, Marx' new society could begin to grow in co-operative harmony. But, far from giving this impression to the world, unions have appeared only in their other guise, that of subversive antagonists of everything harmonious. According to a British friend of unionism:

> The trade unions remain the most maligned organisations in society. If the mass media are to be believed, then trade unions are responsible single-handedly for the disruption of industry, the decline of the economy, and the undermining of social rights and privileges that have traditionally held together the delicate fabric of society.[11]

What is to be made of this contradiction? It was, of course, written into Marx' statement quoted at the beginning of this chapter. Unions are for fraternity (within) and struggles (outside). The unions will explain the situation where the media consistently attack the unions, as the machinations of late capitalism. The branding of the unions as scapegoats for declining economies hides their true colours. *Because of this*, the struggle must go on, especially as capitalism is simultaneously diffusing union potential for radical change through short-term concessions. The unions believe that they must keep up the struggle or else lose any vision of alternative society, simply to become contentedly dependent on the ruling class.

While this may be true, other theorists would point to another (they believe fairer) understanding of Marx – the notion of revolutionary praxis. But does this contain any fewer difficulties?

Revolutionary praxis and its weakness

Marx did not take a mechanistic view of unions pushing capitalism over by brute force – an event which was inevitable given the objective conditions of poverty-amid-wealth and surplus-value appropriation under capitalism. Neither the 'reformer-revolution' nor the 'determinism-or-human-choice' dilemmas would have been real for

Marx. He would have encompassed them in his dialectical notion of 'revolutionary praxis'.

From his early writings onwards, Marx attempted to marry theory with practice. German philosophy, he insisted, had no practical expression. Even the state had an abstractness, in that it did not relate to real people in its practice. (This was partly exaggeration – the state may neglect some aspects of humanity but it can hardly be totally inhuman – and partly semantic sleight-of-hand.) Marx' proposed alternative was a marriage of theory and practice, where theory is truly practical and human. This is 'praxis'. It is properly fulfilled in 'revolution', a word unused by Marx until he had defined praxis.

There are two aspects of revolutionary praxis: the objective organization of conditions, struggling for emancipation from capitalist domination and the subjective change of consciousness in the workers discovering a new fraternal co-operation within their association. Marx did not, theoretically, believe in the 'inevitability' of revolution, for this would have been to understand only the objective and determining conditions as being the motor of history. If pressed, I believe he would have reiterated his critique of this position as in the *Theses on Feuerbach*:

> The materialist doctrine concerning the changing of circumstances and upbringing forgets that circumstances are changed by men and that it is essential to educate the educator himself ... The coincidence of the changing of circumstances and of human activity or self-changing can be conceived and rationally understood only as revolutionary practice.

Praxis goes with revolution; and consciousness is an aspect of praxis. Circumstances are the context of action; but action changes circumstances. Marx did not believe either that history is a river flowing inexorably on, carrying unwilling people with it, or that history is made freely by the conscious activity of people. His notion of praxis makes either view, on its own, redundant.

Consciousness of conditions, as much as the conditions themselves, is vital to revolutionary praxis. However, as we noted before, Marx thinks only of his 'elect' – the workers. He does not seem to believe that anyone but the proletariat could go through this consciousness-changing process (despite the fact that he was an example of such an anomaly!).

All Marx did, on paper, was to indicate the historical possibilities of revolution breaking out. But he was working with so many variables – so many possible routes to revolution – that he tended to scent revolution at every turn. He spent about half his life in optimistic anticipation of imminent revolution! Nevertheless, he did *not* see violent revolution as the only way. A British labouring class, for example, might gain power through the suffrage and democratic means. On 18 September 1872, in Amsterdam, Marx announced that

> The workers must one day conquer political supremacy in order to establish the new organisation of labour ... But we do not assert that the attainment of this end requires identical means. We know that one has to take into consideration the institutions, mores, and traditions of different countries, and we do not deny that there are countries like England and America (and if I knew your institutions better, I would add Holland), where labour may attain its goal by peaceful means.

Nevertheless, under more despotic regimes – which for him included most continental countries – he said that 'force must be the lever of our revolutions'. He consistently refused to make dogmatic assertions on the style of revolution, for this would have made a mockery of the complexities of socio-economic circumstances in different countries, and the level of consciousness of the workers. If society was transformed, for Marx that was revolution, whether gradual or cataclysmic.

This notion of revolutionary praxis also helps us understand his attitude to the Commune. It was not that the working class, or their ideas, were wrong. The failure was rather in the reactionary structure of Napoleon III's Empire. It was a non-proletarian movement and tried to re-enact the events of 1793. Thus Marx spoke only of the potential of the Commune and not about what actually happened.

The Russian revolution, still nearly fifty years away, Marx would have greeted with similar sentiments. It, too, was 'Jacobin' – having recourse to terror to achieve political ends – thus indicating Russia's unreadiness for socialism or communism. Moreover, it used a mechanical interpretation of history, derived from Marx but mediated through Engels, which soft-pedalled the *subjective* (class-consciousness) aspect of revolutionary praxis.

Marx has often been criticized for his dogmatic revolutionary attitude. Ironically, it is his lack of precision and his openness to historical possibilities which has made his ideas more vulnerable to misinterpretation than any other major modern philosopher-activist. He disregarded the possibilities open to his own theory: Avineri correctly describes this as his 'major intellectual blunder'. He did not follow his own favourite motto: *De omnibus dubitandum* (You must have doubts about everything) by applying it to his own ideas. As Avineri puts it:

> Though he thought of open historical alternatives none the less determined by identifiable and explicable causes, he overlooked the possibility that one of those alternatives to which the future development of his own theory was open might be the combination of his philosophical and historical theory with the Jacobin tradition of merely political, subjectivist revolutionary action: Leninism embodied such a combination.[12]

But Marx' tendency to see revolution round every corner, plus his incitement of workers to unite in the struggle, militate against the fine combination of the ripeness of objective conditions and subjective consciousness assumed in revolutionary praxis. It is easier to understand straightforward struggle for a here-and-now goal than to engage in mental juggling of conditions and consciousness. Many would-be disciples of Marx have followed the 'Jacobin' way, where the excitement of the struggle seems to eclipse the goal of a higher quality of life in fraternal co-operation.

War and peace
This is illustrated in much union activity today, where the power struggle seems to have become an end in itself. Arthur Scargill, for example, leader of Britain's Yorkshire miners, concluded after about five years as a miner (age twenty) that 'the *real power* lay either with the working classes or with the ruling classes'. From this he could only see that the power of one had to overcome the power of the other. The workers had to be on top. In a candid interview with *New Left Review* he made clear both his impatience with theory ('we had no time to discuss whether Trotsky said X, Y or Z in 1873') and his basically belligerent perspective:

> We took the view that we were in a class war. We were not playing cricket on the village green, like they did in 1926. We were out to defeat [Conservative Prime Minister] Heath and Heath's policies because we were fighting a government. Anyone who thinks otherwise was living in cloud-cuckoo-land. We had to declare *war* on them and the only way you could declare war was to attack the vulnerable points.[13]

He was referring to the confrontations between miners and government in 1972 (by which time he was union leader), and contrasting this with the famous English miners' strike of 1926.

Again, however, we must stop before joining those who see all this as 'the breakdown of ordered society in Britain'. For this union activity, though it had 'struggle' as a major motif, had as background the conservative Industrial Relations Act of 1971, which represented a government attempt to put legal restrictions upon trade union activities and statutory limitations on pay. It was restrictive and explicitly aimed at greater control. It appears that the unions were not the only ones to think in power-conflict terms. Little wonder, then, that militancy *increased*, resulting eventually in the ascendancy of the Labour Party, armed with their 'Social Contract'.

But they too, with their nationalization programme and economic policy, also seem intent on 'running the economy'. They wish, as much as the Tories, to maintain the upper hand and perpetuate the distinction between rulers and ruled – in the workplace. Instead of making legal restrictions, the Labour government aimed to gain voluntary compliance to the same kinds of policies – with the same end in view. Thus, increasingly, government tries to collaborate with union leaders and to extend the hierarchical organization of the unions. Is this yet another manipulative tactic?

Perhaps advanced industrial capitalist countries really *are* in a war situation. If so, we need peace. And if there is disorder, then we need order; if enmity, then fraternity. But the scriptures, while elevating peace, order and fraternity, never give hope of them *unconditionally*. Christ made peace *through the cross* – that is, on God's terms. The 'vertical' reconciliation (with God) has urgent horizontal implications (for fellow-creatures). Jeremiah the prophet spoke against those who, greedy for gain, made minor concessions to the disadvantaged and described the solution as 'peace' when there was no peace. And what were God's terms for peace? Jeremiah 7 spells them out:

> For if you truly amend your ways and your deeds, if you truly practise justice between a man and his neighbour, if you do not oppress the alien, the orphan or the widow, and do not shed innocent blood in this place, nor walk after other gods to your own ruin, then I will let you dwell in this place, in the land that I gave to your fathers forever and ever.

One biblical word for 'peace' is *shalom*. Now a devalued and meaning-drained word in some circles, it has in its biblical impact the idea of justice: a right reciprocal relationship between persons and between them and God. Biblical peace is a strong concept, not to be equated with water-lapping restfulness, but conditional on God's stringent standards of justice. Likewise *Yasar*, a Hebrew word corresponding roughly to our 'order', has nothing to do with order for its own sake (the idea that a hierarchical chain of command is better than no chain of command, for example) but is inseparable from justice and righteousness.

If it is right for us to see *Shalom* and *Yasar* as goals (which will come in the end through God's activity in bringing about the new community of his kingdom), then how may this be applied to the class-war situation in capitalist (and other) countries? The details of the answer have to do with the meaning of labour, stewardship, the work-community, the activity of the state as God's justice-agent and so on. We have already discussed these in response to Marx' trenchant critique of social relationships in a profit-crazy age. But the fully Christian response is a complex and daunting challenge to a church which has all too often been committed above all to the socio-political *status quo*.

It begins with the good news of God's generosity to undeserving and defiant rebel-creatures in making peace with them through the death of Christ. Only those who unreservedly live out their declaration that 'Jesus Christ is Lord' may be counted as genuine Christians. This includes the practical commitment to deliberately making Christ 'Lord' over every aspect of human life. This is part of the 'good news' from Creator to creatures which is carried by Christ. Christian 'evangelism' (proclaiming 'good news') involves the provocative assertion that Christ is the rightful lord over 'society in all its ramifications'.[14]

This 'social responsibility' calls for a thoughtful, wholly-biblical analysis of socio-economic life, which bears in mind both the ancient cultural contexts of revelation and also the advanced industrial context of today. This problem of interpretation is an undeniably ticklish one but this should not be a deterrent. The fact that a telegram message may have to be decoded in no way diminishes the potential importance of the message.

But even Christian social analysis is inadequate. There must also be a commitment to change in the direction of reformation. Christians may be actively involved at many levels. They may take part in unions, businesses, health and welfare agencies and educational establishments, trying to influence from within. Alternatively, there is scope for 'pilot plants', which take seriously the biblical view of personhood in work, parental responsibility for the education of children, or whatever. The relevance and significance of Christian principles for these areas may then be practised for all to see. Again, Christians may try to obtain a political voice, either through getting elected to parliaments and congresses or through pressure groups such as the American 'Association for Public Justice'.

To say 'Jesus Christ is Lord' is to open oneself to all the dilemmas of a life which is fully engaged with the struggles, injustices and aspirations of the modern world. It is no easy cop-out. But even having said that, immediate realities still confront contemporary world-citizens. Marxists have heard Christians agree that capitalist society is insidiously unequal, that it perpetuates dominance and sub-servience, control and dependence and is based on an underthought which accepts selfishness as being built into the system. They now wait for Christians to explain how they plan to enter the arena of interest-group wrangling and institutionalized power-grasping.

Over against the power-struggling and enemy-trampling of other approaches to political life, Christians begin with a humble dependence on a sovereign God. It is he who initiates change and brings his rule of peace and justice to the world. 'Humble dependence' involves prayer but it makes a mockery of prayer to imagine that responsibilities are completed in a kneeling position. Actions should be evidence of Christians' knowledge of God who, as Jeremiah put it, 'exercises lovingkindness, justice, and righteousness on earth'.

Moreover, the revolution-reform dilemma affects the Christian citizen as much as any other. How does one discern between a situation which is past hope of reform and one which could be judiciously and satisfactorily redirected without cataclysmic upheaval? Christians cannot deny their record of favouring the *status quo*. Neither can they deny Marx' charge that Christianized socialisms have sometimes been merely the 'holy water with which the priest consecrates the heart-burnings of the aristocrat'. But in the late twentieth century there is a resurgence of Christian political concern. The idea of a 'Christian revolutionary' has been mooted and thus cannot be evaded here.

Christian revolutionaries?

Marx firmly advocated revolution. It did not necessarily have to be violent, or to happen at a single stroke, but it had to be revolution. Capitalism has a logic which must be transcended in socialism; it cannot simply be reformed. Some Christians may be overheard today using the same language but prefacing remarks with the 'Christian' adjective. But is there a Christian justification for revolutionary activity, in unions or Third World guerilla movements? Those who think so argue that revolutionary attitudes have a Christian origin and that there is a Christian revolutionary tradition.

Hannah Arendt, writing on the meaning of revolution, deals with the question of the alleged Christian origin of revolution. She suggests that only a *secularized* version of the Christian message is revolutionary, if by that is meant the founding of a new social order. Luther, for example, sees God's word as a permanent agent of change – and the actual revolution (if it is such) is not the important thing:

> The most permanent fate of God's word is that for its sake the world is put into uproar. For the sermon of God comes in order to change and revive the whole earth to the extent that it reaches it.[15]

Arendt will only allow that the Christian notion of the possibility of new beginnings, in the breaking into history of Jesus Christ and the hope of his return, may have influenced the development of revolutionary ideas.

For her, revolution is essentially modern and has developed mainly since the French Revolution. Its characteristics are novelty, beginning, violence and irresistibility. As we have seen, Marx accepted the first two, was ambiguous about the third and elusive about the fourth. Nevertheless, all four *could be* read into Marx' view of revolution. The Christian would be in difficulties over violence, and would repudiate historicism (the idea that somehow history moves forward irresistibly), while maybe still desiring a new beginning, though not placing permanent hope in it.

If it is doubtful whether one can seriously argue for Christian origins of revolution, then the historical record would also tend to confirm this. In general, if movements have genuinely been Christian in inspiration, they have tended not to be revolutionary; if revolutionary, it is difficult to discern their Christian justification.

Robert Banks has convincingly demonstrated the inappropriateness of speaking of a Christian revolutionary tradition.[16] He argues that while there is some anticipation of later revolutionary concepts in medieval millenarianism and in Anabaptism, the actual movements were little more than rebellions and cannot be counted in the same class as modern revolution. Christians have held communist ideas (often overworking the New Testament phrase in Acts 2:44 about having all things in common), have recognized the potential of the poor as agents of change and have had a sense of mission within particular communities: but these cannot be said to amount to a revolutionary spirit.

But what of the 'English Revolution' – was this not motivated by Puritanism? Christopher Hill has admitted that Puritanism was probably the most significant set of ideas which prepared the ground for the English Revolution. Martin Walzer has made the case for specific links:

> The Calvinist belief in the sovereignty of God which cuts through

the metaphysical framework supporting the organic view of the State ... the Calvinist understanding of the church as a voluntary society to which men committed themselves by a covenant and within which equality was shared by all; the Calvinist portrait of the citizen-saint whose ultimate loyalty was to God alone above family, guild, locality, even King; the Calvinist vision of a just world-order in which evil could be restrained and order preserved until its ultimate transformation by God ...[17]

Again, Banks would question the *revolutionary* nature of all this: is it not more *rebellious*, a throwback to the earlier chiliastic movements, rather than the 'call for a radical alteration in the social and economic structure and the belief in the possibility of the realization of this new social order on earth'? True, history contains a worthy record of the Christian impetus to hasten trends already under way, by reform – but not by total, sudden reconstruction.

Individual characters, such as the Leveller Winstanley in the 1640s or the German radical Weitling in the mid-nineteenth century, have taken some kind of Christian commitment as the starting-point for wide-ranging socio-economic reform. In some ways they anticipated Marx, yet at the same time their roots are more in the old millenarian fraternities. (Marx both acknowledged the stimulus of Weitling's concern for revolution and also roundly condemned him to his face for his emotive and unscientific 'preaching' of socialism.)

Banks also mentions Berdyaev, the Russian Orthodox believer who lived through the revolution in 1917 but who was obliged to emigrate in 1922. He was a theologian of revolution – but was far from propounding a theology of revolution in the modern sense. He understood Marx and believed the communist ideal to be vastly preferable to bourgeois civilization, However, he was also extremely critical of Russian 'communism'. He held that there is a Christian interpretation of revolution and that its meaning must be understood in Christian terms.

Revolution is always a judgement on historical Christianity, according to Berdyaev – a judgement on Christians' betrayal of their obligations and a judgement of Christian distortion of the full gospel of Jesus Christ.[18] But while a revolution may be understandable in Christian terms as an attempt to right obvious wrongs about which the church had been silent, utopia is not thus ushered in. The new regime is likely to be as sinful as the old. It can never be complete: 'The chains which fettered energy are struck off. But the slavery of man is not destroyed at the root.' The only 'revolution' countenanced by Berdyaev is a 'personalist revolution', revolution for the sake of man and not for one society or another. This he saw in Christian salvationist terms: spiritual rebirth.

There has always been a positive relationship between the understanding of the kingdom of God and radical social-political activity. When God has been seen as the one who is breaking into history and transforming the world in Christ, this has produced Christian social action – often of a radical stamp. But when seen in passive terms, or underemphasized by the church, there has been an a-political quietism. But Christians, while they have been radical, reformist, even rebellious and anarchic, do not seem to have been revolutionary.

When all is said and done, the question remains as to whether or not there is a *biblical* (as opposed to a merely historical) justification for Christian *revolutionary* activity. José Míguez Bonino, a theologian from Buenos Aires, has noted that 'a significant and growing number of Christians are becoming convinced – not only emotionally, nor arbitrarily, but on the basis of sober analysis – that ... participation in a revolutionary socialist project is an ethically defensible and a necessary action'.[19]

Míguez is sympathetic to such Christian liaison with Marxists: the challenge of revolution is a mutual one. When there is an oppressing class and an oppressed class, where liberal reformism has been a hollow mockery, where the church has historically stood for the *status quo* – in such circumstances, Míguez believes revolutionary activity is called for. While a revolution will *not* bring in God's kingdom, yet the 'greater good' inaugurated by it may be congruous with some aspects of that future kingdom. Revolution may be the only way: Marxism the mode of analysis.

But this position, admirable though it may seem (and Western bourgeois Christians could occupy themselves better than engaging in mere armchair condemnation of someone grappling with tough social realities in an alien environment) nevertheless contains some difficulties. Marxism is a false humanism which, though compatible with Christian commitment to humanity at certain important points, may not be *synthesized* with Christianity.

Marx is wrong about human nature and thus wrong about the solution of human problems. Christianity goes beyond capitalism and beyond Marxism. Marxism tends to glorify the class struggle, (he was thrilled with the heroic struggle of the Commune in Paris), seeing only beyond the struggle (its 'negation' in Marx' terms) the revolution and new society.

Míguez, while accepting the harsh and ugly necessity of the class struggle, does not glory in it as Marx does. Neither does he try to suggest that the oppressed are the only class which can inherit the earth, or that only they may develop a consciousness of the true human condition. He is far more careful about 'using Marx' than many theologians of liberation. He shows a discerning subtlety in his discussion of the faith-commitment of Marxists. In the disturbing trauma which passes for everyday life in many Latin American countries, Míguez' stance is readily understood. The 'choice', however horrendous it may appear, is often between submission to a perniciously unjust regime, or joining with the freedom fighters.

For Míguez, there are no 'third ways'. But it would be too easy to transpose this judgement to all situations. In some contexts, where notions such as 'democracy' retain at least vestigial meaning, third ways and radical reformism may well be the authentic mode of Christian political commitment. If Míguez lived in Canada or Nigeria he might be more gentle with 'third ways'.

But the difficulty with his position lies in his acceptance of Marxism as a method, or mode of analysis. While he is deeply critical of Marxism, he still wields it as a weapon in the struggle. No other tools seem quite fit for the job. Those in Latin America must not be condemned for this. The onus is on Christians in less critical situations to forge alternative tools for the task. For Marxism is ever *more* than a 'method'. From a basic world-view position it must be said that any *unthinking* alliance with Marx is as potentially dangerous as the (traditional Christian) alliance with the capitalist *status quo*.

Abraham Kuyper, a Dutch Christian statesman at the turn of the century, propounded a theory of 'architectonic criticism' of society in *Christianity and the Class Struggle*. There he spelled out the beginnings of an alternative to capitalism and Marxism, on a similar basis to which contemporary Christian social scientists, philosophers and theologians are working today.[20] What is needed is a social-structural critique of the whole fabric of industrial capitalism and state socialism, which shares some of Marx' concerns, but which seeks to transcend both in a more distinctively Christian programme.

What the alternative socio-economic programme might look like obviously partly depends on time and place and must always relate to the existential situation. But it is radical, relating to the life-patterns of creation and to the coming kingdom of God. It involves a radical understanding of the nature of sin and its social effects and of the potential role of biblical people in redirecting our generation towards the ways of God. But no doctrine of inevitable class struggle, or irresistible revolution guides this programme. Rather, it is guided by a Christian ethic of the future. Marx was sadly deficient in that he neglected this. Eduard Bernstein began the work of transcending Marx in an ethical direction. Christian tools are needed – and are being produced – for this central task of the late twentieth century.

The sword and the social revolution

Swept along on a wave of visionary optimism about the Commune, Marx envisaged only a temporary requirement for violence. Perhaps he knew that his writing (of *The Civil War in France*) would give him the notoriety of the 'red terrorist doctor', which is why he might have been vague at this point. But he firmly believed that after the 'state monster' had been replaced with a decentralized communal organization, only a mopping-up operation would be needed to maintain the new system.

> The Communal organization once firmly established on a national scale, the catastrophes it might still have to undergo would be sporadic slaveholders' insurrections, which, while for a moment interrupting the work of peaceful progress, would only accelerate the movement, by putting the sword into the hand of the Social Revolution.

Marxism, because of the historical record of those who have taken Marx' name, is often associated with violence. Marx had no strictures against violence, though on the whole it would seem that he preferred 'peaceful progress'. But class *struggle* does suggest that some force may have to be employed at some stage. Míguez, as one who has had to grapple with this urgent issue, makes some important points.

He reminds us that, biblically, violence is a category more often used to describe the oppressor and all unjust authorities! Míguez also assumes that Christians involved in liberation struggles will do all they can to minimize violence and will never 'suspend ethics' for the sake of the cause.

But there has never been any Christian consensus on these matters. There is the thorny issue of obedience to the powers-that-be, on the one hand, and the justification of violence on the other. Discussion of these problems must always take place in particular contexts, within specific traditions and circumstances. But nevertheless the two main views may be subjected to *biblical* analysis in order to see if they fall short at that fundamental level. In so far as they can be shown to be biblical, yet still subject to contrary interpretation, the Christian community conscience becomes judge. The two views may be brought into focus by the use of examples. The British legal philosopher J. N. D. Anderson takes one position; John Howard Yoder, an American Mennonite ethicist, takes the other.[21]

Revolutionary subordination versus the just revolution

Anderson speaks of the possibility of a 'just revolution', Yoder of 'revolutionary subordination'. The distinction between these two views is also, roughly speaking, the distinction between the Calvinist and Anabaptist attitudes to civil authorities. The Calvinist, who believes that the powers-that-be are to be obeyed when they fulfill their proper function (to 'do good' and be an 'agent of justice', Romans 13:4), will argue for the possibility of a just revolution. This would only be under certain very extreme circumstances, when the government is oppressive and makes the innocent suffer. This is Anderson's position.

Yoder, from an Anabaptist position, contends for 'revolutionary subordination'. Christians, who already enjoy liberty in Christ, should not waste time trying to change wider social structures. Their 'freedom can be realized within (the) present status by voluntarily accepting subordination, in view of the relative unimportance of such social distinctions when seen in the light of the coming fulfillment of God's purposes.'[22] So, when faced with Peter's injunction to 'Submit yourselves for the Lord's sake to every authority instituted among men', the two responses would be somewhat different.

Anderson would say yes, this is right, until the government is so patently wicked that nothing short of a revolution may change things. Yoder, on the other hand, would say that this persistent submission, or subordination, *is* the Christian way of rebelling. It is the way in which Christians share God's patience with the system they basically reject. He would maintain the Christian pacifist stance right through to the end, whereas Anderson would justify violence as a lesser evil and a last resort, when all else has failed.

Both positions are radical, in that they accept the biblical criticism of unjust states but differ on the *nature* of the rebellion permissible to Christians. Of course, there are Christians who are happier with violence as a means of keeping order and changing society and some who refuse to have anything to do with politics at all but Yoder and Anderson make good examples of those who are attempting a consistently biblical third way.[23]

If one did accept Anderson's just revolution, it would have to be stressed (as he stresses) that it is only a last resort and one which may only take place after all other alternatives have been tried and found wanting. In many countries, the 'other alternatives' are the Christian order of the day for Christian political witness. This may be in 'third ways', inside or outside existing political parties but always seeking a just peace and equitable resolution.

I tend to agree with Ernst Gellner when he attacks:

two unutterably foolish contemporary doctrines – one to the effect that revolutions are never desirable, the other, that they are the 'festival of the oppressed'. They are never anyone's festival, though they are, sometimes, indeed, necessary and desirable.[24]

Marx' impatience with the results of compromise with the powers-that-be need not be shared by Christians. For that compromise may lead to the 'greater good' solution, brought about by peaceful negotiation. This may apply to the unions – the original subject of this discussion – as to any area of confrontation with the powers-that-be. The Marxist class-struggle expectation gives rise to a certain belligerence and 'confrontation*ism*'. But the fight for sectional interests at the expense of others, the supposed delights of struggle, the rebellious spirit: none of these are Christian ways.

Christians stand, not only for the justice but for the peace of God in the world. And that may involve more talking than fighting. Even then, the scriptures warn about 'violence concealed in the lips'. Deceptive words are worse than no words at all, as Jeremiah warned. Weary of the violent oppression of unjust rulers, Isaiah once said:

Wash yourselves, make yourselves clean;
Remove the evil of your deeds from my sight.
Cease to do evil,
Learn to do good;
Seek justice,
Reprove the ruthless;
Defend the orphan,
Plead for the widow.

And as I have argued, this may only be on God's terms. Sin is radical, and requires a radical solution. Only the cross of Christ brings the necessary reconciliation to those willing to abandon their old ways. But that same cross also brings with it the possibility of *horizontal* reconciliation, as God's words and ways are brought to the bargaining tables of industrial dispute and to any other place previously characterized by mere confrontationism. Merely human efforts, we must stress, are quite inadequate: the peace-making approach is a fruit of God's Spirit.

Notes and references

1 Shlomo Avineri, *The Social and Political Thought of Karl Marx*, Cambridge University Press, 1968 (London), and 1971 (New York), p. 142.
2 A. H. Halsey, *The Listener*, 16 February 1978.

3 Isaiah Berlin, *Karl Marx: His Life and Environment*, Oxford University Press, 1963, pp. 232–233.

4 David McLellan, *Karl Marx: His Life and Thought*, Macmillan, 1973, Harper and Row, 1974, p. 371.

5 Isaiah Berlin, 1963, p. 255.

6 Quoted in Tom Bottomore, *Marxist Sociology*, Macmillan and Holmes and Meier, 1975, p. 20.

7 Hannah Arendt, *On Revolution*, Penguin, 1973, p. 18.

8 For a useful sketch of the history of the word 'revolution', see Raymond Williams, *Keywords*, Fontana and Oxford University Press, 1976.

9 Johan van der Hoeven, *Karl Marx: The Roots of His Thought*, Wedge Publishing Foundation, 1976, pp. 104 and 106.

10 Hannah Arendt, 1973, p. 62.

11 Tom Clarke and Laurie Clements, *Trades Unions under Capitalism*, Fontana and Humanities Press, 1977, p. 7.

12 Shlomo Avineri, 1968, p. 258.

13 Arthur Scargill's *New Left Review* interview was quoted in *The Observer*, 7 September 1975, p. 7.

14 R. B. Kuiper, *God-centred Evangelism*, Baker Book House, 1961, Banner of Truth, 1966, p. 114.

15 Hannah Arendt, 1973, p. 284.

16 Robert Banks, 'A Christian Revolutionary Tradition?', *Journal of Ecumenical Studies*, 1972, vol. 9, 2, p. 283f.

17 Robert Banks, 1972, p. 291.

18 Nicholas Berdyaev, *The Origins of Russian Communism*, Bles, 1937, University of Michigan Press, 1960.

19 José Míguez Bonino, *Christians and Marxists: The Mutual Challenge to Revolution*, Hodder and Stoughton and Eerdmans, 1976, p. 123.

20 Abraham Kuyper, *Christianity and the Class Struggle*, Piet Hein, 1951. See also these books due out in 1979: Bob Goudzwaard, *Capitalism and Progress*, Eerdmans, and Alan Storkey, *A Christian Social Perspective*, Inter-Varsity Press.

21 J. N. D. Anderson, *Issues of Life and Death*, Hodder and Stoughton and Inter-Varsity Press (Downers Grove), 1976; John Howard Yoder, *The Politics of Jesus*, Eerdmans, 1972.

22 J. H. Yoder, 1972, p. 187.

23 Yoder's argument is theologically questionable at several points. See Richard J. Mouw, *Politics and the Biblical Drama,* Eerdmans, 1976. Mouw makes a much-needed emphasis on the relevance of the *whole* Bible for social-political thought and action.

24 Ernst Gellner, *The Legitimation of Belief*, Cambridge University Press, 1974, p. 172.

Karl Marx' grave in north London

CHAPTER 6

After Marx

His mission in life was to contribute in one way or another to the overthrow of capitalist society . . . his name and his work will endure through the ages.
Engels, Graveside Speech 1883

Marx virtually retired from public life during his last years. By his late fifties, his health was failing, he read more than he wrote, the revolution for which he had spent his life seemed as far off as ever and finally Jenny was to die. And, as Engels said to Eleanor, 'With her the Moor has died too'.

But though his energy was diminishing rapidly, the last decade of his life still contains glimpses of the fiery old Marx. The English socialist Hyndman, with whom Marx had considerable contact during those last years (until the inevitable breach when Hyndman wrote a book about Marxism without mentioning his name!) left these impressions of Marx. He was

> a powerful, shaggy, untamed old man, ready, not to say eager, to enter into conflict, and rather suspicious himself of immediate attack; yet his greeting of us was cordial . . . When speaking with fierce indignation of the policy of the Liberal Party, especially in regard to Ireland, the old warrior's brow wrinkled, the broad, strong nose and face were obviously moved by passion, and he poured out a stream of vigorous denunciation which displayed alike the heat of his temperament, and the marvellous command he possessed over our language. The contrast between his manner and utterance when thus deeply stirred by anger, and his attitude when giving his views on the economic events of the period, was very marked. He turned from the role of prophet and violent denunciator to that of the calm philosopher without any apparent effort, and I felt that many a long year might pass before I ceased to be a student in the presence of a master.[1]

Now that Engels had moved to London, the pair saw each other every day and this association was to determine to a great extent the legacy that would be left for future generations. There was a burst of energy when they attacked a proposal to unite the German socialist parties (the Gotha Programme), and another when Marx helped Engels write against another German socialist economist, Dühring. Engels' role as Marx' interpreter was to prove crucial for the way that his ideas were used in the next few years and as they would eventually help shape the course of twentieth-century history.

The basic ambiguities which characterize Marx' writing resurface in his last invectives. These must be exposed, along with their practical (sometimes tragic) consequences in twentieth-century history. In the end, Marx' proposed solution to the human condition has to be weighed in the balance of history and tested for its truth and adequacy.

Why have so many high hopes been crushed into the harsh realities of ruthless regimes and why have the new people of the classless society failed to emerge – even where capitalism has been officially abolished? What positive gains have Marx' followers achieved and what is yet likely to occur in his name as the world approaches the twenty-first century? Are there any alternatives to the selfish logic of capitalism and the confrontationist fist of Marxism? Marx inaugurated a new era of social praxis. We are still coping with the aftermath.

'I am no Marxist'

Eventually, during the last decade of his life (1873–83), Marx' ideas became widely known in Europe and parts of North America. Some disciples made pilgrimages to visit the two old men in London, especially from Russia and Spain. A huge correspondence was also maintained with German and French socialists, all wanting to find the right way forward from the sage in London. But all kinds of vulgarizations of Marxism also emerged, characterizing Marx in roles to which he could never subscribe. And Engels' own writing, even though Marx approved of it at the time, gave rise to conceptions of Marxism quite incompatible with the central themes of the latter's work. Marx, irritated by these deviations from his understanding of the world, once hotly declared 'As for me, I am no Marxist'!

Of course, the confusion was partly his own fault. He was, like his old master, Hegel, ambiguous, and left a very open-ended dialectic. Besides, his manuscripts were incomplete. Engels had the thankless task of unjumbling mountains of unsorted papers after his death and his particular slant is reflected in the way they were arranged in the end. Moreover, Marx had been writing for a long time and it was easy for certain books to become more important than others, even though Marx may not have given precedence to one over another. Many knew him only through the *Communist Manifesto* (and maybe the first volume of *Capital*), and this became the sacred writing for a mass movement who saw in Marxism a saviour from regimes which denied them the benefits of their labour. It is easy to see how, in such circumstances, his complex thought could be reduced to hard dogma.

Marx showed himself to be a militant socialist revolutionary to the end. He had no truck with what he saw as idealistic nonsense which began with appeal to eternal verities such as justice and ended with glowing scenarios for a harmonious future. He claimed that his materialist analysis had a firm base in science and that any sort of utopianism was beside the point. Marx' final comments on science and on future society are significant, both for what he said and what he left unsaid. They appeared in his angry denunciation of the so-called Gotha Programme in 1875.

The Lassalleans and the party under the Marxist Liebknecht had, despite earlier quarrels, decided to unite under a common banner. It seemed the only way forward after the collapse of international socialism, to provide a broad front against capitalism. Clearly, they suspected hostility to their proposal, for they did not consult Marx and Engels in London. But that only served to increase their wrath!

Simply put, the *Critique of the Gotha Programme* (as their published response was titled) argued that the German socialists were too soft. They were failing to oppose capitalism itself (concentrating on concessions and rights for workers), and its organ, the hated state. Instead of seeing the root of difficulties in the mode of production, these 'vulgar socialists' had accepted the bourgeois notion that 'fair distribution' would solve problems.

> Any distribution of the means of consumption is only a consequence of the distribution of the conditions of production themselves ... The capitalist mode of production, for example, rests on the fact that the material conditions of production are in the hands of non-workers in the form of property in capital and land, while the masses are only owners of the personal condition of production, of labour power.

So, he demanded to know, 'After the real relation has long been made clear, why retrogress again?'

They had similarly missed the point about the state. Instead of declaring themselves to be opposed to the machinery which helped maintain capitalism, they spoke of a 'free state' which gave aid to workers' co-operatives. For Marx, there was no such thing. But he hinted at a transitional stage between capitalism and socialism, during which the 'revolutionary dictatorship of the proletariat' would be in power. This was in line with his notion of dialectical transcendence (*Aufhebung*) – the stages of history which successively supersede each other. But he envisaged this period as a necessary though passing stage, in which wage-labour continues to exist – for everyone – and surplus-value is diverted into investment and services.

But after this definitely limited period, the dictatorship of the proletariat would also be transcended and with it the last traces of the bourgeois state. People will have the opportunity to be fully human once again:

> In a higher phase of communist society, after the enslaving subor-
> dination of the individual to the division of labour, and therewith
> also the antithesis between mental and physical labour, have
> vanished; after labour has become not only a means of life but
> life's primary want; after all productive forces have also increased
> with the all-round development of the individual, and all the
> springs of co-operative wealth flow more abundantly – only then
> can the narrow horizon of bourgeois right be crossed in its entire-
> ty and society inscribe on its banners: 'From each according to his
> ability, to each according to his needs'.

Marx opposed the 'utopians' on the basis of his 'science' because he felt that they were not historical enough. They tended to have abstract notions (such as the free state) which they hoped that they would be able to realize. Marx, on the other hand, had seen things differently, since he wrote in *The German Ideology*: 'Communism is not for us a *state of affairs* which is to be established, an ideal to which reality will have to adjust itself. We call communism the *real* movement which abolishes the present state of things.' He rightly criticized the castles in the air which have no connection with existing social and political relationships and held hope only in a future which grows out of the present. But he never seemed to ap-preciate the fact that there was an unacknowledged utopianism in his own system – the ideal of free and purposeful human labour, un-constrained by others and in mutual solidarity with them. However, his utopianism was not only unacknowledged, it was, as we shall see, incomplete.

It was Engels who made more of a name for himself by opposing utopian socialism. A tract aimed against the German economist, Dühring, which by its very clarity attracted widespread attention and a large following, gave a much stronger version of the 'scientific' pretension than Marx ever preached. It is true that Marx himself, in the last years, became more attracted by the positivism ('fact-science') then popular in England and Europe. And he apparently approved *Anti-Dühring*, even writing a chapter for it. This 'scientific socialism' became the creed of those who followed Engels' clear exposition in *Anti-Dühring*. Objective laws were as apparent in social as natural science, according to Engels, and from them one could build a science of society. His 'materialism' was more associated with the belief that 'matter ·is all that there is' than with Marx' limited 'materialism' which simply meant that he rooted his theories in man's material life of work.

Thus Engels, in his graveside speech after Marx' death, could say 'Just as Darwin discovered the law of development of organic nature, so Marx discovered the law of development of human history'. It was this version which was propounded by Karl Kautsky in the German Social Democratic Party and by Plekhanov in Russia. This (Engelsian) version was to become known as 'Marxist orthodoxy'. How much more vehemently would Marx have declared 'I am no Marxist' if he had heard the 'orthodox' version! It was a long way from the 'unity of theory and practice' of which he had written in the *Theses on Feuerbach*, and devalued the role of consciousness in a way he never did.

The difficulties involved in the 'science' and 'utopia' questions were thrown into high relief by the controversy which was soon to break out in Germany (and the Second International) between Kautsky, who took a hard Marxist economics line, and Eduard Bernstein, who followed but wished to transcend Marx. Bernstein, who had been influenced in his thinking by the English Fabians, believed that the transition to socialism could be gradual and peaceful (as did Marx himself in the case of England). He questioned some of Marx' historical and social observations, arguing that things were not working out exactly as Marx had anticipated.

The class struggle, for example, far from intensifying, was becoming more dissipated and the class lines less clearly drawn than in Victorian England. Frankly, according to Bernstein, Marx' analysis, while setting folk on the right track, was a sociologically inadequate analysis of capitalism. What Bernstein saw then, the West has seen increasingly ever since, that the middle classes have grown, that there has been a real improvement in the condition of the working classes and new forms of administration and control have become prominent. But Bernstein thus made himself an object of scorn from the 'orthodox': Marx' science alone was correct. He earned himself the notorious title (equivalent to 'heretic') of 'revisionist'.

But if Bernstein dared question the scientificity of some of Marx' conclusions, he also alleged that Marx had not gone far enough in his meditations about future society. Of course, Bernstein wanted a socialist society but he also wanted to be sure of the route to it. If Marx' sociology was inadequate, then this had implications for strategy and new theory was called for to show how socialism could grow out of capitalist society. But there was also the question of socialism as a moral ideal, the desires and strivings of human beings. If theory and practice were indeed to be one, then the same standards would have to hold for life in pre-socialist as socialist society. Could those who wish for a harmonious and other-oriented society arrive there through a process of class hatred and violence?

Bernstein did not advance a long way with this ethical analysis of Marxism – on the nature of political action and the actual transition to socialism – and it remains to this day one of the most burning questions that Marxists ought to answer. Engels was wrong simply to oppose 'scientific' and 'utopian' socialism: Marxism must be subjected both to empirical and ethical analysis, judged both for sociological accuracy and the desirability of its utopia.

This, then, was the way in which Marx' followers squabbled over the legacy. Marx only saw the controversies in embryonic form; he did not live to witness any revolutionary changes taking place in his name. Even Engels himself might have been surprised to discover how far his funeral predictions about the continuing popularity of Marx' name and work have come true. But in England, to the close of his years, Marx had little impact. Little was known about him except for his nickname 'the Red-Terror-Doctor'.

However, a member of the English ruling class, Sir Mountstuart Elphinstone Grant-Duff, did once ask him to dinner at his club to probe his opinions on behalf of Queen Victoria's eldest daughter. He was impressed with Marx' scholarly and literary prowess and found him to be quite a gentleman. Curiously enough, Grant-Duff concluded on the one hand that Marx was 'showing very correct ideas when conversing on the past and the present, but vague and unsatisfactory when he turned to the future'. On the other, he decided that 'It will not be Marx who, whether he wishes it or not, will turn the world upside-down'.[2] As we can see with hindsight, however, despite Marx' lamentably vague ideas on future society, he has nevertheless turned the world upside-down. Engels was right about this at least and Sir Mountstuart Elphinstone Grant-Duff quite wrong.

The death of the Red-Terror-Doctor

The Marx household was quieter during the 1870s. Refugees no longer flowed through the house. Marx' daughters found partners. Laura married French Proudhonist Paul Lafargue, travelled at first but eventually settled in London. Jenny married another Frenchman, Charles Longuet, who, after arriving as a penniless refugee, finished by obtaining a lecturing post at King's College. Eleanor, not yet prone to the depression which accompanied her love-affairs over the next few years, increasingly took over hostess duties from her mother Jenny Marx. Lenchen still kept house. Bad health dogged Marx throughout the 1870s. He was constantly searching for cures to pressure on the brain and headaches, in the waters of Harrogate, Karlsbad and other resorts, and in Engels' Dr Gumpert in Manchester.

By the end of the 1870s his headaches were no better, and to add to his pains he had suffered from carbuncles from time to time as well. But he still slept only for three or four hours per night, rising early to read, having lunch at two and never failing to walk and talk with his friend, Fred Engels, during the afternoon.

But suddenly attention was focused upon Jenny. She had cancer of the liver (although this was not recognized until near her death). After six months' suffering, to his intense and irreparable grief, Jenny died in December 1881. Though publishers tried to persuade him to write (they wanted a third edition of *Capital*) he no longer had the heart. He attempted to rid himself of what was now bronchitis by taking a holiday in Algiers but succeeded only in contracting pleurisy *en route* and getting very cold and wet while there. He was lonely and the family were not as supportive as they might have been (Jenny's and Laura's political husbands were seldom at home).

The only matter reported to have excited him at this stage was news of the reception of his ideas in his old hate: Russia. 'I damage a power which, together with England, is the true bulwark of the old society', he crowed. But the final blow was Jenny Longuet's death in 1883, which left his four grandchildren with her unsympathetic husband. She too had had cancer. Marx had been continuing his quest for health in the Isle of Wight but now came home to die. One day, when Engels came round for his daily visit, Marx was half-asleep in his chair and the household was in tears. With Engels beside him, he passed away a few minutes later, on 13 March 1883. He was sixty-four.

The Times newspaper, when prodded from Paris, gave him a brief and inaccurate obituary. He was buried in Highgate cemetery in London, with a splendid laudatory oration from Engels. From that oration it is clear that though the man was now dead, the legend had just been born.

The unexpected revolutions

So Marx died without seeing a revolution burst forth to vindicate his ideas. And although the first major revolution of the twentieth century was made in his name, a question-mark remains over its 'Marxist' nature. For the Russian events of 1917 took place in a context which was, according to Marx' theories about industrial capitalist development as the prelude to revolution, unripe. But this is true of all revolutions made so far this century: they have occurred in non-industrial societies. 'Marxism' has no explanations for this.

So what has Marx to do with revolutions glanced at here, in Russia, China and Cuba? Why is his name linked with Lenin, the inventor of the revolutionary party dictatorship, or Mao, the peasant guerilla and ideological successor to Confucius, or that Robin Hood of the Third World, Che Guevara? At least this: the revolutions were made in his name.

'Peace and bread, peace and land'

Lenin, whose role in the Russian Revolution was indispensable, developed Marxism to his own ends. In effect, he substituted party for class as the motive force of revolution. To make a revolution in an industrially non-advanced society, Marxism had to be modified by a skilful manipulation of its latent potential. Lenin emerged as a dynamo of political action. No literary phrases or bourgeois aspirations for him; he put Marx to work, replacing a crumbling old world with a new one.

The crumbling old world was the Russian Empire. At the bottom of the hierarchy, a mass of peasants, predominating in population statistics and increasingly denied a secure and meaningful existence. At the top, an autocratic traditionalist regime, torn between maintaining their absolute rule over the empire and encouraging industrialization. For in the wake of modernization came a spirit of unease with existing circumstances and a consciousness of inequality which threatened the security of the Tsar. The land was vast and various ethnic groups made up the population. It was hard for anyone to rule Russia, let alone change it.

Things were supposed to have improved when the serfs were emancipated in 1861 but in fact the land repayments, plus their numerical increase meant that their condition still left much to be desired. And agricultural reforms, introduced by Stolypin from 1905 and intended to improve their lot (at least enough to keep them quiet) were singularly unsuccessful. Agriculture was failing and numerous millenarian uprisings by the peasants gave voice to an overwhelming fact: they were hungry.

Stolypin also initiated a wave of industrialization, which induced many peasants to quit the fields for the factories. They constituted ideal raw material for union propaganda and the period 1912–14 was marked by widespread but haphazard strikes and revolts. Very often the one-time landless peasants, now factory workers, were simply sick of autocratic authority and instinctively rebelled. But the Mensheviks (gradualist socialists who opposed party centralism) did control some unions for a time, until the Bolshevik organization (which was as autocratic as Tsardom itself!) eroded their power by appealing more to direct action.

Even so, the power of the proletariat must not be exaggerated. Numerically smaller than that of other world powers, in proportion to the total population, it was tiny. Added to that, it was highly concentrated geographically, being found especially in Petrograd (later Leningrad). In fact, once the Petrograd Soviet had been politically won, the Bolsheviks had a major weapon. The Military Revolutionary Committee of the Petrograd Soviet formally led the Russian Revolution.

It was no accident that the revolution broke out at the end of the Great War. War was the final straw which broke the back of the archaic Tsarist order. Unbearable strains on social control, on top of peasant and proletarian unrest and revolt, were created by the war effort. Subjected to the impact of the German armies, the Russian military, with its chaotic administration, social backwardness and pre-industrial economic support, collapsed. The antique Tsarist army, utterly exhausted from fighting, did not even know how many had been killed. It was perfectly evident to a rising proportion of the Russian population that no one really knew anything. Resentment against the government steadily escalated. The war seemed to have degenerated into a dismal deadlock.

Not a soul knew what would happen. In the cities there was widespread hunger, cold through fuel shortages and inflated prices. Thousands of peasant soldiers had trudged miserably home from the front, illustrating the general and profound war-discontentment. A revolution was there to be made but only one man had sufficient nerve – and he was abroad. Kerensky, leader of the provisional government since February 1917, intuitively grasped this. In March he hysterically announced, 'Just wait, Lenin himself is coming. Then the real thing will start'.[3]

Lenin came. Throwing the ideals of the *Communist Manifesto* to the winds he promised 'Peace and Bread, Peace and Land' to a hungry, war-worn and disinherited people. The choice, barked Lenin, was Bolshevik dictatorship or counter-revolution. The former offered armistice and land-distribution, the only programme to cope with the chaotic ruins of Empire.

Lenin, once an orthodox Marxist, felt obliged to go beyond Marx in order to handle urgent practical realities. As early as 1904 the Polish revolutionary, Rosa Luxembourg, had entitled an essay, *Leninism or Marxism?* because of Lenin's 'ultra-centralist' ideas. Lenin adopted a conspiratorial organization, plus a rationalist and dogmatic version of Marxism, appropriate for his tightly-controlled élitist party system.

He did not believe, however, that revolution was inevitable: his analysis of *Imperialism* attempted to demonstrate that capitalism used war and colonial expansion to maintain profits. Neither did he believe that Marxist class analysis was sufficient; more specific revolutionary tactics were required. These he supplied (in 1902) in *What is to be Done?* This is the central document of Leninism, whose flavour is caught in a paragraph:

> The working class exclusively by its own efforts is able to develop only trade union consciousness . . . Modern socialist consciousness can only be brought to them from without . . . can arise only on the basis of profound scientific knowledge. The bearers of science are not the proletariat but the bourgeois intelligentsia. It is out of the heads of this stratum that socialism originated . . .[4]

Lenin's attitude to morality was to be decisive for Russia's future. Marx' morality, relativist and pragmatic ('if it works, do it') in spirit nevertheless operated within a framework of 'simple laws of ethics and justice by which individuals must be guided in mutual relationships, and which must be the supreme laws of conduct between states'. But he had no foundation for these ideals beyond himself. Lenin, perceiving this, took the openness of Marx' morality to one possible logical conclusion: 'Our morality is completely subordinated to the interests of the class-struggle of the proletariat.' 'Good is what advances the cause of the revolution.'

Lenin explicitly denied all 'morality that is drawn from some conception beyond men, beyond class'. Thus not only the reactionary Tsarist aristocracy but also revisionists, anyone, in fact, who opposed Bolshevik rule, could be mown down in their tracks: eliminated. And even Trotsky, who shared so much in the revolutionary task with Lenin (and after his banishment from Russia under Stalin's regime developed the theory of 'permanent revolution' rather than consolidation) foresaw what would happen: 'The organization of the party takes the place of the party itself; the Central Committee takes the place of the organization; and finally the dictator takes the place of the Central Committee.' In the end, what Lenin said was law.

The terror of birth

For Lenin, terror was essential. To Marx' and Engels' comments about the birth-pangs of socialism he added a horrific dimension. Women are not deterred from giving birth simply because birth turns a woman into a 'tortured, lacerated, pain-crazed, half-dead lump of flesh'. In 1917 CHEKA, forerunner of the KGB, began its secret policing on behalf of the Party and against all dissidents. Its work continues today, condemning people in their thousands to the anguish of labour camps and 'psychiatric' hospitals. Lenin's policies led to the civil war between the Red and White armies, during which the death-toll was far greater than the most pessimistic estimates from the 'Imperialist War' so virulently denounced by the same man.

While the Bolsheviks fought off reaction, the peasants quietly began to take up their age-old dream of village life on the land, virtually independent of the state. But those peasants, whose rising had contributed to the break-up of Tsarism, were rewarded by having their bucolic visions ruthlessly crushed by a regime which 'collectivised' their ancient land in the name of the revolutionary dictatorship of the proletariat. They have, however, partly taken revenge by ensuring that Soviet agriculture has shuffled from crisis to crisis ever since.

On 23 February 1918, *Pravda* announced that there was 'no other method of fighting counter-revolutionaries, spies, speculators, looters, hooligans, saboteurs and other parasites other than their merciless destruction on the spot'. Tsarist executions were a drop in the ocean of blood that followed the inauguration of Bolshevism in Russia. By the time Stalin took over, it was clear that only someone who could manipulate the same sort of apparatus could continue the job. Stalin, in order to build the economic base for Bolshevism, resorted to what Barrington Moore has aptly called 'progress and tyranny'. The details may be found elsewhere. They make grim and awesome reading.

The assessment of all this cannot but begin with Lenin's own attitude to religion. For him, not only did all moral notions tend to cloak class-interest; so, too, did any idea of God. Not for Lenin was Marx' comparatively sensitive reflections on religion ('the heart of a heartless situation' and so on). For Lenin 'Religion is a kind of spiritual gin in which the slaves of capital drown their human shape and their claims to any decent life'. He believed that the subtle idea of God was far more dangerous than sins, violence and plagues, for 'Every defence or justification of the idea of God, even the most refined, the best intentioned, is a justification of reaction'. Thus any 'religious deviants' have been to this day among the most ruthlessly harassed and persecuted groups in the Soviet Union.

But it is not only a sense of solidarity with suffering fellow-believers that makes Christians weep for the Soviet Union. It is the realization that, in turning his back on God, Lenin turned his back on God's ways for political and economic life. There have been great economic and industrial achievements in Russia, but at what cost? Lenin himself admitted in 1922 'our main deficiencies: lack of culture and that we do not really know how to rule'. As Robert Conquest puts it: 'The ability to seize power, and to replace a ruling class or élite by a new one, is not in itself a guarantee ... of the capacity to create a superior, let alone supreme, form of human society.'

Milovan Djilas was right to point out that the gaping hole in Marxist theory is where political liberty should be. Marx' disastrous omission was the failure to recognize the possibility of a socialist *state*. The biblical view makes clear that the state, when it exists, is intended to promote the welfare and justice of all citizens (this is the burden, for example, of Romans 13:1–10). Some Reformation leaders went further, underlining this with an emphasis on the 'checks and balances' necessary for the curbing of factional political power. Political authority, in biblical terms, is derived from God and politicians are ultimately answerable to him (rather than to the electorate, the president, king, queen, chairman, or whoever).

True, in Western so-called democracies there still tends to be a preponderance of resource-controlling interest influencing governments, but this does not mean that the balance of power may never be shifted, or that the state itself is superfluous. The concept of the state, as well as its actual role, must be rethought and reformed. But without the principles deriving from outside the state itself, any Lenin may fill the gap with ruthless, authoritarian expediency.

Against paper tigers

Marx expected the revolution to break out in the West. It in fact went East. Since the early twentieth century, it has moved even further East. Events in Russia did not go unnoticed in China, where in 1918 the son of a peasant was attending a Marxist Study Group at the National University of Peking. His name was Mao Tse-tung. The first Chinese revolution of 1911 had rid the country of the old monarchy, but did not have a dynamic revolution in its place. Could not China follow Russia's example? Mao Tse-tung spent the next fifty-eight of his eighty-two years answering that question. China had a revolution all right, but it was not like Russia's.

It was a proud Mao who announced in 1949 that 'the Chinese people have stood up'. In that year the Peoples' Republic of China was founded, bringing to an end years of civil war and previous centuries of famine, oppression and gross inequality. It was the greatest revolution this century, especially in terms of the numbers of people involved. It was nationalistic, in that a highly-cultured élite set out to vindicate the battered self-respect of a once-great civilization. But it was also a profoundly social revolution made by and for the peasantry. Ostensibly Marxist in inspiration, it was in practice overwhelmingly guided by Mao, especially via his pithily persuasive *Thoughts*.

It is significant that Mao began his thinking about communism for China before understanding Marx. He wanted to see power reside with the people, who needed liberation from landlord oppression, foreign encroachment, ignorance and poverty. China had suffered humiliation through international debt at the turn of the century and this had preceded the 1911 revolution. But the old values of Confucianism still underpinned the élite bureaucracy of 'professional amateurs'.

Mao saw that the Chinese revolution would have to be self-sufficient. First, it could not expect outside aid. Secondly, the old and specifically Chinese culture would have to undergo transformation. Lastly, its potential lay in the villages, not the cities.

Marxism gave the new *literati* an ideology which showed the importance of economic interest groups, inside as well as outside a country. Translated into Chinese terms, this meant that externally, foreign marauders would have to be finally checked and internally, that the exploiting landlords, to whom the peasants mortgaged their lives, would have to go. Such Chinese industry as existed was limited to the coastal cities. Not only unbelievably inefficient, industrial working conditions were also appalling: child labour was common. But urban insurrections were easily flattened and anyway, Mao realized early on that decisive power lay with the peasants. He organized peasant groups from 1925, offering them an alternative to back-breaking and unrewarding toil which did not in any case guarantee a decent standard of living.

Mao's leadership of the communist guerilla army in the 'Long March' of 1934–35 assured him of his post as chairman of the Communist Party in 1935, which he held until his death in 1976. His followers accepted his doctrine of revolution and applauded his aim of outwitting the Nanking leader, Chiang K'ai shek. Guerilla warfare was Mao's *forte* and this, combined with his intricate knowledge of past (largely failed) peasant revolts, ensured his primacy in strategy.

A truce between Chiang and the Communists gave time for the establishment of the remote Yenan University, where Marx and Mao were the students' staple diet. Mao now composed *On Guerilla Warfare* and *The New Democracy*. Thus, while the long struggle against the powerful Japanese wore on outside, Mao trained and retrained multitudes of students from diverse social backgrounds to be future leaders. About one third of China was now his.

Manchuria came to be recognized as the crucial area: control there meant control of China. The Russians stepped in and plundered it (they had joined the war effort after the atomic bombs had been exploded on Japan), and both Mao and Chiang determined to take over when they departed. Mao's highly-disciplined, properly-paid army was set on total Chinese liberation: men, not weapons, were decisive. Also, rampant inflation played against the nationalists, who continued to use money long after the peasants returned to bartering rice and grain. In 1948 Mao took the offensive in the Manchurian cities, with the aim of arriving before United States' intervention. His sweeping victories quite demoralized the opposition. The Peoples' Liberation Army had won. Once Peking was taken, Communists were in control.

Mao knew what to do. Despite the non-recognition of the new Republic by international governments (the USA still supported Chiang in Taiwan) and though the national economy was wrecked, he set about immediate reconstruction. Very quickly, communications were restored, there was peace and monetary stability (there was no inflation between 1951 and 1971!). At long last Mao the guerilla could become Mao the communist leader. 'Land Reform' was objective number one. Land was shared out between the cultivators of every district, the old landlords receiving the same as the rest. They had to become peasants to survive. The ideal appeared noble; its actual execution has left question marks hanging over the issue of ends and means.

On the one hand, Mao gave China what it desperately needed – relief from the cruelty and oppression of the landlords and from fear of famine. Gradually he got peasants working together in mutual-aid co-operatives, so that they shared the risks of harvest-failure just as they shared their abilities and muscle-power. By 1953 whole villages were organized co-operatively and the good sense of Mao's ideas were being demonstrated. In 1960–62 these co-operatives survived dreadful drought which in other times would have wiped out thousands of those who lived on the land. Such co-operatives were quite in line with some of Marx' ideals for worker-solidarity and self-help and in some ways also close to the biblical notion of communally-shared toil and rewards.

On the other hand, getting rid of the landlords involved execution, imprisonment and brainwashing. Village justice condemned to various fates anti-communists, one-time cruel landlords and remnants of Chiang's secret police. Estimates of how many died vary enormously, from the sober and conservative calculation of a British diplomat[5] of 100,000 to 150,000, to the (quite possible) several million.

Whatever the number, Mao was ever confident that his action was right. 'In a great revolution of 600 million people, if we did not kill some tyrants, or if we were too lenient to them, the masses would not agree. It is still of practical significance to affirm that it was correct to execute these people.'[6] Just as there will be no end to the debate over what Marx meant by 'force is the midwife of history', so controversy will continue over Mao's 'Political power grows out of the barrel of a gun'.[7] Are these temperate reflections on historical truth (after all, the English and American revolutions also depended upon gun-power) or incitements to murder in the name of the revolution?

In general, Mao chose the route of brainwashing rather than the torture and execution which has been more popular in the Soviet Union. But rougher 'justice' has played an abrasive role from time to time. In 1956 Mao 'let the hundred flowers bloom' by allowing the free artistic and creative criticism of conditions. But he was soon to regret this leniency when severe attacks were mounted on the very basis of Communist China. People remained far from happy with the strict regimentation of the Party monopoly. The hundred flowers rapidly withered.

The came the 'Red Guard' affair during the Great Proletarian Cultural Revolution of 1966–69. School students of fifteen to nineteen gathered in hundreds of thousands in Peking to denounce 'capitalist roaders' and psychologically to batter Mao's 'enemies' out of office. In the end, the Red Guards themselves became over-enthusiastic and were harshly repressed. Again and again, the difficulty lay in distinguishing the 'real communists' from revisionists, imperialists and other 'paper tigers'. Suspicion and mutual betrayal has come to characterize much Chinese life today, from nursery school onwards. 'Re-education' of such reactionary elements involves large doses of Maoist propaganda, which assumes that there exists only one road to co-operation and socialism: belief in unaided human power.

Mao wished to produce new, unselfish people through his programme of socialist education and cultural revolution. True, China no longer starves or suffers grinding and interminable poverty (and has in fact grown to be a major industrial power in amazingly few years). But as Fitzgerald, a fairly sympathetic observer, has reflected (referring to the Red Guards) 'It is not really clear whether these kinds of experiences did create a new kind of citizen'.

Revolutionary love

'A revolutionary', declared Ernesto ('Che') Guevara, 'is a person possessed by deep feelings of love'. He, along with Fidel Castro, has done more than any other revolutionary to encourage Christian engagement in the socialist enterprise. The context of their activities is, of course, Latin America, with its long association with Roman Catholicism.

Nowadays Protestants[8] as well as Catholics see a need to take up Guevara's famous challenge: 'When Christians dare to give a total revolutionary witness, the Latin American revolution will be invincible, seeing that until now Christians have allowed their teaching to be manipulated by reactionaries.' It is because Che gave up his position in the triumphant Cuban revolution to lay down his life in the Bolivian jungle that he has become the modern patron saint of would-be guerillas.

The simplistic slogans associated with the Cuban revolution do not, for all their attraction, explain *why* there was a revolution. It was a surprising revolution and certainly not 'expected'. Cuba had a high *average* standard of living compared with other Latin American countries, and was more than 50 per cent urban. The Cuban revolution cannot be understood in terms of the triumph of socialism against American imperialism: the story is more complicated.

Sugar production is central to the history of modern Cuba. There was no real prosperity in Spanish Cuba until, in the nineteenth century, it became a sugar island. The economy depended upon slaves. Under the Spanish they were not without personal rights but widespread brutality was still practised, leading to slave revolts in the early days. The population grew with the importing of slaves (who were gradually assimilated) with the result that the majority of Cubans are immigrants of the past 150 years. Sugar production requires extremely hard seasonal work, for which great discipline is needed. The problem for the Cuban revolutionary regime has been how to maintain standards of living without resorting to exactly the same methods to keep the field cultivators working.

Cuba gained independence from the Spanish in 1898 but not a single *Cuban* put his name to the peace settlement. The United States, using the infamous 'Platt Amendment', grasped control: Cuba was her economic colony. American intervention at the beginning of the century did generate a viable economy (with US investment), a communications network and improved health services. Far from representing a free market economy, however, the pre-revolutionary government under Batista maintained a strict control in the interest of the minority. An ugly secret police helped to keep the monopoly, with accompanying vices like gambling and prostitution.

The whole system was geared to fulfilling the American sugar quota (whatever that happened to be) and to benefiting Cuban sugar interests. The majority of Cubans, especially the peasants, were simply not taken into account. Their position, however successful the harvest, remained constantly low. The Batista regime was pitiless and appeared to be hand-in-glove with the Americans. Too often in twentieth-century Cuban history the US ambassador has been more important than the Cuban president. Thus it is not startling to discover that hatred of the United States has been a critically important attitude, not least for Castro.

Castro did not experience much difficulty in persuading the alienated peasantry that their interests were inimical to those of the United States. He simply wanted to 'descend victoriously from the mountains' (with Guevara and other survivors from the landing on the *Granma*) and smash the whole rotten edifice of the Cuban regime. His slogan, 'Patria o Meurte' ('Fatherland or Death') was compellingly nationalistic and left no doubt as to the issues at stake. Recklessly heroic and dramatically convincing, he overthrew the far stronger Batista forces in January 1959.

Castro was utterly convinced of the iniquity of the old order and bent on its total destruction. Quite what to put in its place, however, was another question. Not understanding the mechanics of the Cuban economy (Marx' ghost must have frowned), he entertained grandiose schemes for raising the Cuban standard of living above both that of the USA and the USSR, by minimizing armament production. He also reduced rents in an attempt to direct help especially to landless labourers.

Great strides have undoubtedly been made to reduce ignorance, poverty, disease and lack of work opportunity, and the Cubans have a right to boast of these. But twenty years later, despite massive Soviet investment (which has perpetuated Third World dependence), it is still not clear that Cuba has solved the problem of increasing production (their stated aim) without resorting to virtual slavery and hard discipline. The Americans are still passionately hated but the Russians and Chinese are far from implicitly trusted either. State control lives on, under the triumphantly-patriotic socialist banners but the reign of harmony and love has not yet decisively arrived.

A curious lack of American counter-insurgency assistance in

1957–59 did help Castro, as did the deep international rivalry between East and West. The USSR were eager for a foothold near the US mainland, to extend their tentacles into Latin America and to disrupt the all-pervading American coca-colonization. Cuba was symbolic, too, of socialism-against-imperialism. The fist against American neo-colonialism has since been more provocatively raised in other Latin American countries, as well as in Vietnam, Cambodia and some African countries.

Above all, Cuban experience revived belief in the power of revolution. The romantic Che Guevara took his guerilla tactics to the Bolivian jungle (in 1966) in an abortive attempt to repeat the Cuban experiment. The focus, again, was on the wrongs of the system and not on what might replace the corruption. Unfortunately, Che did not evidence much 'revolutionary love' for the Bolivian peasants, whom he found disappointingly and despicably un-political in their outlook. But by becoming a martyr, he fanned the flames of revolutionary enthusiasm which have not yet died in Latin American countries.

Even radical priests have joined in the battle. Castro believed that there should be a 'strategic alliance' between revolutionary Christians and revolutionary Marxists. Camilo Torres, a martyred priest-cum-revolutionary, followed the Cuban procedure by urging the use of élite guerilla groups in Colombia. Guevara claimed that all Christians should follow this kind of example, thus honouring their 'revolutionary inheritance'. This situation has given birth to the theology of liberation, which is becoming increasingly popular in other parts of the world.

In fact, theology of liberation is no longer exclusively Roman Catholic. From a whole-heartedly biblical stance, Christian liberative motifs are being brought to the fore in discussions of how Christianity is relevant to today's world.[9] At this stage it is impossible to tell where the movement will end. But one matter is clear. While a revolutionary may claim to be possessed by love, expressing solidarity with the oppressed and so on, this cannot be enough, from a Christian viewpoint. In the Bible, love is inseparably yoked to God's law.

One implication of this is that Christian love has to be directed towards enemies as well as 'neighbours'. This is a totally different ball-game. The law is the way of God, the form within which true freedom flourishes. But at the same time it cannot be the way *to* God. Just as, in ancient times, the exodus from Egyptian slavery was followed by the giving of the law, so in the New Testament it is made abundantly clear that no one can please God by rule-keeping. 'Redemption' – the process of being brought back to God and given new life, which in the Old Testament *was* the exodus – must precede proper understanding of the love/law relationship. Only an appreciation of the divine-anger-and-justice-appeasing character of Christ's cross can evoke that love for God which is demonstrated by a willing compliance with his purposes. These purposes have implications for all of life – work, home, political activity, art, everything. We leave them out of account at our peril.

Castro's hatred of political corruption and economic oppression may be shared by Christians, but at the same time, the Christian will point to a better way. While Che Guevara had an inkling of the need for a more radical solution – 'In order to build up communism we must at the same time change the economic foundations *and* man himself' – he died in the jungle without ever finding *the* Way.

Third World Marx

The twentieth century has certainly seen numerous revolutions, too many for us to document here. But this has been almost entirely the achievement of the Third World – China, Indo-China, Latin America and now the rising movement for African socialism. Each has espoused Marxism but on very different terms. China, while paying lipservice to the inspiration of Marxist-Leninism, is Maoist in guidance. Latin America, too, has been influenced by the Soviet Union but Latin American socialist experiments (such as Allende's Chile) have had little in common with Russian Communism. Even Cambodia, while aping some Stalinesque atrocities, is not distinctively Russian. Back in Europe, Yugoslavia too has chosen its own road between Moscow and Peking, though neighbouring Albania is closer to the latter.

Different histories and traditions in Africa make Marx take on different colours there too. Here, it is the failure of the Western-style 'capitalist solution' which has bred discontent and a desire for a fairer Africa. By 1970, nearly half of Africa's independent countries, each launched with a pro-capitalist regime, had fallen to some brand of military dictatorship.[10] Even in Nigeria, where capitalism is strong, there is hope for constitutional safeguards against 'the concentration of wealth or the means of production and exchange in the hands of a few individuals or groups'.

The failure of the middle-class solution led to new policies being adopted by countries such as Tanzania (1967) and Somalia (1971). Julius Nyerere of Tanzania pioneered the 'Ujaama' system of rural socialism based on traditional village co-operation. Varying results have attended these experiments but to many they were at least a preferable alternative after the capitalist dream had turned sour.

But the arrival in Africa of new revolutionaries has catalysed the spread of Marxism even more. In Portuguese colonies especially, where the old colonial powers had refused all reforms, liberation necessarily entailed revolution, which needed a theory and practice. Out of this has grown a distinctive Marxism, which also owes some debt to Lenin.

While aid from other state socialist countries has poured in to Africa (the Chinese railway aid in Zambia for instance, not to mention Russian arms in Zaire and Cuban guerillas in Rhodesia), the Africans have strenuously declined to become stooges of Moscow or Peking. Frantz Fanon, a socialist revolutionary spokesman for black Africa, opposed imperialism, but hoped for a time when black and white would walk hand-in-hand. Communists, as Christians, have to 'de-colonize their minds' when considering Africa. The Africans are determined to analyse and solve their own problems. Help will be accepted from those willing to serve, not to dominate.

The African socialists tend to agree that mass participation is a crucial ingredient to their success. They are trying to build a unity of purpose among the often widely-spread villages and townships, to work together for the same ends. The aim is to establish self-government at grass-roots level, rather than the anonymous hierarchical bureaucracy characteristic of colonial administration. There is also a desire among some to think in terms of continental socialism, transcending the national(istic) barriers which often impede socialist progress. This again is different from the aims of the capitalist effort, which does its utmost to defend narrow territorial interests. The socialists have on the one hand to make it clear that they wish to protect the national interests of these countries which were only de-colonized after the Second World War, but at the same time expand the horizons of socialism beyond national boundaries.

The late twentieth-century awakening of Africa is also a challenge to Christians, who for too long have been associated with the colonial image. If Latin America has its liberation theology, so Africa has a burgeoning African theology, often mixed with Black Theology.[11] Steering a course between the Marxist humanism which often underlies these, and the colonially-superior and socially-unaware theology which characterized some past efforts, is a ticklish but crucial task. Christians dare not ignore the issues of African urbanization, tribalism and the wealth/poverty divide. Whether the decolonialized vacuum is filled by Marxist-Leninist or Christian orientations towards social life will depend to a great extent on the willingness of Christian believers to face the burning issues of contemporary turbulent Africa.

The new revolutionaries

Marx has been appropriated by almost everyone but those for whom he intended his message – advanced industrial societies. The Third World Marx is now well established, especially with the socio-economic analysis of André Gunder Frank,[12] who argues that the coming revolution will be led by the dispossessed of colonialized and imperially-subject countries. He is one of their new theoretical gurus. His thesis is that Western capitalism systematically develops 'underdevelopment' in the Third World, by means of capital invest-ment which is totally controlled by, and in the interests of, the West. 'Aid' is a mere vehicle for subtle neo-colonialism, which has shut its ears to any talk of justice.

But will this revolution (if it comes) be the only one? Will Marx finally champion not the proletariat but some other group? Does he need yet another image for advanced industrial societies? For those who have seized upon revolution as saviour, there are other routes to the goal. Moreover, the goal may also be variously conceived. For many, a single moment of creative destruction will not bring the pan-acea: permanent revolution is required. The obstacle in the road to revolution, it seems, is industrial society itself, which appears to be extremely resilient and capable of resisting all manner of attempts at fundamental change.

Past revolutions have depended upon peasant support, even in semi-urbanized societies. Moreover, insurgents have never been hopelessly under-armed in relation to the opposed regime (even in Cuba). These two factors are missing from modern Western societies. But more importantly, the bureaucratic, centralized state seems to have become indispensable to industrial societies, which make it difficult to even conceive anything outside the existing order – let alone to make a counter-culture.

The 'system' in capitalist societies is so strong that it can afford to tolerate permissiveness, minor rebellion and so on, in the certain knowledge that this will be a safety-valve, allowing the escape of any genuine revolutionary steam. It is thus difficult to imagine what events could possibly precipitate revolution in advanced Western societies. So the new revolutionaries no longer look only to the working class (which tends to have become quiescent and 'incor-porated') but to others who are more obviously 'outside' the system and barred from entry.

The best-known exponent of the new revolutionaries (as I am calling them) is the German-American Herbert Marcuse. The argu-ment of his *One Dimensional Man* is that Marx has to be transcended in the unforeseen conditions of late capitalism. Technological rationality has produced a society which is both efficient and has a high standard of living, making the idea of the polarization of bourgeoisie and proletariat a nonsense. Everything, including art, culture, politics and the economy are swallowed up in the system. People become 'one dimensional', ironed out by a 'comfortable, smooth, reasonable, democratic unfreedom'.

Marcuse attempted to marry Marx with Freud, seeing a complementarity between their approaches with regard to alienation. Sexual repression, for him, takes place in particular social contexts and may be seen as part of a more general inhuman trend towards manipulation and control. Thus the Women's Liberation Movement has huge radical potential which may, when added to that of students, blacks and any other 'alienated' members of society, produce the long-awaited revolution. Marcuse has little sympathy with the Soviet version of 'socialism', for it demonstrates the very same tendencies as the West – anti-libertarian, repressive, alienating. Breaking the culture of the market, being blatantly nonconformist – for Marcuse this was the only hope for the dawn of revolution.

Although Marcuse's slogans were vigorously chanted in the 1960s (he complained that few actually read what he wrote), only one event gave any hope for his kind of approach. 'May '68' in Paris has taken on an apocalyptic character in the thought of the young radicals of today. Here was no peasant or proletarian revolt but a new kind of demonstration by students, industrial workers and professional groups who wanted a say in the making of a self-managed, liberated world.

May '68 was not a revolution. Neither students, nor workers, nor even the Communist Party was in a position to take power. But it was a huge, exuberant and sometimes violent demonstration against the system. A plea for sexual 'freedom' in student dormitories actually sparked things off: the 'system' was repressive. Then came student/police clashes at the Sorbonne and workers occupying Sud-Aviation and Renault plants. Middle-class professionals joined the movement, until a total of six million were on strike in France. Why?

The Situationists, often spokesmen in 1968, summed it up: 'We do not want a world in which the guarantee that we will not die of starvation is bought by the risk of dying of boredom.' A libertarian Marxism (anti-authoritarian) joined hands with a surrealistic plea for creativity and 'liberated' sexuality. Marcuse was partly right. The protest was against alienation. The social trend towards the bureaucratization of everything (analysed by German sociologist Max Weber more than by Marx) seemed to be reducing people to receptors and consumers only. Paris wanted to create, to be multi-dimensional and free!

According to some social thinkers, Marx' notion of class conflict must again be modified (in the light of 1968) to fit the new 'knowledge society' (or 'service society'), where 'experts rule OK'. It is now those in industrial society who do not control knowledge who are alienated (not the non-owners of the means of production). The new revolution is one which must continuously be fought on numerous fronts. The old revolution used barricades to stop horses. The barricades must be transformed and erected against all media and bureaucracy which inhibits liberty. The old revolution stormed the Winter Palace. But the Palace of Alienation is not so easily taken! The revolution must now be fought on many levels and be permanent.

Needless to say, 'orthodox' Marxists take a dim view of this type of rhetoric and regard it as revisionism of the most shameless variety. But Marx is still strongly among the inspirations for the protest against alienation and exploitation in more than one Western country. He has taught several generations how to look for 'contradictions', that the powers-that-be must be confronted and that revolution may purge out the wrongs of a twisted and interest-ruled society. Some still believe in the central role of the proletariat, others in the 'external proletariat' of the Third World.

Yet others place hope in any 'outsiders' of the system: women, blacks and students. Analysis of social conditions with the advent of the social science boom, has exposed 'contradiction' and 'oppression' wherever they hide – in kitchen, classroom, assembly-line, social work office and church-institution. But what is desired in place of alienation and how the revolution will achieve this, are items on an agenda which ever recedes into a hazy horizon.

High hopes and harsh realities

Revolution and the new society are precisely the issues left open by Marx. Revolution was the only way out of the enmeshing chains of capitalist society, as far as he could see. But he was vague about what would follow the revolution. And while his analysis of industrial capitalism was thorough (if somewhat inadequate), he had contempt for those who went into similar detail about future society. Who wants castles in the air? Who indeed! Too often they have been the mere products of social myopia and abstract wishful thinking. We must stick to social and economic analysis, argued Marx. This is the key.

But when Engels entitled his book *Socialism: Utopian and Scientific*, he was deluding himself. Science and utopia are not ultimately separable in this way. He and Marx *did* have some purposes in view when they worked out their theory of society. Facts never 'speak for themselves'. Marx and Engels were speaking for the facts of social life under industrial capitalism (in its developing stages) in the name of its supposed alternative: socialist or communist society. As we have seen, Marx did have ideals for society and its constituent individuals. He believed that work, for example, should be free, conscious and creative, and its products shared for the good of all. In other words, they had a concealed, unacknowledged utopian method, of which, in an age which believed implicitly in 'positive science', they were a trifle ashamed.

In fact, there are good grounds for suggesting that 'science' and 'utopia', far from being incompatible, are complementary partners. 'Science' without 'utopia' produces dogmatic coercion (as in the USSR) whereas utopian ideals without sober social analysis produce, for example, injustice-blind 'democracy' (as in many Western countries). The two are quite reconcilable. The tragedy of Marx' utopianism is that he not only failed to acknowledge it but also (and partly because of this) it remained underdeveloped.

As a result, Marx merely substituted one myth (revolution) for another (capitalist growth). Neither have ushered in the millenium, nor ever will. But this bald judgement does not mean that the way of social analysis plus a guiding ethic (utopian method) is itself wrong. It is the Marxian framework which is questionable. On its own terms (that is, if the theory is tested in historical practice) Marxism has thus far failed to produce the kinds of changes hoped for by Marx. But with a different orientation and a different praxis, 'science' and 'utopia' may realistically be harnessed together for genuine human welfare.

Before commenting on the 'different praxis', we must briefly substantiate the charge that Marxism has failed. As we have seen, in the stages through which capitalism would pass, eventually to become communism, Marx expected certain decisive changes. The division of labour and separation of physical and mental life would be transcended. The fetishism of commodities, in which consumption of goods becomes the over-riding goal of life, would be exchanged for a society where people's real needs, rather than artificially-stimulated wants, would be catered for. The state, for so long the tool of the wealthy and powerful against the have-nots, would also be transcended, along with the whole invidious class structure.

Again, we have stressed that some aspects of Marx' ideal are fully in line with a Christian understanding of what the social world should be. Optimum rather than maximum consumption, as upheld

by John Taylor in *Enough is Enough*,[13] is a Christian virtue. (See for
instance Ephesians 4:28.) Political authority which stands for justice
rather than wealthy interest groups is another fully Christian ideal, as
is the reduction of envy, covetousness and conflict associated with
class division. But Marx thought that these changes would accompany radically-transformed social relationships alone. Get rid of
capitalism and human society will be free to grow.

The 'Marxist' record gives far less grounds for optimism.
Capitalism has been abolished in the Soviet Union, Eastern Europe,
China, Cuba and so on. But China repeatedly castigates the USSR
for its badly-disguised state capitalism, where consumer incentives
and competition are creeping back in. A new form of class structure is
also apparent in Soviet Russia.

But China herself, despite the fight against bureaucratic and
hierarchical encroachment, seems in need of continual purges and
cultural revolutions to rid the country of capitalist tendencies. These
include 'economism', selfishness and even the private accumulation of
capital. In Cuba, the boarding-school system (there is no freedom of
choice whether or not to attend) aims to do the same as Mao's
brainwashing in China – produce a population divested of self-
interest and greed. And as for the state, it is the strongest thing alive
in Russia and though it is less centralized in China, it is no less
powerful there, or in Cuba.

Production itself, associated with that attribute of self-creation
which according to Marx makes a person human, has provided state
socialism with one of its most persistent difficulties. How may the
worker be motivated under socialism? Why does not everyone wish
to work in the interests of neighbour as well as self and share the
fruits of toil? Both sticks and carrots have been tried. The problem is
that sticks are incompatible with freedom (working under military
discipline hardly meets Marx' standards for authentic humanity!),
and carrots are incompatible with selflessness. Neither repression,
nor material incentives are genuinely socialist methods. Both exist
(especially in the USSR and Eastern Europe), and no state socialist
society manages to get its work done without one or the other.

A prominent Marxist ethicist, Eugene Kamenka, has neatly
summed up the basic contradiction: 'We can no longer follow Marx
in the tacit reliance on the essentially co-operative nature of man
freed from economic bonds.'[14] Changing social structure (however
rightly desirable from the viewpoint of a Christian ideal of equality
and liberty) does not change persons. To motivate people, Communist governments either sink to bourgeois incentives, or else play
on the permanent revolution theme. The struggle against paper

tigers, revisionists, or whatever, becomes a holy war where righteousness must prevail in the end. In other words, motivation is either bourgeois or transcendental.

Destroying capitalism has not ushered in an age of freedom, either. True, freedom in Western countries is proportionate to one's access to power and influence (which is related in turn to wealth and income), but the state socialist alternative scarcely seems preferable. The paranoic fear of criticism led to incidents like the Red Guard purge in China: one was only free there to parrot Mao. And collective decision-making? Co-operatively planning for future change? Participation in government? These are virtually unheard of. In *Guerillas in Power* Karol comments, 'the Cuban people deserve more initiative, more self-determination, and more immunity from the abstract manipulation of a remote bureaucracy'.[15] What has gone wrong?

New people: new society

There is no doubt that Marx believed in a new or total person who would emerge in socialist society. The antithesis of the alienated person, he would be free, conscious and purposive in work, which would be done in harmonious co-operation with others.

In 1924, Trotsky wrote:

Man will become immeasurably stronger, wiser, and subtler; his body will become more harmonized, his movement more rhythmic, his voice more musical. The forms of life will become dynamically dramatic. The average human type will rise to the heights of an Aristotle, a Goethe, or a Marx. And above this ridge new peaks will rise.[16]

In 1965, two Soviet ideologists effused 'We have in our hands a truly miraculous method of transformation, our "philosopher's stone" — the philosophy of Marxism-Leninism'. With this, they went on, 'Soviet society is rearing a man whose spiritual and moral qualities are worth more than any treasures in the world'.[16] This alone, supposedly, can eradicate all negative traits such as individualism, bourgeois nationalism, chauvinism, indolence and religious prejudices.

In recent years, the need for the so-called 'new man' has been increasingly seen by Marxists. Mao was explicitly trying to create 'remoulded' selfless people in China. We have quoted Che as wanting to change human nature as well as economic conditions. (During the Khrushchev era in the USSR the Communist Party declared an (unrevoked) aim to be high on the priority list:

> The party regards the education of the new man as the most difficult task in the communist reshaping of society. Until we remove bourgeois moral principles roots and all, train men in the spirit of communist morality and renew them spiritually and morally, it will not be possible to build up communist society.

This aim (curiously worded for materialists of the matter-is-all-there-is kind) has been taken up by Hungary, Romania and other Eastern European countries. Lastly Fanon, though not an orthodox Marxist (who is?), said 'Let us try to create the whole man, whom Europe has been incapable of bringing to triumphant birth'.[17]

But new people stubbornly refuse to arise spontaneously. Evidence flows in to suggest that no socio-economic change produces them. Things have 'gone wrong' because at a basic level the theory is wrong. Socialism searches for a trustworthy, hard-working, selfless, neighbourly and moral man. He can be found in Jesus of Nazareth. As Josif Ton, a Romanian Baptist, has succinctly put it:

> Socialism is fighting against its own interests when it maintains the war against religion. Socialism needs the new man, the moral man. The new man cannot be created by slogans or moral codes of behaviour or laws. Only the spirit of Christ can revolutionize a man, transform him, and make him a new kind of person.[18]

The key to understanding revolution is the idea of self-creation. Here is the titanic atheism of Marx in a nutshell: man can remake himself, he is his only sun. The key to understanding the Christian alternative – rebirth – is God-creation. 'If any man is in Christ, he is a new creation', Paul wrote to the Corinthians.

The old bourgeois life of aspiration and consumer-cravings, rooted in rejection of and rebellion against God, can be turned on its head by Jesus Christ. The whole life – attitudes, words, actions and all – may be forgiven by the innocent victim who was crucified at Calvary in Palestine. For he died, as the Bible incredibly asserts, 'the just for the unjust, in order that he might bring us to God'. No titanic struggle to recreate oneself according to certain standards of ideal humanity. No commitment to completing the environmental transformation before new people can emerge. Authentic repentance, which was the core of his uncomfortable preaching, occurs when a person turns radically away from his or her old life in accordance with the firm but gentle dictates of the risen Jesus. The result is an alternative life-style in which God becomes utterly central and people begin to matter more than things. Following the example of the man-for-others (and especially his words in Matthew 5–7), the radical Christian repudiates consumption for provision, competition for co-operation, lies for truth, fickleness for faithfulness, lust for love, confrontation for reconciliation, boredom for joy, social conformism for Christ-likeness and conflict for peace.

The real new society (resisting manipulation by reactionaries) is the church, the community of God's new people who follow Christ. The church was never intended to be a cumbersome hierarchical structure. Rather, it is-a 'happening', a gathering of like-minded disciples of Christ. They are responsible to declare God's way of peace for mankind – through the death of Jesus Christ – and to be living evidence of the life of Jesus in the here-and-now.[19]

The disciples of Christ know that a new order is coming, when Christ will finally welcome in the age of 'beating swords into ploughshares', and the 'lion lying down with the lamb'. This coming kingdom, because it will fulfill the creation-purposes, is the pattern of Christian hope, our ideal. This utopian vision (*not* blueprint) has solid foundation in the promises of God and clear guidance as to what he desires: justice and peace. Christians pray: 'Your will be done on earth, even as it is in heaven.' But for the present, Christians know that '*shalom*' (God's peace and welfare) in its fulness is not a political possibility. We soberly expect conflict while sin and its social-structural effects remain.

In fact, Christian social analysis seeks to discover patterns of domination, exploitation and unrighteousness, with a view to changing conditions in accordance with the Maker's freedom-frameworks. Thus 'utopia' and 'science' are married. An illustration of this would be the attempt to bring Christ's peace into industry by supporting participatory, co-operative structures and exposing the destructive effects of certain technologies on meaningful human existence. Another would be the concern for stewardship versus exploitation and the profit/growth motive in relationships with fellow-persons and the natural environment. A third would be the examination of the mass media to detect 'Western brainwashing' which encourages spiritual dullness and lack of concern for biblically-directed change in social structure.

In already-existing socialist countries, the lead of Romanian Ton should be followed, in offering whole-hearted and loyal citizenship within the collective (or whatever) system, while simultaneously pleading for the extension of religious toleration (including the chance to show the everyday practicality of faith in Jesus).

Then in countries of the Third World, struggling for liberation from neo-colonial and ethnic-élite power-factions, Christians could be seen to be supporting small-scale, intermediate technology schemes and co-operative agriculture suited to the local environment and conditions (which again would be revealed by a sensitive social analysis). But Christians would also be seen warning against the mere substitution of one myth (revolution) when the other (Western-style growth) has gone sour.

The idea of a communist future is a cruel mirage, when wrenched out of the full-orbed context of a biblical life-style. The new person never breaks out. In the biblical way, new people are called by Christ to live within the present structures as a counter-cultural force. Christian hope is in Christ's recreative work and the future with him after death but this hope gives impetus to action now.

We now live east of Eden but the life-patterns given in Eden still have a compelling relevance now. Christians are truly 'strangers and pilgrims' in the world. Nevertheless we have an eye to present welfare as well as future peace. Jeremiah took God's message to exiles: 'Seek the welfare of the city where I have sent you into exile, and pray to the Lord on its behalf . . .' As Klaus Bockmuhl has commented, this 'exile is engaged in the welfare of the city and the land, even if it is not his own. So he is not determined by his situation, but by God's commission, and in acting upon it he will soon have the effect of the salt of the earth and the light of the world'.[20] We might add, 'whatever he or she does': housewife and social worker, bricklayer and surgeon, teacher and store assistant, if Christian, are equally salt and light.

To focus on inner rebirth and future heaven is emphatically not an individualistic cop-out. These are the distinctive features of new life in Christ. But they are also part of the whole good news of God's ways (born with the creation) for all people. A social gospel, which places salvation-hope in reformed socio-economic structures, is anathema to Christians. But from heart-allegiance to Jesus Christ and in the new community of biblically-directed people, Christians confess Christ as their Lord in every dimension of life: economic, artistic, family, industrial – everywhere.

Recognition, rejection and realization

The Christian response to Marx, as I have tried to stress throughout, should be one of humility. Marxism is a human response to Christian failure to practise the truth in every sphere of life. It highlights the inescapable deficiencies which have too often characterized Christian commitment, especially since the beginnings of industrialism and capitalism.

Marx challenges Christians at several levels. His is a deep and perceptive critique of things as they are, which demands an alternative praxis. Marx' critique probes beneath the surface. His structural-social and historical analysis questions not only the workings of the capitalist system (which is what conventional economics and sociology tend to do) but asks whether the system itself is human.

He also attempted to be comprehensive, and others have filled out his approach ever since. A total understanding of the world is offered, which takes in not only the industrial shop-floor but everything else, from art or religion to science. The critique which shatters illusions about the benevolence of a capitalist *status quo* is based on a view of an ideal person and an alternative society. Praxis is also a way of actively changing the world, in which neither abstract theory nor mindless activism predominate (ideally, at least). Rather, theory and practice are dynamically intertwined.

All this is deeply humbling to Christians who realize that Marx has touched sensitive spots. Why haven't more Christians questioned the very nature of capitalism before now? More than a suspicion is raised about the accuracy of Marx' trenchant criticism that the institutional church has had deep vested interests in capitalism, thus blinding her to its corrosive character. Why has the confession 'Jesus Christ is Lord' failed to embrace all of life? Christians must consider what it means for Christ to be Lord of the long-neglected and strife-torn field of industrial relations, international trade and the pitifully (but involuntarily) dependent Third World, the state in an advanced industrial society and so on.

Christians have an ideal person, Jesus Christ, and an alternative society, the church – but where is the social structural analysis from *this* perspective? And where is the social praxis based on the pattern of the only one who fully practised all that he preached, Jesus of Nazareth? The study of Marx demands of Christians some painful and penetrating reflection and response to these issues.

But two problems remain. The major difficulty is a deep disquiet about the roots of Marx' way. In the last analysis, it is, paradoxically, traceable to the very same soil as capitalism itself. Both are earthed in the radical humanism which flowered in the eighteenth-century Enlightenment. Different plants have appeared on the surface but it is a mistake to imagine that they have not grown from the same ground. Human self-redemption is at the core of Marx' optimistic gospel. But this is also the underthought of capitalism: it simply appears in a different guise. Both agree that human history is a *progress*-report.

Christian praxis cannot simply be planted in the same soil, in order that mutually-beneficial cross-fertilization may occur. At this fundamental, religious level, there is a basic incompatibility. However much Christians have to learn from Marx, there can be no synthesis of the two world-views. Or, to continue the biological analogy, *symbiosis* (growing together) is ultimately out of the question.

The final issue is the verdict of history. On Marx' own terms, everyone has the right to ask why his appealing promises have been unfulfilled anywhere. It is inadequate to argue that Marx has been betrayed. True, he was no champion of bureaucratic collectivism, terror for its own sake, or an anaesthetizing uniformity of culture. But his ideas do not preclude these either. State socialism, as state capitalism, is the fruit of pretended human autonomy from the Creator. Because Marx was also a creature of that Creator, he saw many things. But his blind spots have often proved fatal.

His radicalism was not deep enough. His apparently comprehensive range was limited. His critique is grounded in an incomplete view of personhood and an all too sketchy outline of ideal society, quite detached from God's freedom-frameworks. Hence he failed to follow the perfect orthopraxis of the Creator's Son. Instead, he bequeathed to an unjust world a powerful locomotive of revolutionary activism but only the most frail of ethical-political tracks to run it on.

Marx produced an immensely attractive world-picture of how things came to be and how they could be changed. A theory as attractive as flowers. Beginning with God-rejection, he obscured the chains of human bondage to sin and sinful life-patterns. Because of God's generosity and patience, however, those chains may be broken by the cross of Jesus of Nazareth. Marx' flowers will fade but there will still be flowers.

The biblical response to contemporary industrial capitalism, state socialism and Third World dependency and liberation is complex and fraught with difficulty and dilemma. It often involves transcending the inadequate Christian responses of the past. It may not be credible to an era which has sold out to conspicuous consumption and the demand for rights. But it is an alternative which offers genuine hope, founded in the exclusive claim of Jesus Christ: 'I am the way, the truth and the life.'

Notes and references
1 Isaiah Berlin, *Karl Marx: His Life and Environment*, Oxford University Press, 1963, p. 276.
2 David McLellan, *Karl Marx: His Life and Thought*, Macmillan, 1973, Harper and Row, 1974, p. 445.

3 John Dunn, *Modern Revolutions*, Cambridge University Press, 1972, p. 46.

4 Robert Conquest, *Lenin*, Fontana Modern Masters and Penguin Modern Masters, 1972, pp. 38–39.

5 C. P. Fitzgerald, *Mao Tse-tung and China*, Holmes and Meier, 1976, Penguin, 1977, p. 92.

6 Stuart Schram (ed.), *Mao Tse-tung Unrehearsed*, Penguin, 1974: Mao's 1956 speech 'On the Ten Relationships', p. 77.

7 Mao Tse-tung, *Quotations from Mao Tse-tung*, Foreign Languages Press (Peking), 1966, p. 61.

8 For example, José Míguez Bonino, *Christians and Marxists: The Mutual Challenge to Revolution*, Hodder and Stoughton and Eerdmans, 1976. See also Carl E. Armerding (ed.), *Evangelicals and Liberation*, Presbyterian and Reformed Publishing Co., 1977.

9 See Andrew Kirk, *Theology Encounters Revolution*, Inter-Varsity Press (Leicester), due 1979.

10 Basil Davidson, *Africa in Modern History: The Search for a New Society*, Allen Lane Press, 1978.

11 Byang Kato, 'Black Theology and African Theology', *Evangelical Review of Theology*, 1977, pp. 35–48.

12 For example, Andre Gunder Frank, *Latin America: Underdevelopment or Revolution*, Monthly Review Press, 1970.

13 John V. Taylor, *Enough is Enough*, SCM Press, 1975, Augsburg, 1977.

14 E. Kamenka, 'Marxian Humanism and the Crisis of Socialist Theory', in E. Fromm, *Socialist Humanism*, Penguin, 1967, quoted in Andrew Kirk, 'Communist Society: A Christian Comment on an Alternative Lifestyle for the Human Race', Shaftesbury Project, 1976.

15 Quoted in Andrew Kirk, 1976.

16 David E. Powell, *Anti-Religious Propaganda in the Soviet Union*, M.I.T. Press, 1975, p. 2.

17 Frantz Fanon, *The Wretched of the Earth*, MacGibbon and Kee, 1968.

18 Josif Ton, 'The Socialist Quest for the New Man', *Christianity Today*, 26 March 1976. Documentary material on the situation of Christian and other believers in state socialist countries see *Religion in Communist Lands*, the journal of Keston College, Heathfield Road, Keston, Kent, England.

19 Here the Anabaptist stress on the New Testament church as community (*koinonia*) is needed. See Jim Wallis, *Agenda for Biblical People*, Harper and Row, 1976, Chapter 5. See also the valuable biblical analysis by Michael Griffiths, *Cinderella with Amnesia*, Inter-Varsity Press, 1975, and R. Banks, *Paul's Idea of Community*, Paternoster Press and ANZEA Books, 1979.

20 Klaus Bockmuhl, 'Marxism in Search for the New Man: A Christian Response', Regent College, Vancouver, (n.d.). An English translation of his *The Challenge of Marxism* is forthcoming in the U.S. from Inter-Varsity Press.

INDEX